The Greatest Man
Who Ever Lived

The Greatest Man Who Ever Lived

*Secrets for Unparalleled Success
and Unshakable Happiness
from the Life of Jesus*

Steven K. Scott

WATERBROOK
PRESS

THE GREATEST MAN WHO EVER LIVED
PUBLISHED BY WATERBROOK PRESS
12265 Oracle Boulevard, Suite 200
Colorado Springs, Colorado 80921

Scripture quotations marked (NIV) are taken from the Holy Bible, New International Version®. NIV®. Copyright © 1973, 1978, 1984 by International Bible Society. Used by permission of Zondervan Publishing House. All rights reserved. Scripture quotations marked (NKJV) are taken from the New King James Version®. Copyright © 1982 by Thomas Nelson Inc. Used by permission. All rights reserved. Scripture quotations marked (KJV) are taken from the King James Version. Scripture quotations marked (NASB) are taken from the New American Standard Bible®. © Copyright The Lockman Foundation 1960, 1962, 1963, 1968, 1971, 1972, 1973, 1975, 1977. Used by permission. (www.Lockman.org). Scripture quotations marked (NLT) are taken from the Holy Bible, New Living Translation, copyright © 1996, 2004. Used by permission of Tyndale House Publishers Inc., Wheaton, Illinois 60189. All rights reserved.

Italicized words in Scripture quotations reflect the author's emphasis.

ISBN 978-1-4000-7464-8

Published in the United States by WaterBrook Press and Doubleday, an imprint of The Doubleday Publishing Group, a division of Random House Inc., New York.

WaterBrook and its deer colophon are registered trademarks of Random House Inc.

Library of Congress Cataloging-in-Publication Data
Scott, Steve, 1948–
   The greatest man who ever lived : secrets for unparalleled success and unshakable happiness from the life of Jesus / Steven K. Scott.—1st ed.
      p. cm.
   1. Success—Religious aspects—Christianity. 2. Jesus Christ—Example. I. Title
   BV4598.3.S42 2009
   232.9'04—dc22

                                             2008050064

Printed in the United States of America
2009—First WaterBrook Press Edition

10 9 8 7 6 5 4 3 2 1

SPECIAL SALES
Most WaterBrook Multnomah books are available in special quantity discounts when purchased in bulk by corporations, organizations, and special-interest groups. Custom imprinting or excerpting can also be done to fit special needs. For information, please e-mail SpecialMarkets@WaterBrookMultnomah.com or call 1-800-603-7051.

Dedicated

To Robert J. Marsh—my incredible mentor, my second father, an entrepreneurial genius—a man who loved God and served him and others, selflessly and without fanfare. Your wisdom was a well that never ran dry, and your faith, kindness, and humor gave me what no other man ever has. Your equal will never be found in my lifetime. Oh how we all miss you!

Contents

My sweet wife, Shannon—you inspire me and give me all of the encouragement I need to pursue the projects that mean so much to me. I am soooooo crazy about you!

As always, I am extremely grateful to my wonderful editors, Roger Scholl, editorial director, Doubleday Business, and Ron Lee, senior editor, WaterBrook Press. You two not only make my efforts so much more readable, you make the whole process a pure joy, from start to finish.

Jan Miller, the world's best literary agent—you've always caught my vision and turned my dreams into published realities—thank you for always taking such wonderful care of me and my projects.

All of my Max Partners and Associates—Your love, dedication, and diligence are having a life-changing impact on tens of thousands today, and will make that same impact on millions of lives in the future. You all AMAZE me.

The Greatest Man
Who Ever Lived

——— ⊚⊚ ———

CHAPTER I

What the Greatest Man Who Ever Lived Can Do for You

⊚⊚ Better Than Winning a $100 Million Lottery

If I could show you a secret that would absolutely, positively enable you to WIN $100 million in the next mega lottery jackpot, what would you be willing to do to learn that secret? "Wait a minute," you might say, "how do I know that your secret will really work?" Imagine that I answered your question by revealing, "I won the mega lottery jackpot last year by using this secret, and since then have shared it with my ten closest friends, who also used it to win mega lottery jackpots. In fact, not one person who has tried this secret has failed to win." Suppose I then gave you their names and you were able to verify that all of us had indeed won mega lottery jackpots. Now, what would you be willing to do to learn the secret I've offered to share with you? How much would you be willing to pay me? Would you be willing to take out a second mortgage on your house to get the necessary funds, or borrow from your 401(k) retirement plan? What if I then told you that I didn't want your money or your house . . . I just wanted you to read a book that I wrote in which I revealed the secret? If I told you that the secret was revealed in chapter 7 of my book, and I handed you that book right now, how much time would you let go by before you would read chapter 7? What if you knew the next mega jackpot was only one day away? When would you get around to reading chapter 7 now? With what level of attention would you read each paragraph in that chapter?

That is like the secret I intend to reveal in this book. During the past twenty years, I have made tens of millions of dollars in personal income. Along with my partners, I've had the thrill of starting businesses from scratch (with a few thousand dollars) and building them into companies that have produced billions—yes, billions—of dollars in sales. And making money through one's own hard work and effort is certainly a lot more fulfilling than winning it in a lottery or at the tables in Vegas. Although winning a pot of money in a stroke of luck may give you a greater thrill initially, that thrill is gone almost as fast as it comes, and the personal and financial losses that usually follow such a windfall can be devastating. Moreover, I've never heard of someone winning a mega lottery a second time.

This being the case, if you were my friend, I would much rather give you the keys you need to succeed in business, marriage, parenting, and life than give you the secret to winning a lottery. And if I *really* cared about you, I'd lead you step by step through the process of applying these keys to success to the most important areas of your life.

My business success, like my personal happiness, has been the result of the incredible relationships that have come into my life over the past forty-four years, and the wisdom and benefits that have been handed down to me as a result of those personal relationships. But there is one secret that I've rarely shared. Not *one* of these relationships, nor any of the blessings they have given me, would have come about had I not *first* met the greatest man who ever lived.

๑๑ *Embracing Extraordinary Change*

During my business life I have traveled millions of miles on our nation's airlines. I have spent thousands of hours talking with men and women seated next to me about countless subjects. I've heard them complain about their jobs, their spouses, their children, their bosses, and of course their lives in general. When they find out that I'm that rare person who is happy beyond description, more in love with my wife today than I was during our courtship eighteen years ago, and that I persisted through countless failures to create dozens of successful businesses, they often ask me what the "secrets" to my happiness, my marriage, or my success have been. I tell them that it all started with what I learned from a homeless carpenter I first met one night in 1964. Their eyes usually widen with interest. When I tell them that the carpenter's name is Jesus, their curiosity quickly turns to bewilderment. But as much as they might like to change the subject initially, their curiosity gets the better of them, and they want to hear "the *rest* of the story."

As I begin to describe the life lessons and wisdom I learned from Jesus, their curiosity usually turns to astonishment. "Is this guy for real?" they seem to be saying to themselves. But as I relate the specific ways in which Jesus miraculously changed my mind and heart, guided me in my relationships and business endeavors, and brought purpose, peace, personal success, and joy into my daily experience, they tend to undergo a transformation of sorts. In part because of the fact that I've been so successful in the world of business, they are often interested in what has made me so successful. When they hear how my thinking and attitudes and beliefs were shaped by the timeless teachings of Jesus, their bewilderment turns to amazement, their skepticism to open-minded inquiry. But even when they accept my words at face value, they find it hard to believe that I have become all that I am as a result of my relationship with a man who lived two thousand years ago. From these conversations over the years, I have discovered that there is more misunderstanding about Jesus of Nazareth than about anyone I've ever talked about. Most people regard him as a religious leader, the founder of Christianity. Others view him simply as a great teacher of morality. Some are so unfamiliar with historical texts and documents that they think of him as nothing more than a myth or legend. But regardless of their opinions about Jesus, nearly all of them tragically misjudge the potential relevance of his life and teachings to their own lives. By thinking of him only as one who is "religious," they have failed to discover all that he can do to shape their thinking and inspire their lives. As a result, their lives are often characterized by uncertainty, frustration, failure, anxiety, discouragement, depression, or even despair. The truth is, Jesus was not *at all* about religion—he was *all* about *reality*.

◉◉ *Whom We Walk With*

A young man during the Great Depression walked out of a bank, despondent after he had been turned down for the loan he desperately needed to save his business. As he walked out, he bumped into Henry Ford. Noticing the young man's look of desperation, Ford stopped and asked what was troubling him. The man told him that all the banks he had visited had rejected his application for a loan. Ford simply said, "Come with me." They walked a little farther down the street to yet another bank. This time, as they opened the door, Henry put his arm around the man for just a moment. Henry then called him by name and said, "Let's get together soon," loud enough for those in the bank to hear. He then whispered to the young man, "Go ask the manager for your loan." The young man quickly replied, "But nothing's changed." Henry smiled and said, "One thing *has* changed. . . . The manager saw you with *me* . . . and believe me, young man, that's all he needed to see." Sure enough, the manager quickly invited the young man into his office and promptly made the loan.

A single encounter changed that young man's life. My relationship with Jesus Christ did the same for me, following a single encounter ... not much different from this young man's. Until that night in 1964, I had thought of Jesus as someone who was all about religion. But that night, he became a personal friend to me, who reached out and simply said, "Come with me." From that moment, Jesus no more represented a *religion* to me than Henry Ford represented a religion to that young man. He quickly became my best friend, my mentor and guide, and so much more.

◎◎ From Atheist at Ten to Believer at Sixteen

When I was ten years old, I found out that there was no Santa Claus. I was heartbroken. My parents confirmed that "Santa" was just a figure people had invented to make Christmas more fun. Santa didn't always watch over me, I discovered; he didn't know when I was sleeping and when I was awake. He didn't know if I had been bad or good. When I went to church the following Sunday, I thought, "God is just like Santa. He isn't real. He's just a figure adults created to make us feel better. He doesn't love us or watch over us. He's no more real than Santa." This became part of my emotional geography until I was about sixteen. I kept going to church with my family, but I didn't believe what I heard nor live as if it mattered. When I was eleven, I started going to a different church with my sister and became very involved with its youth group. I joined the choir and became more closely involved with the church. But I didn't believe. It was easy to be religious—I just had to *do* what the religious people around me did. But *believing* in God was a different story.

In high school I became very interested in science. Most scientists seemed to suggest that religion was more of a crutch than a reality. I found it easier to believe that God did not exist. Then, shortly before I turned sixteen, my sister took me to a meeting of college students in a successful businessman's home. The focus of the meeting was the person of Jesus. The speaker that night was a man who was a scientist—the head chemical engineer of one of the world's largest aerospace companies. He too had been an atheist throughout most of his life. But an amazing thing had happened to him. One day he was in a terrible car accident in which he suffered more than a dozen "fatal injuries"—and yet he had miraculously survived. Afterward, he became convinced that only God could have saved his life. He spent the next six years studying the texts of the world's religions, several hours a night, virtually every night of the week. He initially dismissed Christianity because of all of the hypocrites he knew who claimed to be Christians and yet did not seem to live lives of faith. So he started with the Eastern religions. In all, he studied over three hundred religions during the first years of his quest. He became deeply discouraged by them because in every case they had a common theme— man needed to "work his way" up to God to become acceptable to him. Finally, out of despair, he decided to investigate

Christianity, but not from any particular denomination's point of view. Instead, he decided to just read the Bible and see what Christ had to say.

To his amazement, Jesus didn't talk about religion. He talked about relationships—a relationship with God that men and women could embrace by establishing a personal relationship with Christ. Unlike all of the other religions he studied, Christianity (as explained by Jesus) wasn't about man reaching up to God, it was about God reaching down to man—through the loving sacrifice of His Son.

As I listened to this renowned scientist, I was blown away by his words and his conviction. After the meeting, I talked with him further. He asked me, "Do you do anything around the house to help out your dad?"

"I mow the lawn," I replied.

"Why?" he asked.

"Because Dad's got a bad back, and it's a way I can help out."

He asked, "Do you do it so he'll accept you and love you?"

I answered, "No, I do it because I love him. . . . He's my dad."

"And he loves you because you mow the lawn?" he asked.

"No, he loves me because I'm his son."

"How much does he love you?" he asked.

"A lot more than I deserve!" I answered. Then he made a statement I'll never forget. "*That's* a relationship! *That* is what Jesus wants to have with you . . . a relationship . . . not a religion!"

When he told me that, the light went on for me. Nevertheless, my doubts about the existence of God were as strong as ever. When I told the scientist that, he went out to his car and brought back a book. "This man was just like you and me," he said, referring to the author. "A professor at the most renowned university in the world, he didn't believe in God. Then one day, a friend of his gave him a logical argument that he realized he couldn't refute. And overnight, his doubts were erased, and he too became a believer in God and a follower of Jesus." The author was Professor C. S. Lewis, and the book was *Mere Christianity*. That night I went home and began reading this book. When I came to the chapter entitled "The Shocking Alternative," I came to the same conclusion C. S. Lewis had come to—that God *did* exist, and that Jesus was indeed the person he claimed to be. That night I truly met this man named Jesus and accepted him for all he was.

In the forty-four years that have followed that first encounter, everything in my life that I value most has emanated from my personal relationship and daily walk with him. I have experienced countless miracles, in both my personal and business lives. Not that my life hasn't had its share of failures and trials. To the contrary, my own foolishness has created more failures and trials than I can number. While most of my "trials" have been self-induced, a number have come my way that I didn't create or contribute to. But regardless, through every trial, whatever its severity or cause, my relationship with Jesus has seen me through to the other side, bringing levels of peace, joy, fulfillment, and success beyond my wildest dreams.

Jesus did not walk the earth to start a religion. He came to accomplish a specific mission. In the process, he revealed the keys to living a life of unparalleled achievement and attaining the security and strength to overcome even the greatest adversities.

Jesus didn't walk among us simply to add his ideas to those that had already been passed down through the ages by philosophers such as Plato and Aristotle or religious leaders such as Moses or Buddha. He came to earth to accomplish a specific mission—to provide the means by which mankind could become united with God. Both his life and his words provided the means by which that mission would be accomplished. But that is not the focus of this book. After all, there have been countless books about Jesus's spiritual teachings from counselors and ministers and spiritual leaders far more knowledgeable than I. What I have to offer are the ways in which my personal relationship with Jesus and his teachings and leadership have helped to guide and shape my success in business and at home, ways that I think can help you to transform your life as well. In a way, my goal in writing this book is to look at the "by-products" of Jesus's mission—namely, the extraordinary, life-changing principles and values that he proclaimed with his words and demonstrated with his life—by-products that for anyone else would constitute an achievement unparalleled in human history. As powerful as these principles are, they do not encompass the real purpose of Jesus's mission on earth, nor express but a fraction of the totality of his teachings. Nonetheless, as part of *his* teachings, they provide a powerful means to achieve extraordinary success in our lives, in ways that no one in history has matched or approached.

◎◎ Why Are the Teachings of Jesus Critical to Our Future?

For thousands of years, men and women have tried to understand themselves and the meaning of life. Most of us have yet to figure it out. Jesus, on the other hand, had it *all* figured out. His knowledge of our minds and hearts enables him to "tell it like it is" like no one else, before or since. His intimate knowledge of our natural inclinations, our motives, and our strengths and weaknesses, as well as his perfect knowledge of what's best for us now and in the future, makes him the *ultimate* counselor and guide.

◎◎ Your Personal GPS

I love GPS (global positioning satellite) systems. Because I often talk on the cell phone when I'm driving, I can easily get lost, even in my hometown. When I'm out of town, it's literally impossible for me to go anywhere without missing a number of critical exit ramps or turns. GPS has changed everything for me. I no longer have to look at a map, because a nice lady's voice guides me to my destination quickly and efficiently. If I'm in the wrong lane and miss a turn or an exit, she instantly tells me that she's "recalculating" and directs me to my destination in spite of my mistake. How does the GPS system work? Quite simply, the GPS satellites have a perfect bird's-eye view of the car I'm driving, my current location, the destination I'm traveling to, and every street and turn along the way. It can calculate the best route for me to take. Because I have my own mind and will, I sometimes stray from that path (or forget to turn the GPS on). But when I'm lost or stuck in traffic, I turn it on; it picks up my signal and quickly directs me to an alternate route to my destination as efficiently as possible.

Similarly, through the example of his life, Jesus provides us with a "MapQuest" map of the way we should live and the way we should treat others around us. Through his words, he provides us with a GPS system that, when we take the time to listen, guides us step by step through opportunity and adversity in our day-to-day lives. When we fail to heed his directions and end up lost, in a place we did not intend to be, he can offer the directions we need to get from our current location to our ultimate destination. Because the people of his day had no understanding of cars, satellites, or GPS systems, he talked to them in language they could picture and understand. He called himself the "Good Shepherd" and described his followers as his flock. What does a shepherd do? He leads his sheep to food, water, shelter, and safety. He watches over them. Jesus said, "I am come that they might have life, and have it more abundantly" (Jn. 10:10b). He came to give us an *abundant* life. Does that sound like a religious message, or a promise about how to enrich our lives in the

ways that matter most? Like the GPS system, he does not coerce us into following his way. Rather, he simply offers it to
us, so that we decide whether to listen and follow him or ignore his words and go our own way.

We often think our way of doing things is the only way,
and yet most people today are *not* as successful and satisfied
in their lives and careers as they want to be. Most are less
than completely happy with some of the choices they have
made or the lives they live. Most do not feel they have done
everything they might have with their talent and their time.

Now, don't get me wrong, the "abundant life" Jesus offers
us does not refer to material wealth. I've known millionaires,
and even billionaires, many of whom are more miserable
and "empty" than people of ordinary means. As Jesus said,
"One's life does *not* consist in the abundance of the things he
possesses" (Lk. 12:15, NKJV). I have known a great many
people who have thought that their dissatisfaction would disappear when they got a new car, a new house, a new spouse, a
new title, or whatever they had set their sights set on. But
shortly after they acquired what they had worked so hard to
gain, they discovered that it did not provide the fulfillment
they had longed for. As Jesus declared, the best life has to offer cannot be found in a thing. He said, "For what profit is it
to a man if he gains the whole world, and is himself destroyed or lost?"(Lk. 9:25, NKJV). If we are lost in a forest,
on an ocean, or in the desert, does it make any difference
how rich we are or how much we possess? When we're truly
lost, we're lost. When a man is killed in a car wreck, does it

matter if he was killed in a new Lexus or a used Chevrolet? On the other hand, if a person is truly happy, fulfilled, and secure, does it really matter if he or she is wealthy or not? The good news is, when we follow Jesus's principles, leadership, and advice, we don't have to wait a single pay period, much less a year or a decade, to gain greater fulfillment. The abundant life he wants us to experience is available right now. But to receive it, we have to trust in his directions and follow them.

◎◎ Better Than Winning a Lottery?

Is following the words and wise guidance of this "homeless carpenter" *really* better than winning a lottery? Absolutely! Believe me, no lottery jackpot could have created the lifetime of loving and fulfilling friendships and family relationships that I have experienced thanks to Jesus's guidance. No lottery could have created the successful business career that I have enjoyed. Over the last thirty-two years, my projects have generated more personal wealth than I ever could have imagined possible and have enabled me to form friendships with some of the world's most famous and accomplished individuals. None of that would have been possible without the wisdom and example of Jesus. And no lottery ever could have carried me through the greatest trials of my life. And I'm not alone. I have seen the incredible differences he has made in the lives of so many of my friends. To those who have followed his wise counsel and guidance, Jesus has made the fearful courageous, the anxious confident, the hopeless faithful, the worthless valuable, the failed successful, the selfish caring, the hateful loving, the greedy generous, the unattractive desirable, the insecure secure, the sick healthy, and those who were spiritually lost found.

No lottery jackpot can provide all these benefits. And yet Jesus leads us into this *abundant* life with no strings attached. In the chapters that follow, you will learn a number of his keys to significance, success, and happiness—principles that once acquired can never be taken away. Jesus said, "I am *the* way, *the* truth and *the* life" (Jn. 14:6, NASB). He didn't claim to simply offer *a* way or *a* truth *or a* life; he claimed to *be* the pathway itself, the full embodiment of truth and the ultimate source of life. This ultimate GPS can take us down the path to what matters most in life. So buckle up and get ready for the ride of your life.

"He is no fool who gives that which he cannot keep, to gain that which he cannot lose!"—Jim Elliot, martyred at twenty-nine in 1956 in the jungles of Ecuador

CHAPTER 2

Wake Up and Smell the Starbucks

"Do you still not see or understand? Are your
hearts hardened? Do you have eyes but fail to see,
and ears but fail to hear?"

—JESUS (MARK 8:17–18, NIV)

◎◎ More *Real* Than Dr. Phil

When Dr. Phil is counseling someone on his television show,
at some point he usually cuts through all of the distractions,
excuses, and "minor" issues that are voiced and brings that
person down to earth with his familiar admonition, "Let's get
real." The fact is, at any given moment, in any given situation,
we live in two completely different worlds—a world of illusion and a world of reality.

As Jesus was walking through the streets of Jerusalem
with his disciples, they came upon a man who had been blind
from birth. Because of his blindness, the only way he could
survive was to beg for money from the passing crowds—as
he had been doing his entire adult life. As they approached,
Jesus's disciples asked him, "Who sinned, this man or his parents, that he was born blind?" They assumed that the only

way God would permit such a terrible thing to happen to a child was if the parents had done something terrible, or if God knew the baby would do something terrible in the future and punished him in advance of his deed. Because they believed that God was both loving and just, they saw the situation from *their* perspective—that the man's afflictions were punishment for his sins. Jesus corrected their misunderstanding: "Neither this man nor his parents sinned," said Jesus, "but this happened so that the work of God might be displayed in his life" (Jn. 9:3, NIV).

How many times had that poor man's parents asked, "Why did this happen to our son? What did *we* do that brought this on?" For his entire childhood the man had been deprived of all the wonderful things other kids with normal sight could experience. He had never seen a sunrise or sunset. He could never play the way other kids could play. He could never see his mother's comforting smile or his father's reassuring face. And when he became an adult and his parents could not afford to support him, he was relegated to a life of begging on the streets. "What a tragedy," we think. People at the time looked for reasons for his affliction. But Jesus explained to his followers that this man's plight did not occur as punishment for some action of his or his parents'. Instead, he told them, it served a larger purpose—to reveal to the world the work of God. Jesus then healed the man of his blindness. In a matter of minutes, word of the healing began to spread throughout Jerusalem. The man and his parents were called before a group of the top religious leaders, who grilled them about what had happened. When he insisted that Jesus had healed him, they verbally attacked Jesus. This young man stood up to them and gave one of the most inspiring defenses of Jesus recorded in the Bible. And as a result, he did indeed help to display the work of God to the world. Ridiculed and kicked out of the meeting a short time later, he met Jesus face-to-face and became a devout follower of his.

The blind man and his parents lived under the illusion that his birth defect was a terrible tragedy, and even worse, a punishment from God. They and the community they lived in assumed that was the case because it was the only reason they could think of to explain the young man's affliction. The point is, when we make assumptions about God's intent, we are likely to be wrong—because our own understanding and perspective are so limited. What the boy and his parents were blind to was the *reality*—his blindness had in fact been a gift, one that ultimately brought him to Jesus. Not only did Jesus restore his sight, but his affliction helped lead him to Jesus. What he experienced had literally separated him from the crowd and had transformed him into a man of tremendous influence for the rest of his life, and to countless generations after his death.

Too often we focus on the illusions that appear to be important, but in reality are not. For example, we live with the illusion that we have "all the time in the world," and we respond by procrastinating. We waste time instead of doing the more important things that we should be doing. The illusion is that we have an unlimited amount of time. The reality is that our time is extremely limited, even irreplaceable.

We live under the illusion that money is our most precious possession, and that time is our least precious. The reality is that our time is far more precious than money. The money we spend or lose can usually be replaced. On the other hand, lost time can *never* be regained, not a single minute. The average American lives for 3,952 weeks. If you are fifty years old, you've already lived 2,600 of those weeks. Most people treat their time as if it were a clock that will never stop ticking. In reality, their time is like the countdown clock at a football game . . . except there are no time-outs. From the moment we're born, the clock starts its countdown, and it never stops. Every minute, day, and week that passes is a minute, day, and week gone from our lives that can never be replaced. The fact is, we are not guaranteed another moment, much less an endless expanse of time.

Time and money are just two examples of how we are often blind to reality. Think of the words we speak, or neglect to speak. We convince ourselves that cutting, condescending, or hurtful words don't impact the person we're speaking to. Our spouses, children, employees, or peers will "get over it." The reality is that the hurtful words we utter often do severe damage to the other person and may never be forgotten or easily remedied. Many psychologists believe that verbal and emotional abuse inflict deeper wounds than physical abuse, and are much more difficult to recover from.

Or think of parents who have kids playing sports. Kids play to have fun. Parents and coaches, on the other hand, treat the games or matches as if their children were vying for college scholarships or trying out for the pros—as if a child's future rides on his or her performance. I've seen parents screaming at their own kids, as well as at the kids on the opposing team. One of my sons had a baseball coach who wanted him to "crowd the plate," to let himself be hit by a pitch, in order to advance a runner on first base. My son was nine years old at the time. And when the coach on the other team protested, the two got into a verbal exchange that almost turned into a fistfight.

Professor Greg Smalley of John Brown University recently told me that in a marriage, when an argument *escalates*, the escalation is not about the issue that started the argument. That's only the illusion. The reality is, the escalation takes place because there is a deeper issue that lies festering, unresolved. And as the argument spirals out of control, the real issue rises to the surface, with all the anger and resentment and fear that person has been holding back.

Most of our days and weeks are focused upon the illusions of life rather than on the realities. And as a result, our more fundamental concerns often go unaddressed. As a result, we do not accomplish the things that matter most to us. And our lives hold an undercurrent of discontentment, frustration, stress, disappointment, and failure. Our creativity, productivity, and sense of achievement are limited, and our sense of fulfillment and happiness is compromised.

☙ A Mirage Will Never Give You a Drop of Water!

Growing up in Phoenix, I've seen lots of mirages in the desert. Before I knew what a mirage was, I could have passed a lie-detector test swearing that I saw a pond of water on the highway ahead. The illusions of our daily lives are similar, because we behave as if they reflect reality. For example, I lost my first eight jobs after college. At the time, I believed that losing these jobs meant that I was a failure, that I would never be successful in business. In fact, my third boss said as much when he fired me. "Steve," he said, "you are the single greatest disappointment in my entire career—you will *never* succeed in marketing. You've got twenty minutes to clean out your desk!" Since the man making these statements was the senior vice president of marketing, and I was only a twenty-three-year-old assistant product manager in the marketing department, I believed him. I accepted his judgment of me and my capabilities. His illusion became my belief. It wasn't until job number ten, when I started a new company with my mentor, that I was able to break free from that illusion and believe that I *could* achieve extraordinary success. In our new "start-up," I also dispelled the illusion that I could succeed on my own; I realized that to achieve extraordinary success, I needed to effectively partner with my mentor and others. In a matter of months our new business grew from nothing to millions of dollars per month in sales—all as a result of the very marketing skills that my ex-boss had claimed I didn't possess. When a person begins to see the true reality of any given situation, illusions can no longer prevent or limit his or her success. This is true in business, marriage, parenting, and every other arena in our lives.

๑๑ Dispelling Illusion with a Light Switch

The $64,000 question is, "What can we *do* to see, understand, and respond to the reality of each situation, and *not* be deceived or distracted by illusion?"

Have you ever walked into a room that was totally dark? It's very easy to become disoriented. I've walked into walls, broken my toes on doorjambs, tripped over toys, and banged my shins on chairs and tables. Walking in darkness, you are *not able to see* the reality that surrounds you; it is also conducive to creating further illusions. But if we turn the lights on, we can instantly see everything in its proper perspective. The walls, the tables and chairs, the toys on the floor are clearly visible. And once seen, they are easily avoided.

Jesus said that the world in which we live is filled with darkness. Our natural inclination is to "walk" in that darkness. Consequently, we are easily misled. We believe and embrace illusions about ourselves and others. We misjudge our worth, our abilities, and our potential. We misunderstand the words, actions, and motives of others. We mistakenly value unimportant things and ignore the things that matter most. And in relationships, rather than accepting our own responsibility and mistakes, we are quick to blame the other person.

In John 8:12, Jesus told us, "I am the light of the world. He who follows Me shall not walk in darkness, but have the light of life." In other words, the wisdom and insights that Jesus offers can illuminate every area of our lives and can expose the illusions that we have lived by and reveal the reality behind them. The advice and counsel he gives can empower us to achieve higher levels of success and fulfillment than we could imagine.

◎◎ The Difference Jesus's Light Can Make

People often ask me, "How can your relationship with Jesus make a difference in your career or professional life?" The fact is, Jesus's insights and wisdom have changed everything about my business life. I look at people and opportunities from a different perspective. Too many managers look at employees and potential customers as a *means* of achieving an end. If the employee fulfills their assigned role, the manager or owner embraces them—if they don't, he fires them. In a nutshell, he *uses* people. It is not uncommon for such a person to put a higher value on projects and "things" than on people. To my embarrassment, I've been guilty of this myself. A few years ago, I fell in love with a beautiful, fire-engine red, four-passenger Mercedes convertible that I saw in a showroom. I drove it home that night. A few months later, my three-year-old son decided to take his tricycle out of our garage and go for a ride. It got stuck between my new car and our second car, so he decided to force his way out of the garage. As he pushed it forward, the tricycle gouged a six- or seven-foot gash into the side of the car. At age three, my son didn't think anything of it, other than that he was proud of how strong he was. When I discovered the gash a couple of hours later, I was in shock. I grabbed Ryan, took him out to the garage, and yelled at him. As he realized what he had done, his eyes filled with tears. He started crying . . . not because he had made a scratch on Dad's car, but because the biggest hero in life, his father, was disappointed and angry with him. It was at that moment that the words of Jesus came to me: "For one's life does not consist in the abundance of the things he possesses" (Lk. 12:15, NKJV). I had fallen into the trap of believing that my $80,000 thing was more important than my *priceless* son. The *reality* was, the scratch could be fixed, and the car itself was replaceable. My son is *irreplaceable*. His personal esteem is worth far more to me than any possession. A friend once shared the following two diagrams with me. The one on the left is how most people treat people and things, while the one on the right reflects the reality that Jesus revealed.

The diagram on the right should become a model of how we prioritize our behavior in any situation.

In March of 1976, I was coordinating the launch of a national television advertising campaign for Ambassador Leather, an Arizona-based catalog company. I flew to Omaha, Nebraska, to meet the owner of a call center that would be taking the orders in response to our commercials, which were due to

begin airing soon. When I travel, I usually rent a car at the airport. This time, however, I was picked up at the airport by the
owner of the call center, taken to dinner, and then dropped off
at my hotel. I didn't want to be stuck at the hotel without a car,
so I asked the hotel staff if their driver could take me back to
the airport so I could rent a car. On the way to the airport, the
driver casually mentioned that Pat Boone was in town and was
performing at a concert that night. I asked if he was staying at
the hotel, and the driver replied, "I'm not supposed to tell."

When I came back to the hotel, I was tired and started
toward my room. I had always wanted to meet Pat Boone but
realized he was at the concert and probably wouldn't be back
until much later. Besides, I was a twenty-six-year-old kid, and
he was one of America's greatest entertainers. How could I
possibly meet him? But then a statement that Jesus had made
instantly came into my mind, so I wrote a note to Pat. I went
up to the hotel's front desk and said to the clerk, "Pat Boone
is at the concert right now, but would you please leave this
note in his box and make sure he gets it when he returns?"
She smiled, took the note, and placed it in his box. A few
minutes after midnight, my phone rang. When I picked it up,
the voice on the other end of the line said, "Steve? . . . Pat
Boone." We talked for two hours and then met for breakfast
the next morning. By the time breakfast was over, we had become friends.

A week later, a businessman I respected more than any
other, an entrepreneurial genius, Bob Marsh, made me an incredible offer. "If you could find a product that you and I

could market on TV, we could start our *own* television marketing company." The next day I called Pat Boone and told
him that I was looking for a unique product and that if he
found one, I could go into business with the one man on
earth I most wanted to work with. And I would make Pat the
spokesperson in the national television commercial that we
would create to sell the product. He promised to keep his
eyes open for one. One week later, he was invited to a
Passover dinner at the home of a Beverly Hills rabbi. At that
dinner, the rabbi's sister-in-law, who was a doctor, told Pat
about an acne product she had created. She went to her
car and pulled out a couple of bottles for Pat to give to his
teenage daughters. They began using the product and loved
it. So Pat called me at my office and told me about the product. I asked for samples and began handing them out a few
days later. Everyone who tried it loved it. Bottom line: I quit
my job at the catalog company and moved back to Philadelphia to start a television marketing company with Bob
Marsh. Pat and his daughter Debby agreed to be in our commercial to market the acne cream for no up-front fee (something that was unheard of in entertainment circles). So I
produced a commercial with Pat and his daughter. That two-
minute commercial turned Bob's and my little start-up company into a multimillion-dollar business within a few months.
We went on to create dozens of companies and hundreds of
television campaigns to sell our services and products. During the next thirty years, our companies produced billions of
dollars in sales and affected the lives of millions of families.

What is my point? Until that night in Omaha, I had never

written a note to anyone I didn't know, much less a celebrity. My assumption was, "Pat Boone probably won't respond to a note, so why even bother?" And until that night in Omaha, Pat Boone had *never* responded to the hundreds of notes from strangers left for him during his multidecade singing career. Had I followed my normal routine, I would have rented a car at the airport when I landed and never would have heard from the hotel limo driver that Pat Boone was in town. Had Pat not responded to my note, we never would have met. Had Pat not gone to the Passover dinner, he never would have met the rabbi's sister-in-law, the doctor. Had Pat not agreed to be in our commercial, and agreed to do so for no up-front fee, we could not have afforded to produce the commercial. All of this happened as a result of following specific teachings of Jesus. For example, Jesus said that if I would *knock* on doors in faith, they would be opened; if I would *ask* in faith, I would receive; and if I would *seek* in faith, I would find. His teachings taught me to open my eyes to the opportunities in front of me, and courageously walk through doorways that would have otherwise intimidated me.

◉◉ The World's Ultimate Counselor

In Proverbs, King Solomon warns us that without counsel our plans will fail, and that with a multitude of counselors they will succeed (Prov. 15:22). I've had the benefit of a wonderful coterie of counselors, advisers, partners, and mentors in both my personal and business lives. Without their counsel and wisdom, I would have experienced far more failures and far fewer successes, and much less fulfillment. But even the best counselors are limited in what they can offer. They may know more than we know, but their information, too, is limited. In contrast, Jesus's teachings are not based upon theory, human logic, or reason, or upon human experience, but rather upon truth. Jesus understood in a way none of us can the hearts and minds of men and women, their natural inclinations, their strengths, and their weaknesses.

⊚⊚ Why Is It Critical to Discover, Embrace, and Respond to Realities?

When my son Devin was fifteen, he told my wife, "I hate Dad's cell phone. . . . I wish I could throw it into the trash!" When Shannon told me this, I realized that I had fallen into the trap of believing the illusion that business was more important than giving my undivided attention to my son when we were together. The illusions I had believed were (1) It really didn't matter to him that I was on the phone; (2) It was critical that I handle business affairs whenever they intruded upon our time, even when I was with my children; and (3) My kids could wait, and business couldn't. But the realities that I was ignoring were (1) Devin is a million times more important to me than a fleeting business need; (2) My time with him is limited and precious; and (3) Diverting my attention away from him for the sake of being overly solicitous to a client or business associate was sending him the *wrong* message about my feelings for him and was hurting him.

Jesus warned his followers *not* to allow the needs of adults to crowd out the needs of children. While it was my wife who brought the situation to my attention, it was Christ's words that convinced me I needed to change my behavior.

Throughout my life, the words of Christ have illuminated my path in business and in life. Having met countless people in my business and personal life, I can assure you that focusing on the illusions that surround us is the norm in life, rather than the exception. Here are a few of the common illusions we embrace:

ILLUSION	REALITY
Success is measured by material wealth, job titles, and social status.	Success is evidenced by the positive difference we make and the fulfillment we bring into our own lives and the lives of others.
Love is a feeling.	Love is a decision to act in someone else's best interest.
You have to be "in love" to love, and be loved.	You love because you choose to love, not because you are loved or in love.
The business of adults is more important than kids.	Kids and adults are equally important, but the vulnerability of children gives them a higher priority.
People who are wealthy or successful are more important than those who are not.	All women and men are equally important.

I'll be happy when I get a . . .	True happiness is not a function of getting, but a function of giving and serving.
The future matters more than the present.	Focusing forever on the future robs us of the power of the present.
My past failures mean I cannot succeed in the future.	Past failures can provide the wisdom and insights necessary for success now and in the future.
What I can achieve is limited by education, knowledge, skills, talents, and money.	What we can achieve in the future is determined by the strategies we utilize and the diligence and energy with which we pursue them.
This is as good as it gets.	We can make our lives richer and better.
I'll do it tomorrow.	If you put something off until tomorrow, you'll probably never do it.
Loving "things" is part of life.	Loving things is a waste of affection and time.
Using others for personal gain is par for the course.	Serve others—never use them.

These are just a few of the hundreds of illusions and realities that Jesus illuminates with his words and insights. For every illusion he exposes, he reveals a reality that will bring us higher levels of success and greater degrees of happiness and fulfillment. In the chapters ahead, you'll discover the how-tos of using the power of his wisdom and the example of his daily life to improve and enrich every area of your life.

Understanding Changes Minds— Action Changes Lives

TURNING UNDERSTANDING INTO ACTION

1. List the illusions that you embrace in your life. (First, list as many illusions as possible that you hold in your attitudes, beliefs, or behavior. Next, list those illusions that you hold in your relationships with friends, spouses, or children. Finally, list those that are true of your business life.)

2. For each illusion you identify above, identify a corresponding reality that you have overlooked or been blind to.

3. List specific things you can do to change how you think or respond.

CHAPTER 3

The Six Keys from the Life of Jesus That Can Transform an Ordinary Performer into an Extraordinary Achiever

⊚⊚ From Twelve to Hundreds of Millions

Until the age of thirty, Jesus's days were spent in a carpenter's shop. When he began his ministry, he went into the villages and countryside owning nothing more than the clothes on his back. He never traveled more than a couple hundred miles from his home and never entered a big city. Three and a half years after he began proclaiming his message, he was arrested at night and executed the next day. During his brief ministry, he preached to tens of thousands, but most of his time was spent teaching the twelve men who left their livelihoods to follow him. When he was crucified, only one of the twelve had the courage to stay with him. One betrayed him, and the other ten had fled for their lives. If ever there was a scenario for failure, this was it: spend three years training twelve men, and have all but one of them run away as soon as you're in serious trouble. And here is the most amazing thing of all. All of this happened in an obscure part of the world that the ruling Roman Empire really didn't care that much about. And it happened at a time when there was no Internet, television, radio, newspapers, magazines, or even printing press to help spread Jesus's message. If ever a story and a message should have died in obscurity, *this* is it! But it didn't.

Within a year of his death, his eleven followers had multiplied into thousands. In the next few decades, those thousands turned into tens of thousands, and those tens of thousands ultimately grew into hundreds of millions over the centuries. At the time of his execution, it seemed like his life had been a terrible failure. And yet in the months, years, and centuries that followed, he has become recognized the world over as the *greatest* man who ever lived. What happened?

◉◉ The Human Side of Christ

As a Christian, it's easy to say that the growth of Christianity is the result of God performing His miraculous work on earth. Although I believe that to be true, there are behaviors that Jesus exhibited and strategies that he used and actions that he performed that helped to create these extraordinary outcomes. The value and power of these behaviors, strategies, and actions are easily overlooked when we simply attribute his unparalleled success to his divinity. There are just as many stars in the daytime sky as there are at night. And yet in the daytime they remain unseen because of the brightness of the sun. In much the same way, the divine nature of Jesus's words, behavior, and works is so blindingly brilliant that the awesome starlight of his humanity is easily missed. For years, I overlooked these human aspects of his life and their implications and value to my life. And yet they have the power to effect extraordinary change in our lives and help us to achieve extraordinary success at work and at home.

What do I mean by that? Let me illustrate my point. The New Testament teaches that on one occasion Jesus miraculously fed a crowd of thousands from a single serving of fish and bread. *That's* a miracle. But the crowd had been following him for three days, with little or no food. Have *you* ever followed *anyone* around for three days, just to watch what he or she did and listen to what he or she said? Witnesses wrote that when he spoke, his words, his manner of speaking, and the authority with which he taught *amazed* the crowds. Shouldn't we ask what communication techniques he used? In what manner did he speak? How did he teach with such authority? Jesus wasn't merely a great communicator—he was in fact the greatest communicator to ever walk the earth. Since communication is the number one challenge in business, the number one problem in marriage, and the most important tool in parenting, can we not learn more effective ways of communicating from the greatest communicator who ever lived?

Jesus told his followers, "Learn from me" (Matt. 11:29). He didn't mean for us to simply learn from his words. He was telling us to learn from *him* . . . from his life, his behavior, his attitudes, his actions, his manner, and his words. Of course, we are to learn from his teachings—that is his preeminent call—but not to learn from the *examples* of his daily life is to overlook life-changing and life-empowering lessons that we may never see anywhere else. His meaning, his mission, his methods, his message, his manner, and how he accomplished his missions, should *all* be carefully examined and learned from.

You may be thinking, "Can I *really* learn life-changing strategies and skills by looking at the life of a man who lived over two thousand years ago?" Well, here is what one of the greatest military geniuses of all time, Napoleon Bonaparte, said about Jesus:

> I know men; and I tell you that Jesus Christ is no mere man. Between Him and every other person in the world there is no possible term of comparison! Superficial minds see a resemblance between Christ and the founders of empires, and the gods of other religions. That resemblance does not exist. . . . Everything in Christ astonishes me. His spirit overawes me, and his will confounds me. He is truly a being by Himself. His ideas and sentiments, the truth which He announces, His manner of convincing, are not explained either by human organization or by the nature of things. . . . The nearer I approach, the more carefully I examine, everything is above me—everything remains grand, of a grandeur which overpowers. . . . One

can absolutely find nowhere, but in Him alone, the imitation or the example of His life. . . . I search in vain in history to find the similar to Jesus Christ. Neither history, nor humanity, nor the ages, nor nature, offer me anything with which I am able to compare it or explain it.

◉◉ Meaning, Mission, Message, Manner, Method, and Mission Accomplished

When you look at these six aspects of Jesus's life, you'll see a level of purpose, drive, perseverance, and congruity never seen before or since. His "whys" for doing what he did created a degree of purpose that resulted in an unwavering commitment to achieve his goals. His mission was a perfect reflection of his meanings. His message, which he proclaimed with his words and demonstrated with his life, perfectly reflected his mission and meanings. The methods he employed to accomplish his mission and the manner in which he performed those actions—and handled every situation in his life—were also in perfect congruity. There was no hypocrisy or inconsistency between what he said and what he did or *how* he did what he did! He never had to hide behind the situational ethic of "the ends justify the means," because he refused to compromise his means to achieve his ends.

These six aspects of his life emanated from the very core of who he was. They gave him the incomparable human tools to accomplish his missions on earth.

❦❦ Why We Settle for Mediocrity

The vast majority of us today rarely achieve better than mediocrity. Of course, we would all love to be wildly successful in
our jobs and lives—yet surveys show that 80 percent of us
would change our jobs or careers if we were able to do so.
Less than 5 percent of the population earns an income they
are satisfied with. Moreover, most people fail to achieve the
financial independence they work their entire lives hoping to
achieve. By the time we turn sixty-five, only 5 percent of us
are financially independent. The other 95 percent of us must
continue to work just to make ends meet, or become dependent upon government assistance and the charity of family
and friends.

When it comes to success in our personal lives, most of
us do not fare much better. Nearly everyone who marries believes at the time that they will remain married to that person
for the rest of their lives. They believe that their mutual love
and hard work will enable that relationship to last a lifetime.
And yet the fact is, at least 52 percent will divorce. And of
those who remain married, most would not consider their relationship ideal.

Why is mediocrity and failure the norm for most people,
rather than the exception? Is it because we are poorly educated? Is it because of our parents' social and financial standing? Is it because we're not smart enough? In each case, the
answer is no. The vast majority of people are as smart and
educated as those people who have achieved extraordinary

success. But the one-tenth of 1 percent of the population that actually *do* achieve extraordinary success do so by using *strategies* that the other 99.9 percent of the population do not use. What the world's most successful people have in common is: meaning that drives their mission; the ability to effectively communicate their message; and methods or strategies that help to create extraordinary outcomes. As a result, they *accomplish* their missions. Unlike Jesus, however, too often they use a manner that achieves success but *fails* to achieve fulfillment and happiness for themselves and others. Those who achieve extraordinary outcomes in their work often experience devastating failure in those areas of their lives where they don't apply these same strategies and methods.

By following the example of Jesus's life they will achieve not only extraordinary success but lasting fulfillment and happiness. By doing so, they will be able to provide unlimited blessings to their families, friends, and others they work with and influence.

◎◎ It All Starts with *MEANING*

Why did Jesus do what he did? Most of us know *what* he did, and what he did captures most of our attention. And yet his "whys" are just as important as his "whats." "But how on earth can we ever know his whys?" you might ask. The answer is simple—he told us. Why are his whys so important? Because they serve as the foundation that gives strength and purpose to our mission. If you have ever seen a foundation upon which a single-story house is built, you've noticed that there's no hole in which the foundation is set—it is simply a flat slab of concrete upon a well-graded piece of ground. On the other hand, if you've ever seen the construction of a high-rise building, you know that the higher the building, the deeper the hole in which the foundation is poured. The same is true in life. The deeper your whys, the higher and more secure your accomplishments will be. The vast majority of us have very shallow whys; often we don't even know our whys at all. Thus, the vast majority of us rarely accomplish the extraordinary. We build lives of mediocrity—OK jobs, OK careers, OK marriages, and OK families. On the other hand, those people who have deeper whys, and know and understand their whys, nearly always achieve greater success. When their whys in their business pursuits are deep, they can achieve extraordinary success in their careers. When their whys in their marriages and families are deep, their marriages and family relationships are secure and fulfilling.

Jesus had an infinitely deep why—to save humanity and bring us closer to God. He had equally deep and secure whys for *everything* he did. In fact, his whys were so deep that when he was given the choice of abandoning his mission to save his life, he stayed true to his mission and sacrificed his life. His why was so deep he wouldn't let *anything* deter him from accomplishing his purpose.

What are your whys? How deep are they dug? In the next chapter, you'll discover Jesus's whys and see how they empowered him to accomplish the impossible. Then you'll learn how to discover your own whys—and how to create even greater and more secure whys in every important area of your life.

Jesus didn't just "go with the flow" or "make the best" of each day. Because Jesus had clearly defined purposes, he knew exactly why he was here and where he was going. Today, most people have no idea why they're here or where they are going. Like a raft on a river, they just "go with the flow," wherever the rivers of life and livelihood take them. Because they haven't discovered their whys, they've never embarked on a genuine mission. And without a mission, they will have little purpose and few significant goals.

◎ A Message That Reflects Your Life and Advances Your Mission

Effective communication is *not* simply about speaking or writing well. Effective communication results when your listener or reader clearly and accurately *understands* what you're saying and *feels* what you are feeling. Persuasive communication goes one step further, providing an incentive to act upon that understanding and feeling. Gary Smalley states that one of the most common complaints of both women and men is that their spouse "just doesn't get it": "No matter how many times I tell him, he just doesn't understand." But the truth is, when the person you are addressing "doesn't get it," it's usually not their fault, but yours—*you* have failed to *effectively* communicate your needs or desires. But it doesn't have to be that way. Whenever Jesus wanted someone to understand what he was saying, he had no trouble communicating it. And when he wanted to motivate them to action, he *persuaded* the other person, rather than trying to manipulate them. In chapter 6, we'll take a closer look at how Jesus was able to communicate so effectively and persuasively and see how we can apply these same techniques to our own important relationships at work and at home. How effective are these techniques? Using them, I was able to motivate more than twenty-five million people to call our call centers to order our goods and services. And each time, I had only two minutes to communicate my ideas to the viewers and persuade them to take action. That's how powerful these techniques are.

The fact that Jesus was the most effective and persuasive communicator who ever lived does not mean that every person he spoke to did exactly what he wanted them to do. Some people simply did not *want* to know or respond to his message, under any circumstances. Jesus was not interested in trying to manipulate these folks. He simply held up truth like a beacon of light, to reveal the best paths and actions people could take. But the choice was theirs. Similarly, there are times when we effectively and persuasively communicate, and yet the other person reacts differently than we had hoped.

◎◎ Acting in a *Manner* That Reflects Your Meaning

If the *manner* in which you act is not consistent with your meaning, your mission, or your message, you'll never achieve the success you would otherwise achieve. In other words, *how* you do what you do is as important as *what* you do. What you *do* is as important as what you say. Moreover, *how* you say what you say is as important as *what* you say. Jesus talked about loving your neighbor as yourself and loving your enemies. Do you think his message would have been believed if he himself had not loved others?

More often than not, our missions and our messages are ignored or rejected, not because they aren't valid or worthy but because our actions or manner contradicts the message we proclaim. By looking at the life of Jesus, we can learn how to underscore, enhance, and empower our mission and message rather than detract from or interfere with it. As you incorporate his attitude and actions into your life, you will be able to influence and empower and love others to a degree you have never before experienced.

In 1969, I became friends with a fellow student at Arizona State University, Jim Shaughnessy. Jim and I were as different as night and day. He was an All-American football player, and I didn't have an athletic bone in my body. But over the next few years, we became best friends. Apart from my immediate family, he has been my best friend for more than forty years. Among other things, Jim is truly the most loving and generous person I know. He can make whomever he meets, regardless of their age or the circumstances of their meeting, feel like they are truly awesome. As a result of the way he treats people, there must be at least a thousand people around the world who would name Jim as their best friend in life. Watching the way Jim treats children, I learned how to express my love of my children in ways that I would have otherwise never known. By watching his way of making complete strangers feel valued, I have learned how to treat everyone who crosses my path. His *manner* of loving others is so exemplary that all I need to do to make anyone feel loved and valued is to think to myself, "How would Jim act with this person?" As a result of Jim's example, I have had the chance to make thousands of people feel loved and valued.

But as good as it has been to have Jim's example in my mind, it cannot begin to compare with the example of Jesus.

◉◉ Creating Miraculous Results in Minimum Time

As I've discussed in earlier books, I flunked out of my first eight jobs after college. I started my own business twice and failed. I couldn't succeed at anything, no matter how hard I tried. But on job number nine, along with my mentor, I was able to create a television ad campaign that doubled my employer's annual sales, from $30 million to $60 million, in the three months that I worked for that company. And on job number ten, my mentor and I created a company that ultimately grew into more than a dozen multimillion-dollar companies achieving billions of dollars in sales. My "hit rate" became the highest of any television direct-marketing company in the world. My campaigns generated more than 25,000,000 calls. In one campaign alone, my commercials generated more than 125,000 calls per week. What was the difference between all of my failures and the incredible successes that followed? The answer is simple. In the first eight jobs and my first two businesses, I used methods or strategies that *didn't* work. On jobs number nine and ten, I used methods and strategies that worked phenomenally well. The only thing that changed was that I was using effective strategies that I hadn't used previously.

Most people use methods that *don't* work. The result is they're stuck in the status quo. Whether in their business lives or personal lives, they experience little (if any) significant improvement. What is worse, their methods never change. They just keep doing the same things, over and over again. They may do them with more intensity, commitment, or consistency, but the methods remain the same. *Doing more of the same never brings about change!* The only way to bring about significant change for the better is to use different methods or strategies that are substantially more effective. The methods Jesus used are the same methods that have made an incalculable contribution to the successes I have experienced.

∞ Purpose-*Driven* Is Not Enough

One of the greatest and most successful books published in recent years is *The Purpose Driven Life*, by Rick Warren. It clearly illustrates the vanity of going through life aimlessly. It wonderfully articulates the reasons for and benefits of living a life that is driven by purposes of true value. I learned an enormous amount from it, and I recommend it to everyone I know. The next two chapters are going to focus on finding your whys and on clearly defining your goals or missions. But although Jesus agreed with the need to live a purpose-driven life, he offered no reward or accolades for being "purpose driven." Instead, he put a much higher value on achieving a purpose-*accomplished* life. He taught that a person should be judged not just by their words or efforts, but, like a tree, by the "fruit" that their life actually produces.

As an employer, I don't want my employees to simply *try* to produce extraordinary outcomes—I want them to actually produce those outcomes. I don't want my assistant to *try* to make people who call us feel welcome, I want her to make them feel more welcomed and valued than they ever could have expected. And she does just that! The same is true in my marriage and parenting relationships. I don't want to just *try* to be a good husband and father, I want to *be* the absolute best husband a woman could ever have and the absolute best dad my children could have. Yes, I want to be mission driven, but more important, I want to achieve "mission accomplished." Jesus was the ultimate example of a "mission accomplished" life. His missions were the most critical missions ever undertaken. And from the beginning of his life to the end, the opposition and adversity he faced would have stopped anyone else. When we study *how* he overcame that adversity and what he did to accomplish his missions, we see life-changing examples that we can apply to ourselves. Like it or not, others will ultimately judge us by the goals we actually accomplish in life. Even more important than how others judge us is the ultimate sense of fulfillment we will experience when we *accomplish* what we set out to do in life. And that fulfillment is something that no title, no amount of money, and no praise can ever replace.

Understanding Changes Minds—
Action Changes Lives

1. Create a list of the most important areas of your life.
2. Create a second list, prioritizing those areas. (Try to prioritize them not according to what you *think the order should be*, but according to what it *is* in light of your actions and behavior.)
3. Create a third list, prioritizing those areas according to the priority that you think they *should* have.

MEANING That Motivates: Finding Your "Whys"

"He is like a wise man building a house, who dug deep and laid the foundation on the rock. And when the flood arose, the stream beat vehemently against the house, and could not shake it, for it was founded on the rock."

—JESUS (LUKE 6:48, NKJV)

On July 4, 1776, the American colonies declared their independence from the strongest nation in the world. The American colonies had almost no money to supply their tiny army and navy. And yet, knowing their action would result in their homes and their homeland being invaded by the greatest army and navy on earth, they courageously decided to go their own way and declare their independence. England initially believed it could squash the American upstarts in a matter of weeks, with minimal losses. But the British were wrong. Five grueling years later, the world's most powerful military was defeated by a ragtag military force a fraction of its size. How could this happen?

For nearly fifty years scientists and engineers all over the world raced to create the world's first practical electric lightbulb, one that would give off sufficient light while lasting a reasonable length of time. Thomas Edison and his small staff of engineers and technicians set their sights on inventing a practical electric lightbulb within three years. How could they hope to accomplish in three years what the world's foremost scientists and engineers hadn't been able to do in fifty years? And yet Edison and his team did it.

When James J. Braddock challenged the heavyweight champion of the world, Max Baer, virtually no one believed Braddock could win. In fact, most feared for his life. Baer was younger, stronger, and so powerful in the ring that two of his opponents had died from the massive brain injuries that he had inflicted. Braddock, on the other hand, was an impoverished "has-been" who had never fought anyone of the caliber of Baer. Plagued by arthritis, Braddock was made a 10–1 underdog by the oddsmakers.

But on the evening of June 13, 1935, the sports world and an audience of thirty thousand boxing fans were shocked when Braddock won a fifteen-round, unanimous decision to become the heavyweight champion of the world. How did he do it?

The answer to all three of these "against all odds" stories is the same. The inferior American army and navy beat the vastly superior British army and navy because the "why" for the Americans was infinitely deeper than the "why" for the British forces. Americans were fighting for their independence and for their very survival, as well as the survival of their families. The British, on the other hand, were three thousand miles away from home, fighting for a king back in London living in royal luxury. Their own homeland and their families were not threatened. The only thing at stake for them was the sovereignty of the British Empire.

Thomas Edison's why, too, was much deeper and more compelling than the whys of the engineers and scientists who had gone before him. They were all simply trying to invent a lightbulb. Edison, on the other hand, was trying to invent a device that would create a universal demand for electric power—power that he intended to provide to every household, farm, factory, and office in the world. His electric lightbulb was simply a means to an infinitely greater end, one that he felt certain would transform the world.

And James Braddock's "why" was also measurably deeper and stronger than Max Baer's. Baer was simply fighting to hold on to his crown. Win, lose, or draw, at the end of the fight he would return to his mansion and continue to enjoy the benefits of his past success. When *Braddock* was asked by reporters, "What are you fighting for?" his reply was simply "Milk." His family was destitute. Not only were his kids living in squalor, but he literally didn't have enough money to buy his family food. In other words, he wasn't fighting for fame, glory, or a bigger payday. He was fighting for the very survival of his family.

In Luke 6:48, Jesus tells us if a foundation is dug deep enough, and anchored into a rock, the structure built on that foundation will survive any storm. Said another way, the deeper and more solid a person's foundational whys, the more sure that person will be to succeed at what he or she undertakes.

As you will see in the next chapter, the missions that Jesus undertook were the toughest ever undertaken by anyone in history. And his adversaries did everything they could to sabotage his efforts. But each of his missions was built upon whys that ran so deep and were built on such a solid rock that they could not be deterred or defeated.

◉◉ The Whys upon Which Jesus Built His Life and His Missions

When someone tells me of a project they are taking on, I often ask them, "What is your why for doing that?" Most of the time a blank look crosses their face; they ask what I mean by "your why." After I explain, they tend to come up with superficial answers, such as, "I guess it's because I want to make more money." Jesus was never so vague or superficial. Here are just a few of the whys he identified for taking on his missions.

Jesus's Whys

- He was commanded by God to do and say what he did and said.
- His love for his Father and his desire to obey and please Him
- His desire to "glorify" God to all mankind
- His love for mankind
- His desire to provide eternal life to his followers
- His desire to serve mankind and sacrifice his life as ransom for those who would follow him

• His desire to finish what he knew to be the work of God on earth

As you look at his whys, you notice that the whys that motivate most of us are missing from the list. Nowhere do you find money. Or material possessions. Or sexual fulfillment. Or the approval and applause of others. Nowhere do you see any hint of self-gratification at all. Even the fear of death is missing.

As you look at the nature of his whys, it becomes clearer *how* he was able to accomplish his "*impossible missions*," despite the temptations and adversity he faced. When Pilate said to him, "Do You not know that I have power to crucify You, and power to release You?," Jesus replied, "You could have no power at all against Me unless it had been given to you from above." At any time, Jesus could have abandoned his mission and saved his life. But his whys were too profound— he felt not even the slightest temptation to do so. Was he looking forward to the horrific execution that was in store for him? Of course not! If there had been any other way to fulfill his mission, I'm sure he would have gladly taken it. But there was no other. His only choice was either to fulfill his mission completely or to abandon it totally . . . and his *whys* gave him everything he needed to see it through to the end.

◎◎ What Your Whys Can Mean to You

To accomplish our day-to-day tasks, most of us don't need a why . . . we need only a to-do list or a calendar. But to accomplish a major project or a life mission, we need a why for a number of reasons. Our levels of energy, creativity, productivity, perseverance, and passion will all be determined and empowered by our why. The greater the mission, and the more difficult and time-consuming it is, the deeper our why must be to help us achieve our goal successfully. Less difficult, shorter-term missions, on the other hand, do not require a deeper why. Here are a number of whys, arranged according to their depth and profoundness.

1. *Personal Gratification.* This why stems from our desire to satisfy our feelings, from our romantic yearnings to our passion for a hobby, a project, or a relationship. This is the most common why in our personal lives and at work, but also the least stable and empowering. It drives a lot of good behaviors, as well as a lot of negative behaviors. It can encourage us to accept a good outcome in place of an extraordinary outcome. And it quickly evaporates in the heat of even the least adversity.

2. *Money and Material Possessions.* This is another common why for most of us. It is what drives so many of our careers in the workplace, and it influences or determines many of our decisions and priorities in our personal lives as well. It produces more drive and commitment than personal gratification, but it fails to produce the kind of commitment that will sustain us through adversity.

3. *The Approval or "Applause" of Others.* This is one of the greatest motivational whys for children and adults. In early childhood we desperately seek the approval and applause of our parents. During adolescence the need for approval and applause of our peers begins to replace our need for approval from our parents. For many adults, however, this external approval remains the most powerful why in their lives. I've worked with dozens of America's most famous entertainers: Academy Award–winning actors, Grammy Award–winning singers, and Emmy Award–winning television stars. For many of them, this is the *primary* why in their lives. It drives them to succeed but at the same time leaves them feeling terribly insecure.

4. *Fear of Failure, Fear of Criticism, Fear of Consequences, Fear of Loss.* Fear is one of the most powerful motivating forces of our behavior. It is certainly a more powerful why than the first three I described above. But although fear can create significant short-term results, it can also produce very negative long-term consequences. When a person's why is fear, they may "get the job done" or accomplish a specific mission. But the stress created by fear is destructive to us and to our relationships, and it can undermine our long-term effectiveness.

5. *Our Survival Instinct.* This is one of the greatest forces there is to ensure our survival in the face of

danger or to succeed at a *single* goal. However, it is only a mediocre why for achieving long-term goals. Like most fears, it can spur a person to get a specific job done, but *not* in the most productive and beneficial way. Such thinking is driven by a "whatever it takes" mentality and rarely produces sustainable or repeatable long-term outcomes. It certainly won't produce a template for future achievement or create a pattern of achievement that will foster a lifetime of excellence.

6. ***Personal Achievement.*** This is the first of the foundational whys that is anchored deeper into bedrock. This *why* is different from that of self-gratification, although one of its benefits is personal gratification and fulfillment. When the desire to do well in one's life or career is built into our inner being, it can drive a lifetime of achievement. Each time we complete a mission, the fulfillment we experience drives us to succeed at our next mission. The more we achieve, and the more we excel, the more this becomes woven into the fabric of who we are. Thomas Edison developed a specific technique to instill a powerful drive for personal achievement into himself, his staff, and every project he pursued. We'll look more closely at this technique in a moment.

7. ***Love.*** This why is anchored even deeper into our bedrock. But the kind of love I'm referring to is *not*

sexual or romantic love. When most of us think of love, we think of a feeling. *That* type of love is often built upon sand rather than anchored into a rock. Feelings can change in a moment. The kind of love I'm talking about is best defined as a total commitment to honor and value another person—to value them equally or above yourself and your own personal needs and desires. This kind of love drives us to do whatever it takes to complete the task at hand, and to complete it in the best manner possible.

8. *Family.* Today's family relationships are all over the board—from loving and committed ones to dysfunctional and hurtful ones. When we are truly committed to loving our family, our family can become one of the most powerful and driving whys for long-term achievement, in the best possible way.

9. ***Connection to God.*** When people are truly connected to God, they endeavor to serve God with a loving, devoted, and obedient heart. This is without a doubt the strongest-anchored why that I know of to drive a mission and to achieve extraordinary accomplishments no matter what it takes. Many people are religious, but people who consistently *act* on faith and a sense of purpose are rare. This is a love that is characterized not by a feeling, but rather by a commitment of the head and the heart to live a life every day that is in line with their faith.

In 1976, the man I admired most in business, Bob Marsh, invited me to be his partner in a new marketing company. Our first project was Acne Staten, the product Pat Boone brought to me. If it succeeded, Bob and I would have a chance to build a great business together that could change both of our lives. On the other hand, if that project failed, Bob could lose his media company, his home, and everything he had spent a lifetime building. His employees would all lose their jobs as well. If we failed, I would lose my "new job," and the greatest business opportunity of my life. But this was not what drove me. I was *really* driven by one why, and one why only. I loved Bob Marsh! He was like a second dad to me. He was betting everything he owned on me and my ability to create a two-minute television commercial that would succeed, one that would sell enough of our product to pay for the television time and generate enough profit to launch and build our new business. More than anything in the world, I wanted to hit a grand-slam home run that would pay him back for the love he had shown me.

That why was deep enough to drive me and my partners to succeed for the first twenty years of our business. But when Bob became less active and retired from our business, the power of that why began to dissipate. My whys became more superficial—personal gratification, the admiration of my partners, and money. During those years, I still hit home runs, but I also experienced a growing number of strikeouts. Since one home run generated enough profit to pay for a lot of strikeouts, our business grew, but sometimes it was a roller-coaster sort of growth.

Then, in 1995, our company experienced two marketing disasters that brought us to the brink of collapse. We lost millions of dollars and had only enough money to try one last project. If that project failed, we would be out of business, and each of the partners would lose just about everything we owned. Worse than that, we would lose the opportunity to continue working with one another. We were as close as a family, in some ways even closer. We held a partners' meeting where the partners laid out six possible projects. I was asked the critical question: "Which one do you want to do?" My answer was, "If we can make the Total Gym more attractive, lighter-weight, and collapsible to fit under a bed, deliver it to consumers fully assembled, and get Chuck Norris and Christie Brinkley to be our spokespersons, then I'd choose the Total Gym."

We were able to achieve all of those things, and I wrote and produced the first Total Gym infomercial in 1996. We ran the show on a handful of television stations in our market test. The sales were disappointing and certainly not good enough to take the multimillion-dollar risk of rolling it out into a national campaign. It looked like we were doomed. But we *couldn't* let it die. Our whys were deeply anchored into a bedrock of love for one another. One of my partners, Dave Marsh, came up with two radical marketing ideas that we wanted to test. We swallowed hard and spent six months testing and verifying the effectiveness of Dave's ideas—they both worked! Our million-dollar loss was turned into a billion-dollar winner. *That* is the power of a why that is built upon a foundation that is anchored deep into the rock. And *love* is one of the most deeply anchored foundational whys.

◎◎ Discovering *Your* Whys, and Creating Deeper Ones

What are the whys that drive your career, your performance in your job, your marriage, your relationships with your children, and your relationships in the larger world? Are they deep enough, anchored into bedrock? At the end of the chapter I've suggested an exercise that may help you identify your whys. Once you discover your why for a specific aspect of your life, or for a mission or project, ask yourself if you can deepen it. If you can't, and it's a more shallow, superficial why, consider replacing it with one that is more meaningful and better anchored.

For more than thirty years, one of my roles in our company has been to search for "breakthrough" products to which our company could acquire the marketing rights. Once we acquired the rights to such a product, I would create a marketing strategy, contract with a major celebrity to be our product spokesperson, and then produce television commercials and infomercials to market that product to millions of people. Throughout my career, one of the whys that drove my efforts in business had been personal achievement. I loved hitting home runs, and I hated striking out. But in 2006, all that changed for me.

While working on a side project (marketing a piece of software that protects children from Internet predators and

pornography), I met one of the world's leading medical research scientists. In the course of our conversation, he told me
about his development of a nutritional supplement, one that
offered extraordinary benefits in the area of antiaging and optimal health. I began taking it, and I found that within a couple
of days, it made a significant difference in my energy level. I
knew I had found my next product. We formed a new company, Max International, to market it. At this point, my why
was the same as it had been on other business endeavors—
namely, personal achievement. I saw this product as a potential
marketing home run.

My assistant's husband had been a serious baseball player
until he finally retired from semipro baseball at the age of
thirty-seven. At the age of forty-one, he developed a number
of ailments linked to cellular inflammation that severely limited his physical activity. His energy level was so low he was
falling asleep at his desk during the day and unable to sleep
well at night. For three years, he had the energy of a wet noo-
dle and would tell you that on a one-to-ten scale, his quality
of life was less than a one. A month after I started taking the
supplement, I gave him a couple months' supply, believing
that it would significantly increase his energy level. As it
turned out, it did a whole lot more than that. Within a few
weeks, he was like a whole new man and told me he was feeling better at forty-four than he had felt at twenty-four. A few
months later, he was playing baseball again, for the first time
in seven years. He was pitching an average of seven innings
a game. And he hit two home runs, including one that was

almost four hundred feet. His team won the state amateur baseball championship, in which he pitched ten innings.

His experience completely changed my why. At this point, we had less than a few hundred people on the product. Yet I had just seen a near-miraculous transformation. I wondered, "How many more people's lives would be radically changed if we took this product to the masses?" What had simply been a wonderful business opportunity had now become a cause! My why was no longer about personal achievement; it was about transforming people's quality of life. In the months that followed, as more and more people tried the supplement, we continued to hear more amazing stories. People were seeing an increase in their energy and focus, as well as experiencing quicker recovery times from exercise with a lot less soreness. The list of benefits seemed to grow every month. Finally, my why became so broad and deep, so overpowering, that I retired from the company I had co-founded in 1976—a flourishing company that had made me tens of millions of dollars in personal income. Why? Because my new why was anchored so much deeper into the bedrock of my heart. Bringing the supplement to the awareness of the public wasn't just about my own personal success—it was about making a significant difference in the lives of millions.

◉◉ You Don't Have to Wait for a "Miracle Product" to Deepen Your Whys

The good news is, you don't need a once-in-a-lifetime break-through supplement to deepen the whys in your life. Any why in life can be deepened or exchanged for a deeper, more powerful why, just by using the technique that Thomas Edison used. In addition to creating the lightbulb, Edison created an effective means of generating power and transferring it to our homes. He created recorded sound and movies and patented the modern system for making cement. In all, he created more patented breakthroughs than any individual in history. What was his secret to achieving such unparalleled success? It was his technique for discovering and deepening his whys.

Edison started with a clear vision for what he wanted to accomplish in a project (or mission). To do this, he would write a description of what he wanted to create—and what it was intended to accomplish—on a single page of his journal. He would then make a small line drawing of that idea on the page. (Edison did very little "pure" research—research solely to uncover a scientific truth. Every one of his inventions and breakthroughs was aimed at creating a machine or device or process that would change and improve our lives.) His next step was what I call the "deepening" of his whys. He would make a detailed list of all of the broad ramifications of achieving his mission. While his idea or project description rarely took more than a single page, his list of broad ramifications usually took a number of pages. Here is my paraphrase of his "broad ramifications" pages for his mission of creating a practical, affordable lightbulb.

If I create a practical, long-lasting, and affordable electric lightbulb, then every home, factory, office building, and farm in America will want to replace its dangerous and higher-maintenance kerosene lamps and gaslights with electric lightbulbs. If every home, factory, office building, and farm in America wants lightbulbs, then they will need electric power lines in their homes and buildings to turn on those lights and keep them on, allowing me to create the means of generating that power. And once they have electric power in their homes and offices to run their electric lights, they will be interested in other electric appliances, tools, and machinery to reduce their labor and increase their efficiency and productivity, allowing me to invent those electric devices. If I can provide electric lights and machines and electric power in America, it will transform our lives. And then I can duplicate that throughout Europe, Asia, Africa, and South America.

By deepening his why, Edison, instead of just inventing an electric lightbulb, saw a way to use this invention as a springboard to transform life in the twentieth century, by putting electric power into every home, farm, factory, and office building throughout the world. This broader and deeper why not only fueled his passion and the passion of his staff and investors but gave him the determination to never give up, regardless of his failures or the adversity he faced.

The good news is, we can apply this same technique to any important endeavor in our lives. For example, when we planned the launch of a study-skills video series, *Where There's a Will There's an A*, our initial why was an economic one. We created three programs, one for middle school and junior high students, one for high school students, and one for college students. At the time, my daughter had been kicked off the cheerleading squad at her high school because her GPA for a quarter had dropped below the minimum necessary to be on the squad. When I told her to take three hours to watch this seminar, she replied, "Dad, when are you going to understand that I'm an athlete and an artist, *not* a student?" I told her, "When are *you* going to understand that *I'm* your parent!" So she went to her room to view the seminar. Three hours later she came down and said, "I'll never get another B on a term paper again . . . nothing but straight A's!" I asked her what had happened. She replied, "Now I know what my teachers want and how to give it to them." The professor who created this series told me it could literally turn a D student into an A student in a single semester, and at that moment I became a believer. In a single quarter, my daughter's grade point average shot up from a 1.9 to a 3.4.

The next week, I listed the broad ramifications of the success of our video series. Our whys were transformed from mere economic ones to the whys of making an incalculable difference in the lives of millions of middle school, high school, and college students. It created a much deeper, more powerful and sustainable commitment from all of us. If this simple series could transform my daughter into a confident, successful student, what could it do for other "low-achieving" students? And if they were more successful in their academic pursuits, what kind of a difference would this program make in their future lives as adults? What a difference this product could make in the future lives of so many. (My daughter, for example, went on to get her degree in secondary education and English and a master's degree in counseling.)

Having deepened our whys, we became totally committed to making this project work, no matter what. We recruited two prime-time television stars to become our spokespersons for the program, John Ritter and Michael Landon. The program was incredibly successful; millions of lives were forever changed. One college football player who viewed this seminar not only improved his grades but followed the seminar's directive to start a small business *before* you graduate to learn and sharpen your entrepreneurial skills. He started a small business to sell "sports underwear" to his fellow athletes. By the time he graduated, his company, Under Armor, was already generating a profit. Today, he's one of the wealthiest young men in America.

Husbands and wives can strengthen their emotional whys by listing the ramifications of a marriage that is loving and mutually satisfying and comparing them with the consequences of a marriage that fails. Their why for creating a successful marriage will deepen dramatically, drastically reducing their risk of failure and divorce. This simple exercise takes only a few minutes a day but can produce the kind of commitment, creativity, and perseverance that can power anyone to a lifetime of success.

✸ What You Value Most

What are our greatest whys, the whys that make up the foundation or the very core of who we are? In the New Testament, Jesus revealed that he had two foundational whys upon which all of the other whys in his life were founded. They not only were central to who he was but were literally woven into the very fiber of his being—every strand of his DNA. First was his unique, perfect relationship with God, his heavenly Father. His second core why emanated from *who* he was. He was the light of the world, the bread of life, the literal fulfillment of the moral laws of God. He said, "*I* am *the* way, *the* truth and *the* life" (Jn. 14:6, NASB). That empowered his missions, his messages, his actions, and his teachings; they flowed *naturally* from who he was.

So what are *our* foundational whys?

Some of our core values are noble; others are self-serving. Whatever your core values, be aware that your whys will or will not support every aspect of your life. The way you tackle a project at work or the way you raise and guide your children will reflect the core values you hold most dear, or your lack of those core values. In the days and weeks following September 11, 2001, many of us reexamined our values. Many realized for the first time how short our lives here on earth really are. We looked at our families, our careers, and our priorities in a new light. And yet, over time, it is easy to forget the priorities of those feelings, decisions, and commitments. The abiding lesson of Jesus's life is that the values you base your daily life upon inevitably impact your future and the hopes and dreams of those you love. That is why it is so important that each of us discover our whys, deepen them, and search for a way to transform them into whys that truly reflect who we are, who we want to become, and what we want to achieve with our lives.

What Do You Want? What Do You Value Most?

Through the years, I've found that people are quick to tell you what they love and what they hate. But ask them what they *want* and they have to stop and think about it. They can quickly tell you in general terms—more money, a better marriage, a lower golf score, a better job, and so on. However, few will give you specifics, because they haven't taken the time to figure them out. For example, in their careers, almost no one can tell me where they want to be in three years, five years, or ten years. And without a specific destination, they certainly haven't planned a route or schedule to get there. On the other hand, superachievers—those who strive for their impossible dreams and achieve them—know exactly where they want to go and how they want to get there. They usually create a map and a timetable for reaching each intermediate goal along the way.

When I've asked businessmen or businesswomen what they value most, they nearly always say their family, their friends, or their health. But there's a real disconnect between what they *say* and what they do. Most people's day-to-day priorities, what they think about, how they act, and how they spend their time do *not* reflect their stated values. Nor do their priorities help them to achieve what they've said they want most. Most people's daily and weekly routines reflect the demands and priorities of others or follow the path of least resistance and "go with the flow." When our daily activities do not reflect our values and efforts to achieve what we really want, we end our days and weeks and years frustrated and unfulfilled. As you examine the life of Jesus, you'll discover that his words, actions, and daily activities perfectly reflected what he valued most. This enabled him to make the most of every minute of his life. As a result, he had no inner stress to contend with; he experienced no depression or anxiety over tasks undone. Instead, he experienced the true contentment and fulfillment of working with a clear sense of purpose; his daily life was in perfect congruity with his whys.

To experience greater levels of achievement and more contentment and fulfillment, we need to find the whys that will motivate and sustain our actions and work. We live in the most advanced, educated, civilized age in the history of mankind. We have more wealth, more health, and more material possessions than any other people in history. And yet we consume more antidepressants and more antacids and spend more time in the offices of therapists than ever before. By discovering and deepening our whys, I believe we have the opportunity to bring our lives and careers into line with our values. If we do this, we will be more successful in everything we do. Our daily stress will lessen, and our depression will give way to fulfillment and joy. In John 10:10, Jesus stated that one of his missions was to provide us with a more fulfilling life than we could ever achieve on our own. He said, "I am come that they may have life, and that they may have it more abundantly." Given a choice between an abundant and fulfilling life and one of mediocrity and discontentment, which one would you choose?

Understanding Changes Minds—Action Changes Lives

IDENTIFYING AND DEEPENING YOUR WHYS

1. Personal gratification
2. Money and material possessions
3. The approval or "applause" of others
4. Fear of failure, fear of criticism, fear of consequences, fear of loss
5. Our survival instinct
6. Personal achievement
7. Love
8. Family
9. Connection to God

WHAT DO YOU WANT? WHAT DO YOU VALUE MOST?

1. The above list represents some of the "whys" that motivate and drive our behavior and ultimately determine our level of success, significance, and fulfillment we achieve in any endeavor or on any project.

    a. Use this list to determine your *current* whys for your most important endeavors or projects.

    b. You can use this to gauge those projects that are most dear to you, and those in which you desire to see the most success.

    c. You can use this same list to examine what drives you in the most important areas of your life that you prioritized in the exercise in chapter 3.

2. How can you deepen your whys for your most important endeavors, projects, or areas of your life by relating them to items 6, 7, 8, or 9 on the list?

3. For your most important endeavors, projects, or areas of your life, write out the "broad ramifications" of succeeding— and the broad ramifications of failing.

CHAPTER 5

━━ ෨෨ ━━

The Sense of MISSION That Gets You Where You Want to Go and Makes You What You Want to Be

"Behold, I send you out as sheep in the midst of wolves.
Therefore be wise as serpents and harmless as doves!"

—JESUS (MATT. 10:16, NKJV)

"Steve, what is this?" Mike Siegal, president of Ambassador Leather, looked a little confused as he read my resignation letter.

"Mike, I have a chance to start my own company with an entrepreneur that I really admire."

He looked at me as if I had just made the dumbest decision of my life. He said, "A start-up? You're leaving *us* for a start-up? Are you nuts? Don't be stupid. . . . These things *NEVER* work out!"

When he realized I was committed to leaving, he asked if doubling my salary, giving me a company car, and making me vice president of marketing would change my mind. This was the ninth job I had held since graduating from college five years earlier. In the first eight jobs, I had failed eight out of eight times. Now, on job number nine, at the age of twenty-seven, I was being offered *all* of my career goals, and I had worked on *this* job for only three months! What had transformed me from a chronic failure to an "overnight success"? And whatever it was, was it just a once-in-a-lifetime fluke or the beginning of a whole new, lifelong path of repeated, extraordinary successes?

What brought about that "overnight success" was a new approach to the way that I viewed and pursued every aspect of my business life. As it turned out, my overnight success was *not* a once-in-a-lifetime fluke. The same approach that worked on my ninth job worked on my tenth, as well. I *did* leave Ambassador Leather, and the opportunity to achieve all of my career goals, to pursue that "start-up" on job number ten. As it turned out, job number ten lasted for thirty-two years. During that time, my partners and I built more than a dozen multimillion-dollar companies from scratch, achieving billions of dollars in sales. During that time, I undertook scores of projects, and in every case I followed the same strategy that I had applied to job number nine. Simply stated, I treated every project as a mission, and as such applied a particular routine to the all-out pursuit of accomplishing it. Was every project a home run? Not even close. But our batting average became the highest in the television marketing industry. We hit more home runs each year than any other company in television . . . for nearly three decades.

◉ Missions Create Direction, Movement, and Momentum

Because I treat every project as a mission, I have been able to get a lot more done in a lot less time than I ever could have done before. Right now, I'm working on writing, directing, and producing three television shows, writing two books, and engaging in numerous speaking tours for my newest company's regional sales events. Treating a project as a mission has become as normal to my business life as eating, breathing, and sleeping are to my personal life. In fact, it became so much a part of my normal routine that I wrongly assumed that *everyone* did it. But as I began to consult with a number of executive and sales teams of some of our nation's leading corporations, I discovered that being mission driven was more the exception than the rule. Now, before you quote me your company's mission statement, let me tell you that most mission statements are merely public relations documents. Mission statements are usually vague and very general. They have absolutely nothing to do with creating corporate, executive, managerial, or employee missions. And when it comes to the way *individuals* pursue their work, careers, and personal lives, being mission driven is even *more* rare.

◉ The Ultimate "Mission-Driven" Man

Jesus provides the greatest example I have ever known of someone *mission driven* throughout his life. He devoted his life to fulfilling his missions. Our first glimpse of this aspect of his life can be seen when he was only twelve years old. He had become separated from his mother, Mary, and Joseph for three days in the city of Jerusalem. When they finally found him in the temple, they were astonished to see him conversing with the teachers, amazing everyone with his questions and his understanding. Moreover, he was answering questions the teachers were asking *him*. When his mother scolded him for the worry he had caused her, he replied, "Why did you seek me? Did you not know that I must be about my father's business?" (Lk. 2:49, NKJV). Already, he was doing the work that his Heavenly Father had commanded him to do.

On the night of Jesus's arrest, his disciple Peter drew his sword to try to stop the guards from arresting him. Jesus told Peter, "Put your sword into the sheath. Shall I not drink the cup which My Father has given Me?" (Jn. 18:11). At any time he could have said "enough" and bailed out—but he didn't. He wasn't about to let anyone—his disciples or the Roman governor of Judaea—keep him from fulfilling his mission to sacrifice his life. But that was only *one* of his stated missions. In all, Jesus identified twenty-six missions that he set out to accomplish during his lifetime. And he fulfilled every one of them! Among them were:

Please his Father and do *His* will—every day
Reveal his Father to the world
Finish his Father's work on earth

Fulfill the laws of God perfectly

Save the world

Seek and save those who are lost

Give his life as a ransom for many—lay down his life for
his sheep

Call the "unrighteous" to repentance

Give abundant life to his followers

Heal the sick and give sight to the blind and hearing to
the deaf

Raise the dead

Set people free from the power and consequences of sin

Provide the *way* to God

Preach the good news to the poor

Heal the brokenhearted

Not one of his missions was self-centered, self-gratifying, or self-promoting. On the contrary, *all* of his missions were about serving others, while sacrificing himself to achieve God's ends.

To accomplish all that he did during his brief life, Jesus had to be mission driven. How can we expect to achieve all that we are truly capable of without being similarly mission driven and focused? I've studied the lives of countless high achievers, people who achieved their "impossible dreams"; every one of them was driven to achieve very specific goals. And yet the remaining 99 percent of the adult population are *not* mission driven. At the end of every year, their cry is "Where did this year go?" And in nearly every aspect of their lives, they start their new year right where they started the year before—at the same weight (or worse), earning the same salary (plus or minus a little), with the same unresolved marriage problems . . . and so on.

Jesus not only conducted his own life from a mission-driven perspective but demanded it of his disciples as well. He told them, "Do you not say, 'There are still four months and then comes the harvest'? Behold, I say to you, lift up your eyes and look at the fields, for they are already white for harvest!" (Jn. 4:35). In other words, don't procrastinate your pursuit of your mission. Open up your eyes and start accomplishing what you set out to do . . . right now!

෨෨ Without a Vision, You Cannot Have A Mission!

When I teach the importance of missions to business executives, the first question they always ask is, "*How* do I figure out my missions?" King Solomon, in the book of Proverbs, wrote, "Without a vision, the people perish" (Prov. 29:18). You can't embark on a mission without first having a vision of what that mission is. For Solomon, a vision wasn't something mystical or vague or abstract like a piece of modern art. It was more like a road map. A vision includes a clear and precise understanding of what you want to accomplish, where you are right now in relation to that goal, and the precise route and timetable for getting from where you are to where you want to be. Having this kind of clear and precise vision in each important area of your life is so critical that the absence of such a vision guarantees that you will achieve little more than mediocrity in that area of your life. Only by gaining a clear and precise vision of where you want to go and designing a specific route to get there can you achieve extraordinary success.

The first step in creating a vision is to answer the question, "What do I *really* want to achieve in this area of my life, or on this project?" Don't limit your thinking to what you can *afford* to achieve, have *time* to achieve, or have the know-how or talent or abilities to achieve. Rather, ask yourself, "If I could achieve *anything* I want, what would it be?" Once you realize what you want to achieve, write down some of the specifics around it. This "statement" should be a paragraph to a page in length—no more. The more specific you are, the better. For Thomas Edison, this was the first step in every project he undertook. List your "whys" for wanting to achieve your goal. Then broaden and deepen those whys by listing the broad ramifications of fulfilling that vision.

∞ Create a *Vision Map*

Next comes the most important step in the process—creating a vision map. Since a true vision and mission involve a specific destination, creating an effective map and timetable is critical to achieving it within a set period of time. Now, I doubt that Jesus consciously created a vision map to accomplish his missions. His daily progress in moving toward the completion of his missions was as *natural* to him as breathing is to you and me. But as ordinary people with endless distractions screaming for our attention, few of us are focused enough to effectively organize an important mission without first mapping it out. The people whom I have studied who have achieved their impossible dreams have nearly always done so with the aid of this kind of map. Edison, Rockefeller, Ford, Warren Buffett, Bill Gates, and other brilliant and driven individuals have all used this approach. To date, I haven't found a single high achiever of the past two hundred years who *didn't* follow this approach in one way or another in pursuing and achieving his or her dreams. It is a common thread among those who achieve *extraordinary* accomplishments.

First, list all of the intermediate goals that have to be accomplished in order to achieve your vision. Then take each goal and identify the steps needed to achieve that goal. Now take each step that requires the completion of *more* than one task, and break those steps into specific tasks. When you've done this, you will be able to see everything that needs to be done to go from where you are now to where you want to be. You have a road map to every task, step, and goal that has to be accomplished along the way.

The last step is to create a schedule. If you have a deadline that you're working against, start with that deadline, and then create a target date first for each goal, then for each step, and finally for each task. If you are *not* working against a deadline, you can start your scheduling from the bottom up—beginning with the first task of the first step that needs to be taken, then moving to the second task, and so on. At the end of this approach, you will have a completion date for the mission derived naturally from the completion dates of all of the tasks, steps, and goals leading to your ultimate goal. This may sound complicated, but believe me, it is not. I've illustrated it fully in Appendix 1.

Because a picture is worth a thousand words, let me illustrate the first two steps of the vision-mapping process with an example from my past. In 1996, my partners and I decided to undertake a project in which we would market a piece of fitness equipment for which we had acquired the marketing rights. At the time, the equipment was a piece of strength-training equipment used by professional sports teams and medical rehab facilities. Our hope was to market it to consumers as a premier home-fitness unit. The name of the product was Total Gym, and our hope was to recruit Chuck Norris and Christie Brinkley as our spokespersons. Chuck had been using the professional unit for eighteen years and loved it so much he had it shipped all over the world to every filming location to which he traveled. Christie had never used it before, but we knew she worked out to keep in shape, and we believed that if she tried it, she would fall in love with it. Here's a visual example of the first two steps of creating a vision map of my vision for marketing the Total Gym. The remaining three steps of this process are illustrated in Appendix 1 of this book.

◎ Vision-Map Example: Total Gym

Step 1: Clearly define your vision/mission.

Vision

Redesign the Total Gym into an attractive and practical piece of home fitness equipment, and create a marketing program that will sell millions of Total Gyms to consumers in America and throughout the world.

Step 2: Convert your vision into specific goals that must be accomplished in order to achieve your mission.

Vision Goals

1. Redesign the Total Gym to make it more attractive and practical for home use. Shorten it and take at least twenty-five pounds out of it. Change it so that it comes fully assembled and can be folded up small enough to be slid under a bed.

2. Recruit Chuck Norris and Christie Brinkley to be our television spokespersons, at endorsement fees that we can afford to pay.

3. Produce a thirty-minute infomercial and two-minute and sixty-second commercials to sell the Total Gym directly to television viewers.

4. Create a market test to test consumer response to the infomercial and commercials.

5. Create a media plan to guide the media purchases.

6. Find a marketing partner that can distribute the Total Gym through retail stores that sell fitness equipment.

7. Create the marketing collateral material to send to interested consumers and include with each Total Gym sold.

8. Create the program and scripts for the inbound telephone call centers that will be taking the orders.

9. Create newspaper ads to support the sales of retailers.

Whenever I teach on this subject, someone always asks: "Do I *really* have to do this in writing?" The answer is no, you don't. You have to do this in writing only if you want to achieve an *extraordinary* outcome or a high level of success. The fact is, most things we do in life do not require extraordinary success. I enjoy skiing with my family, but I have no aspirations to become an extraordinary skier—I just enjoy cruising down a mountain. So I don't vision-map my hopes for skiing. My wife and I are planning a family trip to Disneyland. We want to have lots of fun with our kids, but we certainly don't need to create a vision map for that. At the same time, I'm currently working on three multimillion-dollar television projects and two books, and all must be completed by the end of the year. My partners and publishers are risking millions of dollars on these projects. They are expecting me to produce extraordinary outcomes. There is absolutely no way on earth that I could meet my deadlines if I *didn't* create my vision maps. Yes, creating a vision map requires a little bit of time and effort. But when it's done right, it can pay back that little investment tenfold, a hundredfold, a thousandfold.

◎◎ By Definition, Your Most Important Missions *Must* Be Accomplished!

We live in a day when it's politically correct to pat people on the back for just "showing up." As well-meaning as that may be, it's counterproductive. My partners and I started a new company eighteen months ago that launched a newly patented nutritional supplement. In this brief time, our little start-up has grown from a handful of sales associates to over seventy thousand. Six months ago, I received an e-mail from a member of our management team suggesting we throw a party to celebrate our first year in business. I rejected the idea, because reaching the one-year mark is *not* a significant accomplishment. Our company has become one of the fastest-growing companies in business history. Our associate ranks and sales volume will soon reach a major milestone. We will have over one hundred thousand associates creating sales of more than $10 million per month. When we have achieved *that*, we will throw a party. Our mission was never to simply survive our first year—so celebrating a one-year anniversary is not a significant accomplishment. On the other hand, one of our missions *is* to provide our product to as many families as possible, as fast as possible, and when we hit sales of $10 million per month, that will be a major step in achieving our mission. *That* will be an accomplishment worth celebrating.

Jesus didn't offer words of praise for people who used their talents and gifts to "just get by." In fact, he gave a startling parable to show his disdain for such waste. In the parable, a business owner gave three different amounts of money to three of his managers to invest while he went on a lengthy trip. The amount of money he gave to each was based upon their own investing abilities. When the owner returned, he asked all three managers to give an account of what they had *achieved* with the money he had given them. The first, who had been given the most, had doubled the money through wise and aggressive use of it. The second, who had been given substantially less, also doubled the amount of money that he had been made responsible for. The third, who had been given much less than the other two, had simply buried the money in a safe place so he wouldn't lose it. In response, the business owner rewarded the first and second managers with praise and an extraordinary promotion. Both of these men had accomplished their missions, getting high return on their boss's investment. But the owner told the third manager that he could have deposited the money in a bank and would have at least earned interest. He called him deceitful and lazy and fired him on the spot.

What Jesus was getting at is that there are no rewards for "just showing up." Praise, promotion, and reward are given to those who effectively use what they've been given to accomplish the missions they've undertaken. As you identify and map out your missions, if you determine they reflect your whys and are important enough to pursue, then they are important enough to accomplish! So the question becomes, "What must I *do* to succeed and *accomplish* my missions?" (I'll address that in more depth in chapter 9).

๑๑ Reality Check: Does Your Mission Reflect and Advance Your Meaning?

I have known many businessmen who have made fortunes in business but have suffered devastating failures in their family lives. One reason for this disparity is that while they've been mission driven and mission focused in their business pursuits, they *haven't* been in their family relationships. But there is a second reason that is an even greater cause of their personal failures. It is a reason that is almost second nature for most men, and it can all but ruin their chances for lasting happiness and fulfillment. Simply stated, their missions are *not* reflective of their personal values. Unfortunately, my own past is a perfect example of this.

After I graduated from college in 1970, one of my three most important whys was: "Provide everything my wife and children need for a fulfilling life." For five years, my various "missions" and activities reflected this why. However, chronic failures in my career resulted in a low income that provided only a modest lifestyle. We had no savings and mounting debt. My desire to provide for my family's needs was concentrated more on trying to provide their *material* needs and desires and less on their emotional and spiritual needs. This subtle shift in focus resulted in a new *unstated* mission that became my number-one priority: make more money to better provide for my family. But I continued to fail. In 1976, my failures turned to success when I partnered with Bob Marsh, and I began to treat each business project as a mission. Our first project was a grand-slam home run and moved me from an annual income of $18,000 to over $150,000. I was twenty-eight years old, and overnight I was making more money than most of America's corporate presidents at the time. As I experienced the euphoric thrill of my first *real* success, my highest-priority whys began to change. And the change was so subtle that I didn't realize it until many years later.

Even though I was totally unaware of them, two *new* whys became the invisible driving force in my life, fueling my success. My incredible mentor, Bob Marsh, had become like a father to me—the most inspiring, encouraging, and loving father a young man could have. My number-one why shifted from "providing for my family" to "trying to hit home runs" as a way of expressing my appreciation and love for Bob and for the opportunity he had given me. I delighted in seeing his pleased expressions, his verbal and emotional "attaboys," and the unconditional love that he so freely gave to me. My number-two why was a desire to experience the thrill of hitting marketing home runs. My third why was a driving desire to avoid losing what we had gained, by achieving even greater successes. My original highest-priority why had been replaced, and yet I didn't realize it. I could have passed a lie-detector test affirming that my whys had not changed. And here's the problem. My new whys did *not* reflect my true values. I loved my family more than anything else in life, and I wanted to share God's love with others. But those values had been sabotaged by my new whys. There was nothing innately wrong with my new whys; in fact, in many ways they were positive and beneficial. But what *was* wrong was that they had become my highest priorities. As a result, my family life and my relationship with God suffered.

Jesus's highest-priority missions were a perfect reflection and undiluted expression of his whys. His mission to lay down his life and give it as a ransom was the perfect expression of one of his whys—to make a way for those who had rejected God to be reconciled to Him and experience a joy-filled relationship. When our whys do *not* reflect our highest values, we lose the *power* to achieve those things that matter the most to us. We may still accomplish our specific goals, but those accomplishments fail to make us as happy. On the other hand, when our driving whys are in concert with our highest values, we gain more power to accomplish those missions more rapidly, and to do so with a greater level of fulfillment and happiness.

◎◎ Identifying Your Values

A couple of years ago, I was filming a DVD mentoring series entitled *The Master Strategies of Super Achievers*. The most emotional moment in this filming came when my business partner, Greg Fullerton, shared the stage with me and led me through an exercise that brought my core values to the forefront of my heart and mind. Greg was one of the founders of Franklin Quest, the predecessor to the FranklinCovey organization. In front of the group I was teaching, Greg asked me if I had ever been on the outside observation deck atop the south tower of the World Trade Center. I told him that I had, on a number of occasions. He then asked if I had ever looked across the 110-story precipice at the roof of the north tower. Again I answered, "Many times." He then asked me to close my eyes and imagine that I was once again atop the south tower, gazing at the top of the north tower across the courtyard, only this time there was a twelve-inch wide I-beam that stretched from the corner of my tower to the corner of the other.

Greg told me to keep my eyes closed and then began asking me questions. "If I offered you twenty-five million dollars to try to cross that I-beam to the other building, either walking across or crossing with your hands, would you do it?" Picturing the 1,300-foot drop below, I instantly replied, "No." He then raised the offer. "How about if I give you $100 million and assure you success in everything you have ever hoped for?" Once again, I instantly said no. "A *billion* dollars?" he asked me. "No." Finally he asked, "Is there *anything . . . anything at all* that I could offer you that would get you out onto that I-beam?" "Absolutely nothing" was my reply.

Greg went on, "Now picture a very big, scary-looking

man on the roof of the other building, clutching your five-year-old daughter, Hallie. Holding a megaphone in one hand, he yells out, 'You've got one minute to get across that beam, or I'm throwing your daughter over the side.' You can tell he means business, and Hallie is crying in terror. She yells out, 'Daddy, Daddy, Daddy!' and the man begins counting down, 'fifty-nine . . . fifty-eight . . . fifty-seven . . .'"

As Greg began the countdown, I vividly pictured my precious little girl terrified and crying, and I "lost it," totally lost it, in front of the group, with the cameras still rolling. Greg yelled, "Well . . . are you coming?" Totally lost in the moment, I instantly yelled back, "Yes, yes, yes!" In front of a room full of people, my six-foot-three-inch partner came over and kindly put his arms around me as I opened my tear-filled eyes. As it turned out, I wasn't the only one in the room who was shedding tears. Patting my back, Greg said, "I'm sorry, Steve. But *now* you know what you *truly* value most— more than money, more than business success, more than anything else in life." And he was right. I would have tried to cross that beam for Hallie, or any other member of my family—and I would have tried it instantly, without thought. All I could think about in that vision was my terrified daughter; I couldn't get out on that beam fast enough. In just a few minutes, I had come to the realization of what *really* mattered and what did not. Every member of my family was infinitely more important than my bank account, my job, or any project I'd ever worked on. And yet my life and daily behavior reflected a very different set of priorities.

✎ Settling for *Good* Can Rob You of the *Best*

Granted, we cannot quit work and devote 24/7 to focusing on our families, but we can make adjustments that *will* provide a better reflection and expression of our real priorities. For example, when we're with our spouse or children, we can *really* be there for them—turning off the cell phone, the news channel, or whatever else diverts our attention away from them. We can say no to a golf date or a weekend business meeting. We can get home from work on time and avoid doing work at home until the family is in bed. Most of us don't waste our time pursuing or doing worthless or hurtful activities. Unfortunately, many of us *do* spend a lot of our time doing good things, rather than using our limited time to do the *best* things. But with our *mission* in mind, there are countless ways we can replace *good* uses of our time that don't reflect our highest values with *great* uses of our time that do.

When Jesus was at the height of his popularity, and thousands of men and women wanted just to get near him, a woman named Martha invited him into her home for dinner, and he and his disciples accepted. As Jesus began teaching to those who were in the house, Martha's sister Mary sat near Jesus's feet, listening intently to his every word. Martha, on the other hand, was focused on serving everyone. She complained to Jesus that her sister wasn't helping her serve and asked Jesus to tell her to do so. Instead, Jesus gently reproved Martha, telling her that she was worrying about too many things and focusing on the wrong things. Her sister, he said, had made the *better* choice. Both Mary and Martha would have every day and every night for the rest of their lives to serve the needs of their guests and deal with the daily distractions of life. But in a matter of minutes, Jesus would leave their home, and they would never again on earth be able to interact with him so intimately. Martha had forever lost a once-in-a-lifetime opportunity, sacrificing the *best* use of her time for a *good* use of her time.

A young, rich businessman, too, had a face-to-face encounter with Jesus. He took that opportunity to ask Jesus the single most important question any of us can ask. He asked, "What shall I do that I may inherit eternal life?" Imagine being able to hear firsthand, from the mouth of the *only* person who could give you the absolute truth—the answer to this greatest of all questions. Jesus responded by telling him to "keep the commandments." The man asked which ones, for there were over six hundred commandments given in the Old Testament. Jesus answered with six commandments. The man quickly replied that he had kept them all from the time of his youth, and asked, "What do I still lack?" Jesus then told him to go sell everything he owned, give the money to the poor, and "come, follow me." Jesus had just offered him the chance of a lifetime. He had invited him to leave behind his wealth and comfortable furnishings, which had become his master, and become a companion, apprentice, and disciple of Jesus himself. But the wealthy businessman chose his house and his riches over following Jesus, and traded eternal life for the temporal pleasure and security of his estate.

Now, Jesus was not saying that everyone who followed his teachings had to sell everything they had. That is not the case. But this young, rich man was confident he had kept all of the commandments of God perfectly. These commandments included one that said you must not serve any other "gods" besides God, and another that said you should love your neighbor as yourself. Yet he showed by his response to Jesus that he loved his wealth and possessions more than he loved God and more than he loved his "poor" neighbors. He had mistakenly believed that he had kept God's law from his youth; the reality was, he had been breaking it daily. He had substituted his worst values for the *best* that Jesus had offered.

How often do we let "good" rob us of the best? Do our missions reflect our greatest values, or do they reflect values that are less important? By identifying your foundational values and building your whys upon those values, you will become much more focused on pursuing the best in place of accepting good. As your missions begin to reflect your highest values, you not only will accomplish everything important that you set out to do but will experience greater joy and fulfillment than you have ever known.

Understanding Changes Minds— Action Changes Lives

VISION-MAPPING

1. What are the most important endeavors or projects you currently want to accomplish?

2. Write a clear and precise statement of your vision for each of those projects or endeavors.

3. Which are the most important or urgent that you wish to accomplish with the greatest degree of success?

4. Purchase a loose-leaf notebook and tabbed subject dividers to create a vision-mapping journal.

5. Following the example in this chapter and in the appendixes, begin to vision-map your number-one priority project or endeavor.

Note: Vision-Mapping Journals with all of the necessary preprinted forms are available at my Web site, www.stevenkscott .com, for the convenience of my readers.

CHAPTER 6

—— ෨෨ ——

A MESSAGE That Communicates

"The heart of the wise trains his mouth and adds
persuasiveness to his lips."

—SOLOMON (PROV. 16:23, NASB)

෨෨ Being Heard, Understood, and Appreciated

Imagine a speaker so captivating that a crowd of thousands
listens intently for hours, even days, without so much as taking a break for a meal. Imagine a speaker so inspiring that his
words ignite a miracle-working faith in the hearts and minds
of his listeners. Imagine a speaker so enlightening that even
children can grasp his life-changing principles. Such were the
experiences of those who listened firsthand to the inspiring
and empowering words of Jesus.

Today, communication is the single greatest challenge in
business, marriage, and parenting. People often ignore or reject our ideas, not because they're bad ideas, but because they
are ineffectively communicated. Those with whom we communicate are often distracted, complacent, or cynical toward
us or our message. If you study the words that Jesus spoke

and the communication techniques he used, you will quickly discover that he was much more than just a great communicator. He was the *greatest* communicator who ever lived. No matter whom he addressed, he was able to get his listeners to pay attention and to understand what he was saying. Whether his audience was an individual or a crowd of thousands, an adult or a child, the highly educated or an illiterate peasant, he communicated in such a way that he was able to capture their undivided attention and bring a crystal-clear focus upon the issues he was addressing. His messages and the manner in which he communicated them so powerfully persuaded and motivated his listeners that they embraced his words and followed his guidance, even to the point of death.

What's the longest speech or talk you have ever listened to? How long were you able to stay focused on the words of the speaker? How soon after you started listening did your attention begin to wander? On one occasion, a crowd of more than five thousand men listened to Jesus teach for an entire day and into the evening. Most women will tell you that they have a hard time keeping their husbands' undivided attention for even a few minutes, much less an entire day. Yet Jesus was able to do this repeatedly. On another occasion a crowd listened to him in the desert for three days. How could he communicate in such a captivating, life-changing manner?

For Jesus, effective and persuasive communication involved much more than merely words. We mistakenly think that communication is merely the act of talking or writing. This critical misunderstanding prevents most people from becoming effective and persuasive communicators. In reality, what we *say* makes up only a small *portion* of how we communicate. And speaking (or writing) is only one of a *number* of critical steps that must be taken to effectively and persuasively communicate with others.

∞ The Ultimate Mentor's Communication Skills

Because ineffective communication is the number-one challenge in so many of the most important areas of our lives, our lives would dramatically improve if we could be better communicators. As you look at the manner in which Jesus communicated, you will discover seven steps that he took that helped him to reach the hearts and minds of men and women so powerfully. By learning to use his methods and techniques, we can become more effective and persuasive than most of us would have imagined possible. In business, our peers, bosses, and customers will understand what we're saying. Moreover, they will *value* what we say and be persuaded to do what we show them to be in their best interest. In marriage, our partners will not only understand what we're saying but *feel* what we're feeling. In our relationships with our children, we'll be better able to motivate them to do what is right, and to *want* to do so. And they will be able to freely share how they feel, without fear of being belittled, ignored, interrupted, or misjudged. We will be able to achieve a deeper level of intimacy in all of our relationships.

◎ The Incredible Power of Persuasive Communication

For thirty-two years, I have successfully sold our company's goods and services directly to television viewers through the commercials and infomercials I've written and produced. During the first ten years of our business, we used two-minute commercials to sell our products, with "800" numbers displayed on viewers' TV screens for the last twenty seconds of those commercials. In other words, I had only one hundred seconds of communication to grab viewers' undivided attention, present a problem they could identify with, show how my product solved that problem better than anything else, overcome their resistance and excuses for not ordering, and persuade them to interrupt what they were doing to go to their telephones and order the product or service. How was I able to do it? By using the same communication methods and techniques that Jesus used. Thanks to what I learned about effective communication from the life of Jesus, I was able to achieve a record-setting number of responses—a number that has never been equaled in the history of television advertising. More than twenty-five million people ordered our goods and services in response to the various two-minute commercials I created.

To put that number into perspective, visualize the crowd of people who attend an NFL football game. To see twenty-five million people, you would have to attend every single home game your team plays for the next fifty-two years. Now imagine getting all of those people, every single one of them, to *buy* what you want to sell them. Remember, you have only one hundred seconds to grab their undivided attention, reveal a problem they can identify with, overcome their resistance, and get them to hand you a credit card to make that purchase. *That* is the incredible power of the communication methods and techniques that I learned from the world's greatest communicator.

What is effective and persuasive communication? To me, it is when the person I'm communicating with *understands* what I'm saying, *feels* what I'm feeling, and has been persuaded to *act* in response to my communication. Manipulation is an attempt to *force* or deceive the other person into acting in *my* best interest. Persuasion is an attempt to *convince* the other person to do what you truly believe is in *his* or *her* best interest—or the best interest of a group, a project, or a family. Needless to say, it's dangerously easy to cross over the line that separates persuasion from manipulation.

What Jesus Did to Effectively and Persuasively Communicate That Most of Us Don't Do

The first and most important step in communicating with others is gaining an accurate understanding of your listener's frame of reference. Jesus did this consistently, whether he was speaking to an individual, a small group, or a crowd of thousands. We see this in his use of parables to illustrate his important points. He would tailor the stories to the frame of reference of the individual or audience he was addressing.

The single greatest obstacle to effective and persuasive communicating is our failure to understand our listener. We mistakenly assume that their perspective or interpretation of a situation or issue is similar to ours. Usually, that is not the case. Every person responds and reacts to situations from their own background, set of circumstances, understanding, and feelings, and they are different from anyone else's. We make a critical mistake when we frame our message from our own perspective, rather than from the perspective of the person we're talking to. It's not at all about you, your needs, or even your message—it's all about your listener! Ask yourself what their needs and desires are. What stands in their way physically, intellectually, or emotionally to hearing, understanding, believing, or responding to your message? Jesus not only understood the hearts and minds of people generally, but knew and understood the specific needs of the individuals he was talking with.

"How can I *possibly* know the other person's frame of reference?" you might ask. The answer is that you need to do your homework *before* you communicate. The best way to find out a person's frame of reference on any given issue or situation is to ask them. And when you ask them, you need to ask in a way that creates a safe environment for them to answer openly and honestly. This is not the time to evaluate or even comment about their answers. You're on a fact-finding mission. A single word of criticism or judgment can defeat your purpose and cause the other person to withhold how they really feel. If they become concerned about your response, they are likely to say only what they feel it is safe to say—what you want to hear! So instead of learning their true frame of reference, you only hear them trying to fit into your frame of reference, defeating the very purpose of your questions.

If you are unable to learn your listener's frame of reference through direct questioning, talk to others who may be able to give you the insights you need. If you're trying to communicate with a group of people, learn everything you can about the demographics of that group. While we may never have the intimate awareness of a person's heart and mind that Jesus did, we can at least gain some understanding of their perspective before we speak. And that understanding can make all the difference in the effectiveness of how we communicate.

My company's first product that I had to sell was a topical antibacterial cream for acne sufferers. Because I had terrible acne throughout my youth, I already knew the frame of reference of teenagers with acne and the frame of reference of their parents. So writing an effective and persuasive commercial turned out to be easy.

On the other hand, when I wrote my first commercial for our weight-loss product, I didn't have firsthand knowledge of what it was like to try to lose weight. I had been skinny my entire life. When I graduated from college I weighed only 145 pounds, even though I was nearly six feet tall. How could I possibly understand the heart and mind of a person who was overweight or obese? So I talked with overweight people.

I talked with professionals who dealt with overweight adults. My spokesperson for this particular product was Richard Simmons. I listened to Richard for hours as he told me what he had been through as an obese youngster and young adult. He told me story after story of the people whom he had helped to lose weight. I asked to hear the stories of the people he introduced me to. By the time I wrote my first weight-loss commercial, I completely understood the frame of reference of our potential customers. When my partner later took over that project, he did the same kind of research. As a result, Deal-a-Meal became a major hit that helped millions of people shed unwanted pounds.

I recently had a meeting with a woman who is one of America's favorite actresses. In fact, a few years ago she won an Academy Award for best actress, and I have long been a fan. I was talking with her about a project I intended to write and direct. I listened to what she had to say for a few minutes and then foolishly started to try to move her from her point of view to mine. Unfortunately, I had not listened to her long enough, nor with the focus and sensitivity that she deserved. I not only spoke prematurely but talked far too much! At the end of the day, she rejected the project. Later, my friend who had been in that meeting with me gave me a well-deserved dressing-down for how little I listened and how much I talked. As Solomon tells us in the book of Proverbs, a man who speaks before he has adequately listened is a fool; an "abundance of words" inevitably leads to error (Prov. 18:13 and 10:19, respectively).

As important as it is to discover the other person's frame of reference in business, it's even more important in marriage and parenting. We are sometimes too quick to speak our minds to our spouses and children, with little regard for their personal frame of reference. Using the practice of thinking about the other person's frame of reference is the first step in transforming even the worst relationships into strong, enduring ones.

∞ The Power of Truth

One advantage Jesus had over us was his perfect knowledge of truth. He never had to guess about anything. He never had to stop and wonder what the other person was *really* thinking or if there was a hidden agenda behind their statements or questions. He didn't have to stop and figure things out. He already knew. Some of those who came to Jesus with a burning question in their heart or on their mind would throw up a smoke screen to mask the real issue. His enemies used trick questions to try to show that he was *not* who he claimed to be. But Jesus was never fooled by smoke screens or tricks. He was never tempted to react to the world of illusion; rather, he used his knowledge of truth to illuminate reality.

An elderly religious leader, Nicodemus, approached Jesus under cover of night to ask him a question that only God or someone with a direct pipeline to God could answer. It was the most important question anyone could ever ask. But Nicodemus began the conversation not with his question, but with the smoke screen of flattery. He said, "Rabbi, we know you are a teacher who has come from God—for no one could perform the miraculous signs you are doing if God were not with him." But before Nicodemus could go further, Jesus cut through his smoke screen and specifically addressed the question that Nicodemus desperately wanted answered. Jesus replied, "I tell you the truth, no one can see the kingdom of God unless he is born again." The conversation continued, and in a matter of minutes, Jesus revealed the ultimate truth about what it would take for anyone to gain eternal life. But he could have never done any of this had he not first known the truth—about Nicodemus, about the burning question in his heart, about eternal life, and about God's plan (Jn. 3:1–21).

Obviously, we can't know the truth in the way that Jesus did. But though we do not have his perfect knowledge, it is incumbent upon us to make an effort to *learn* the truth about those we are addressing and the issues we want to discuss with them. We need to gather the facts about an issue and then craft our message accordingly.

Back in 1996, when I was writing the first infomercial to launch the Total Gym, I needed to learn the facts about strength training and aerobic exercise. At the time, most adults knew the benefits of aerobic exercise, but few were aware of the much greater benefits of strength training or resistance exercise. In my research, I discovered some startling facts that had been uncovered by a number of medical studies. For example, running would change only the *shape* of a person's body if they jogged thirty miles per week or more. But only twenty minutes of strength training, three days a week, could *radically* change one's body shape. Most people over sixty could *double* their strength through only six months of very moderate resistance exercise. I discovered that strength training alone affected all twelve "biomarkers" that determine a person's true biological age, and that anyone could turn back the biological clock and slow the aging process with just fifteen to twenty minutes of strength training a day. Aerobic exercise only raises your metabolism *while* you're doing the exercise, but a twenty-minute strength workout raises it for an entire day. And the lean muscle you build with strength training can even burn calories while you sleep!

I was able to be so much more effective and persuasive in that first infomercial by learning these simple truths. According to the industry reports that monitor America's infomercials, the Total Gym infomercial campaign I wrote became the number-one fitness infomercial of all time.

Knowing the power that knowledge of truth brings to a conversation, I am always amazed at how much of our communication is based on everything *but* truth. Whether in business or politics, truth seems to be intentionally avoided in our conversations. Last year two executives from a call center told me how much they could do for one of my businesses if I would let them participate in one of our campaigns. They went on to quote "industry statistics" that not only stretched the truth but defied it! I had never heard so many ridiculous exaggerations authoritatively presented as facts. Had I been new to the industry, I might have been wowed by their statistics. But having been one of the pioneers of direct television advertising, I knew their hype was an outright lie and dismissed it.

That same truth in communication is too often neglected in our personal relationships as well. It's not that we lie outright, but rather that much of our communication is based upon our feelings about the issues, rather than on concrete information or the facts. And so we fall into exaggeration, superlatives, and hyperbole. "You *always* do this" or "You *never* do that." We assign or embrace "false beliefs" about the motives of our friends, spouses, and children, rather than attempting to discover their real motives. "If you *really* loved me, you'd . . ." or "Your work is obviously *more important* than your family is," and so on. We magnify the negative and minimize the positive. And our ignorance of and setting aside of the truth can chip away at our relationships. It doesn't have to be that way. By making the truth the foundation of our messages, we can not only eliminate such faulty and destructive communication but replace it with communication that builds and fortifies relationships.

◎◎ *Illuminate the Issues*

How much of our communication with others involves trying to convince them to do something we want them to do or to get them to believe something we want them to believe? While there is nothing inherently wrong with this, it's important to think about whose interests we are serving. Even when our motives are not self-serving, trying to convince others to do what we want them to do may "put the cart before the horse." Before you try to convince others to do what you want them to do, you should first consider what is truly in *their* best interest. Will your efforts empower them? Will they help them to achieve what is truly best for *them*?

Jesus was neither a salesman nor a manipulator. He was not trying to convince anyone to do anything. Instead, Jesus focused on *illuminating* the *truth* about issues, events, questions, and concerns. His words made it possible for his listeners to see the truth. But what they did with that understanding was their choice. Of course, he hoped that his listeners would make the right choices and decisions, but he did not try to coerce or manipulate them. Rather, he focused a penetrating spotlight on false beliefs and life's illusions. This is why he claimed to be "the light of the world." Those who would follow him "would not walk in darkness, but have the light of life" (Jn. 8:12). Over and over again we see him exposing false values and revealing hidden truths.

A perfect example of this can be seen when a man called out to Jesus from a crowd, saying, "Teacher, tell my brother to divide the inheritance with me." This man thought the issue was about fairness or generosity. But as Jesus showed, that wasn't the real issue at all. First, Jesus stated that he was not the judge or arbiter of this matter. He did not have all of the necessary facts to render a fair assessment of who should have what. Then he revealed the *real* issue that both the man and his brother should be more concerned about. He said, "Watch out! Be on your guard against all kinds of greed; a man's life does not consist in the abundance of his possessions" (Lk. 12:13–15).

Although our natural inclination is to try to convince others to do what we want them to do, following that inclination can produce terrible consequences. We may come across as arrogant and condescending. Such efforts can cause others to dig in their heels and reject our ideas. Instead of bringing us together, our efforts may drive us apart.

The first objective of any important conversation should be *illumination*; that is, shedding light on the issue at hand, helping a listener to understand the issues so they can make a choice based on the realities of an issue. Most people don't do this, because it requires them to *prepare* before they speak. They must take the time to learn the truth about an issue and then frame their message to reveal that truth in a manner that enables their listener to see it. And doing this requires that you state your message in a way that plays to the listener's frame of reference.

๑๑ Getting Your Listener's Undivided Attention

Understanding your listener's frame of reference, knowing the facts about an issue, and *illuminating* the issues will result in effective and persuasive communication. Among the skills or techniques needed to help you to illuminate an issue is that of gaining the undivided attention of your listener. At the beginning of a conversation, your listener's mind and focus may be elsewhere. They might be thinking about something that happened a few minutes ago, or a problem they are trying to solve. You need to bring their focus into the present moment. Jesus was able to "hook" his listeners successfully, whether his audience was rich or poor, educated or uneducated, whether they were servants or kings, individuals or enormous crowds.

What do I mean by "hooking" the other person's attention? Think about a fish swimming down a pristine mountain stream. He's enjoying a warm, sunny day, swimming in any direction he wants to swim. Then he sees a scrumptious bit of food floating nearby. He quickly snaps it up, only to discover he's "hooked." No matter where he was going or what he was doing, he's now going in a completely different direction . . . where the fisherman wants him to go.

A communication hook does the same thing. It captures a listener's attention so that you can take them where you want to go.

Jesus was sitting by a well in Samaria when a woman walked up with a water pot to draw some water. Jesus looked at her and said, "Will you give me a drink?" Whatever the woman had been thinking about before, she instantly focused on Jesus. First, she was shocked that he had talked to her, for he was a man and a Jew. In her culture men didn't talk to strange women. Moreover, Jews did not talk to Samaritans, as Samaritans were looked down on. And yet this Jewish man was not only talking to her but asking her for a drink. She answered,

"You are a Jew and I am a Samaritan woman. How can you ask me for a drink?" Jesus replied, "If you knew the gift of God and who it is that asks you for a drink, you would have asked him and he would have given you living water." She noticed that he didn't have anything to draw the water with and said, "You have nothing to draw with and the well is deep. Where can you get this living water?" Jesus replied with an answer that astonished her. He said, "Everyone who drinks this water will be thirsty again, but whoever drinks the water I give him will never thirst."

In the conversation that followed, he told her things about her past that no stranger possibly could have known. She was so astonished and excited by their short conversation that she forgot the reason she had come to the well. She left her water pot and ran home to tell the men in the town that she had found the Messiah.

Without any attempt to coerce, persuade, or manipulate the woman, Jesus, in a matter of minutes, had so effectively and persuasively communicated his message that she became a devout believer. And it all started with Jesus "hooking" her attention. His "hook" was one of the most effective hooks one can use—a specific question, in this case, "Will you give me a drink?" A specific question always captures the other person's attention. A generic question, such as "How are you?," can be answered with a noncommitted answer like "Fine," without ever really capturing the other person's attention. If I ask you, "What did you have for breakfast this morning?" however, you have to stop whatever you were thinking of before and think about your answer. That is why a *specific* question is such an effective hook. Jesus used two other hooks that are extremely effective—strong, "sticky" statements, and personal references. Jesus's statement, "Everyone who drinks this water will be thirsty again, but whoever drinks the water I give him will never thirst," is such a powerful, memorable statement that the listener can't help but be caught up in Jesus's words. A "personal reference" is referring to someone that your listener knows. If Mary Jones is a good friend of yours, and I say, "I was talking to Mary Jones yesterday, and she said something that really surprised me," my use of that personal reference has hooked your undivided attention. Just saying her name creates a picture in the listener's mind of the person he knows, and my statement about her is likely to create a strong sense of curiosity.

Some years ago, I wrote a script for our Lori Davis hair care line, in which the singer Cher appeared as my spokesperson. In the script for the infomercial, I had Cher ask a specific question to hook the audience's undivided attention, a question that nearly every woman in America could relate to. Cher asked, "Have you ever looked at your hair in the mirror and wanted to cry?"

Using a hook to get a person's undivided attention is a powerful tool. But because most people have short attention spans, a second technique is needed to heighten their attention whenever you want to make an important point. Here again, Jesus was an absolute master. To keep his listener's attention, he used a technique that Gary Smalley calls "salting."

Of course, Jesus didn't consciously think, "Now, here's a great communication technique I can use." Everything he did he did naturally. His manner of doing things flowed from his inner nature; it was a natural function of who he was. But most of us are *not* born communicators. To become effective communicators, we need to *learn* the skills and techniques of effective communication. Once we've learned them, we need to practice them enough and use them enough that they become second nature to us. Salting, like hooking, is extraordinarily effective in communicating with others. In my case, I use this technique with everyone from my seven-year-old daughter to my investors and bankers, from individuals to large audiences.

So what is salting? You've heard the adage, "You can lead a horse to water, but you can't make him drink." As it turns out, that isn't really true. I can make a horse drink every single time I lead him to the water, and so can you. All we have to do is salt his oats before we take him to the water. Salted oats will do for a horse what heavily salted popcorn will do for you. It will make him very thirsty. Similarly, we can "salt" our conversation by creating curiosity about what we're going to say, *before* we say it. Let's go back to our example of Jesus's conversation with the woman at the well. We can see him salting his statements a number of times. For example, look at the incredible dose of salt in this statement: "If you knew the gift of God and who it is that asks you for a drink, you would have asked him and he would have given you living water." He makes her thirsty to hear what he has to say with comments like "If you knew the gift of God." Who *wouldn't* want to learn the "secret" of "the gift of God," and this "living water"? His next two statements add even more salt. He says, "Everyone who drinks this water will be thirsty again, but whoever drinks the water I give him will never thirst."

By the time he is ready to illuminate the truth for her, she is not only ready but eager to embrace it.

A while back, I was invited to speak to five thousand business owners on various topics discussed in the book of Proverbs. I told the audience that in one particular statement, Proverbs reveals the number-one reason that relationships decline and ultimately fall apart. It is the reason married couples "fall *out* of love," and ultimately divorce. It's the reason that relationships between parents and their children disintegrate. And it's the number-one reason employees leave their companies to take jobs with other companies. Equally amazing, this one statement also reveals the fastest and most effective way to reverse that failure and bring the relationship back to where you want it to be. By the time I quoted this particular proverb, nearly every man and woman in the audience had pulled out a pen and something to write on. Why? Because they had been adequately salted. And in case you've been adequately salted, this revealing statement is found in Proverbs 13:12. It reads, "Hope deferred makes the heart sick, but desire accomplished, *it* is a tree of life."

So you now know how to "hook" your listener's attention and "salt" your conversation with statements and questions that will create curiosity. Next, I want to show you a communication technique that will instantly enable the person you are speaking to to clearly understand what you're saying and *feel* what you're feeling.

◎◎ Use "Word Pictures" to Stimulate the Other Person's Vision and Feelings

"A picture's worth a thousand words," right? Wrong! In communication, the right picture will accomplish what *no* words can, not a thousand, a hundred thousand, or even a million words . . . unless your words create a picture. When Jesus wanted to clarify a point, or make an important point in a way that his listeners would never forget, he used words that created a picture. And he often used his listener's frame of reference as the source of the picture he created. For example, when Jesus was walking along the shore of the Sea of Galilee, he saw two brothers throwing their fishing nets into the sea. He said to them, "Follow me, and I will make you *fishers of men*" (Matt. 4:19). They instantly understood what he was saying and left their nets in the sea and followed him. With the woman at the well, he used the image of water and a fountain. In some cases, his word pictures were as simple as a single phrase, and in others, he used more lengthy stories or parables.

Why are word pictures so much more powerful and effective than mere ideas? A declarative statement or abstract thought activates the left side of the brain; a word picture, on the other hand, activates the right side of the brain. The right side is both the "visualization" side of our brain and the seat of our emotions. A word picture not only enables the listener to visualize what the person is saying but also enables him to *feel* what the speaker is feeling. The most effective and powerful communication method a speaker can use to deliver a clear vision and powerful feeling is a good emotional word picture.

The nutritional supplement that my company markets is radically different from any nutritional supplement in the world. The product enables the cells of the body (trillions of cells) to produce more of the body's most important antioxidant, a tripeptide called glutathione. The more glutathione the cells produce, the more energetic and healthy they become. Many of our distributors and customers couldn't understand *why* this is so much better than simply drinking juices rich in antioxidants or taking antioxidant vitamin supplements such as vitamin C or vitamin E. No matter how I explained it analytically, many still didn't get it. I finally came up with a word picture that enabled everyone to clearly understand the difference.

Here is the word picture I came up with to describe the process. (I'm going to withhold the name of the nutritional supplement here, as my goal is not to convince you to buy our product, but rather to show you the power of word pictures to convey a message simply and unforgettably.) When you drink a juice rich in antioxidants or use an antioxidant vitamin supplement such as vitamin C or vitamin E, you are ingesting an antioxidant that can put out *some* of the oxidative fires in some of your body's cells. Picture a forest fire in which millions of trees are ablaze. Now picture a helicopter carrying a large bucket of water. It dumps that water on a patch of dozens of trees, instantly extinguishing the fire among them. That's effective on that patch of trees, but the rest of the forest—millions of trees—is still on fire. That's what you're accomplishing when you ingest an antioxidant. You're putting out some kinds of oxidative fires in some of the cells but not putting out most of the fires in most of the cells. On the other hand, I pointed out, when you take our supplement, you are giving every cell in the body the nutrients it needs to manufacture more of its own antioxidant, glutathione. It's like having every tree in the forest tapped into an underground lake and turning every branch of every tree into a sprinkler system. Every tree puts out its *own* fire. Glutathione is millions of times more powerful than vitamins C or E in its ability to put out oxidative fires and defeat the free radicals that attack our cells. Giving each cell a greater reservoir of glutathione provides your body with a level of defense that no ingested antioxidant could even begin to provide.

When I shared this word picture at our company's convention, every distributor at last understood the difference between our product and every other product on the market. Moreover, they could use this same word picture to explain that difference to their customers. And that is exactly what happened.

I use word pictures regularly with my wife and my children.

My twelve-year-old son recently said something that hurt the feelings of his seven-year-old sister, who came crying to me. He defended himself by saying that he didn't see what the big deal was—all he had said was that she was "annoying." He couldn't understand why that would make her cry. Borrowing one of Gary Smalley's word pictures, I told Sean that sometimes we say things to other people that we think are just "little pebbles." We toss these little pebbles at someone thinking that they won't do any damage. Unfortunately, what is a pebble to us may be a giant boulder to them. So even though we don't mean to hurt them, they *feel* like they've just been crushed. I told him that I've made the same mistake a number of times. It doesn't matter that *I* think it's just a pebble. If it's a boulder to the other person, then I've got to realize that and try to undo the damage that was done by my words or actions. Sean then looked at Hallie and asked her, "Hal, when I said that, did it feel like you got hit by a pebble or a giant rock?" She said, "A giant rock." He felt terrible and told her how sorry he was. That is the power of a good word picture . . . to clarify a message and convey a powerful feeling.

◎◎ Focus on the Real Issues, Not the Smoke Screens

Today, as in Jesus's day, people sidestep the issues that drive their behavior and communication. They often communicate in ways that minimize their risk of being rejected. Or they talk out of frustration, fear, personal hurt, or even guilt. As a result, they throw up smoke screens to hide their real feelings, or communicate in ways that vent their frustration, fears, or hurt. Unfortunately, we then get drawn into their game by *re-acting* to their misdirections. We address their words, rather than the real issues behind them. In a nutshell, we get caught up in the fray. Jesus did not. He was quick to cut through such smoke screens and focus upon the real issues behind them. For us to do this, we have to (1) know the real issue that is driving the other person's behavior or comments, (2) let them say what they have to say *without* reacting to it or challenging it, and (3) patiently ask questions to try to uncover the real core issues.

Here again, Jesus was a natural at this. We are not. For us, discovering the *real* issues takes time, patience, probing questions, and the ability to listen. For most of us, that runs contrary to our nature and the way we behave in both our personal and professional lives. And yet it is absolutely necessary when we have something important to convey. Solomon said, "He who holds his tongue is wise" (Prov. 10:19, NIV). He also said, "He who answers before listening, it is his folly and shame" (Prov. 18:13, NIV).

∞ Be Interactive

It's much easier to lecture someone than it is to genuinely interact with him or her. Unfortunately, people forget most of what they are told in a lecture. On the other hand, when we interact with another person, they retain far more of what is said. In a 'sense, they take ownership of the communication. Consequently, their interest, focus, and commitment increase. Jesus frequently used dialogue and interactive communication.

The Pharisees were strict religious leaders. Desperate to quash Jesus's influence, they put together a plan to trap him using his own words. They came up with three trick questions designed to put him in a no-win situation—questions that could only be answered in ways that created division, controversy, and anger among those who were following him. They asked these questions in the presence of a crowd, knowing that no matter how Jesus answered, his answers would turn a portion of the crowd against him. Their first question was "Is it lawful" to pay taxes to Caesar? If he answered no, he would be guilty of treason and could be executed by the Roman officials who governed Judaea. If he answered yes, then he was advocating paying homage to the Roman emperor Caesar. Because Caesar claimed to be a god, paying homage to him would violate Jewish law and would be viewed as blasphemy. This would give the Pharisees and the crowd the right to stone Jesus on the spot.

Jesus realized what they were doing and condemned their efforts, calling them hypocrites. But he did *not* dodge their question. Instead, he answered it in an interactive fashion. He asked them to show him a coin, which they did. He then asked, "Whose image and inscription is on the coin?" They answered, "Caesar's." He then gave the Pharisees an answer that amazed them and astonished the crowd. He said, "Render therefore unto Caesar the things which are Caesar's, and to God, the things that are God's" (Matt. 22:17–21). His implication was unmistakable: since Caesar's image is on the coin, give the tax money to him—and since man is made in God's image, give yourself totally and unconditionally to God.

The Pharisees went on to ask him two more questions intended to entrap him. Again his answers defeated their efforts, and they never tried to trick or entrap him with words again. It became obvious to them that his wisdom, reasoning, and ability to communicate were not only infinitely superior to theirs but even greater than those of Solomon.

So how can we make our communication interactive? Ask questions of the other person, or try to role-play with your listener.

Gary Smalley teaches couples an interactive communication method he calls "drive-thru talking." Imagine yourself at a fast-food drive-through window. You say, "I'll have a double-decker, extra mayo, no mustard, a large order of fries, and a medium root beer." You hear a voice repeat back, "That's a double-decker, no mayo, extra mustard, a medium order of fries, and a large root beer." You reply, "No, no! Extra MAYO, NO mustard, a LARGE order of fries, and a MEDIUM root beer!" After two or three times back and forth, the employee taking your order finally understands *exactly* what you want.

In the case of a couple, one person shares his or her thoughts and feelings, *uninterrupted* by his or her spouse, who listens until the first person is finished. The listener then repeats back exactly what he or she thinks the person is saying, in his or her own words. The other person then corrects him or her if he or she has gotten it wrong, saying something like, "Almost, but not quite. What I'm saying is . . . ," and then gives a word picture to help clarify what he or she means. They go back and forth until the listener completely understands what the speaker is saying. Most of the time, according to Gary, the listener doesn't fully understand what the speaker is saying until they've gone back and forth two or three times. And yet, almost miraculously, in a matter of minutes they progress to a very clear, near-perfect understanding. Once that takes place, they switch roles, and the listener becomes the speaker and vice versa.

๑๑ These Communication Techniques Can Make All the Difference

After graduating from college in 1970, my first job was as a management trainee for a life insurance company. I was told that on average, it takes a life insurance agent at least three one-hour appointments to sell a life insurance policy. This was not just our company average, but the industry average. Six years later, I began selling products directly to consumers on television. We sold low-priced items such as skin-care products, books, and household products. One day, my partner ducked his head into my office and asked me if I thought I could create a two-minute commercial that could sell life insurance directly to consumers. My first thought was, "If it takes professional life insurance agents three one-hour appointments to sell a policy, how on earth can I sell a policy in a hundred and twenty seconds?"

At the time, no one had successfully sold life insurance through a direct-response television commercial, although a number of the giant insurance companies had tried. But after thinking about it for a minute or two, I told my partner that I thought I could. The communication techniques I had been using for a little more than a year were already breaking all previous response records in the television marketing industry. Could I use these same techniques to sell life insurance? I believed that these techniques were so powerful and effective that they could do it. We launched our first campaign with Senator Sam Ervin as our spokesperson. It worked so well that in the next ten years our two-minute television campaigns, featuring more than a dozen celebrity endorsers, generated millions of leads and sold hundreds of thousands of life insurance policies. Yes, these techniques work miraculously *wherever* they're applied—at home, at work, with listeners of any age and any background.

Rather than being frustrated by the fact that the people you talk to may not clearly understand what you're attempting to say, keep in mind that *that* is the norm. As Jesus said, when people see, they often don't see, and when they hear, they often don't hear. If they're going to understand—if they're really going to "get it" and catch your vision—you have to become a more effective and persuasive communicator. By using the techniques that Jesus used, and practicing them regularly, I can guarantee you that you will become more effective and persuasive than you ever would have dreamed possible.

Understanding Changes Minds— Action Changes Lives

SUPERCHARGING YOUR MESSAGE

1. Think about an important issue that you recently communicated on your job or at home—to your boss, your spouse, or one of your children. Write down a summary of what you said.

2. Describe the "frame of reference" of the person you were communicating this message with. If you don't *know* that person's frame of reference, that means you made your first mistake by communicating from *your* perspective rather than his or hers.

3. Thinking of *his or her* frame of reference, create an opening statement with a strong "hook"—either a strong statement, specific question, or personal reference.

4. Write out the most important points you wanted to communicate—then write "salting" statements or questions that you could have used to create a heightened level of curiosity about each point *before* you communicated the point.

5. Write either simple analogies or emotional word pictures that clearly communicate or reinforce your main points— that can create an understanding of the importance of

taking the course of action you wanted that person to take.

6. Was your communication "lecture style" or "interactive style"? Can you think of ways you could have made it more interactive?

CHAPTER 7

—— ෨෨ ——

A MANNER That Moves Men and Women

"But Jesus stooped down and wrote on the ground with
His finger, as though He did not hear."

—JOHN 8:6 (NKJV)

Jesus boarded a boat with his disciples and set out across the
Sea of Galilee. As he slept below deck, a furious storm arose,
and the crashing waves upon the deck began to overwhelm
the boat and terrified all the men aboard. His disciples scram-
bled below the deck and woke him up. Panicked, they cried,
"Save us!" Jesus calmly asked them, "Why are you fearful, oh
you of little faith?" He then got up and "rebuked the wind
and the sea," and immediately the wind ceased and the sea
became perfectly calm. All the men on board were astonished
and began to talk among themselves, saying, "What manner
of man is this, that even the winds and the sea obey him?"
(Matt. 8:23–27).

While their comment focused upon Jesus's miraculous
power over the seemingly relentless forces of nature, I am
more interested in the *manner* in which he *acted*—the *ways* that
he did what he did. For it wasn't just *what* he did that set Jesus

apart from ordinary men, but *how* he did it. For example, notice that he peacefully slept during a raging storm. And when he was awakened from his deep sleep, he didn't react to the panicked behavior of his terrified disciples or to the threatening waters or to the storm itself. In fact, he was incredibly calm, so much so that he dealt with his disciples first, *before* he dealt with the storm. Why? He first dealt with a concern that he considered much more dire than the storm, namely his disciples' lack of faith, and the fears that their lack of faith produced. Rather than *reacting* in agitation to a tense situation, he *responded* calmly to the needs of those around him. This kind of exceptional behavior runs contrary to human nature and our natural inclinations. But for Jesus, it was perfectly natural. It was *typical* of the manner in which he acted throughout his life, whether talking to his disciples or addressing a mob. For Jesus, this manner of behavior was perfectly natural because it reflected his nature. His actions flowed from deep within his innermost being. Ordinary humans are not so fortunate. What was quite natural for Jesus is unnatural for us. However, by learning from and following his example, the *manner* in which we behave can bring about miraculous changes to our own lives, our relationships, and our success in everything we do.

◎◎ Our Manner Can Either Accelerate Our Successes *or* Speed Our Failures

The manner in which Jesus acted and communicated always *enhanced* his message, rather than hindering or contradicting it. More often than not, we experience failure of varying degrees not because of our lack of intelligence, our inexperience, or even our incompetence, but because of the *manner* in which we act. In relationships, many of our mistakes, missteps, conflicts, and outright failures are *not* the result of bad intentions or devious motives, but instead are the direct result of the manner in which we behave. Speaking out or acting in an ill-considered way can become an insurmountable obstacle in our relationships, preventing others from hearing what we are trying to say or from grasping what we are trying to accomplish.

For years, American Telecast has marketed products that were created by brilliant inventors, and our spokespersons have been major celebrities (including Academy Award–winning movie stars, Grammy-winning musicians, Emmy-winning television stars, and pro sports Hall of Famers). Creating and maintaining good relationships with such people is critical to the success of every project we undertake. We always come to the table with great intentions and well-thought-out plans. And the celebrities and inventors we work with come to the table with the hope of creating a successful project (as well as a desire to avoid tarnishing their images). And yet I have seen a number of meetings end in disaster, simply because of the *manner* in which our ideas were presented or because of the manner in which others reacted to our presentations. An individual with a direct and candid communication style can be perceived as uncaring or even rude by an overly sensitive artist. Personally, I love dealing with someone who has such a style, because it allows me to quickly cut to the chase and deal with the real issues at hand. But I've seen a number of VIPs become irritated or upset and nearly kill a deal because they see such speed and directness as impatience or rudeness.

A while back, one of my companies was introduced to a new product that represented a major breakthrough in its category. The product was developed and patented by a major university, and clinical trials were conducted by another university. The results were astounding. Our management team spent months negotiating an exclusive license to market this product; it had the potential to generate hundreds of millions—or even billions—of dollars in revenue. But negotiations broke down and we lost this extraordinary opportunity. Why did they break down? Neither side *wanted* them to break down. They did so in the end because of the *manner* in which the two negotiating executives acted. Both had limited patience and became abrasive in their conversations. Fortunately, the deal was later put back together by one of the other executives in our company. This time, both parties were intently focused upon the manner in which they acted toward each other as they worked out the details of the deal. Unfortunately, the delay caused us to lose two months in our production schedule—and those two months cost us millions of dollars in lost sales. The breakdown and delay easily could have been avoided and millions of dollars in sales could have been saved. We didn't need to change the language or terms of the deal; all we needed to do was to change the manner in which the negotiators acted and spoke.

∾ An Amazing Demonstration of Godly Manner in Human Action

One day, as Jesus was teaching a group of people in Jerusalem's temple courtyard, a band of religious leaders pushed their way through the crowd and sat a woman down in front of him. They told him that she had been caught in the act of adultery. They said to him, "Now, Moses, in the law, commanded us that such should be stoned. But what do you say?" Jesus knew that they were trying to trap him with another "can't win" question. If he told them, "Obey the law," they would have killed her on the spot and demonstrated to the crowd that Jesus had no compassion or mercy and therefore could not be the Messiah. On the other hand, if he said, "Leave her alone," then he would have been telling them to break the law of God and would have been guilty of blasphemy. They would have been within their rights to focus their attention upon him and stone him to death. But instead of reacting to their urgent demands for an answer and being drawn into their trap, he acted as if he didn't hear them. He simply stooped down and began writing words in the dirt. When they continued asking him for the answer, he finally acknowledged their question, stood up, and said, "He who is without sin among you, let him throw a stone at her first." Then he stooped down and began to write more words in the dirt. The

Apostle John wrote that the men were "convicted in their conscience," and without saying another word, one at a time each man dropped his stone and walked away (Jn. 8:3–11).

In a single moment, Jesus had said and done something in a manner that caused the men to search their consciences and *convicted* them beyond reason or doubt. What on earth had Jesus done to evoke such a powerful outcome in every one of these men? After all, these callous, self-righteous hypocrites had come with stones in their hands, ready for blood. They believed that they had the right to stone the woman to death. Their leaders were equally hopeful that they could expose Jesus as a false prophet. I'm sure some of them hoped that they would get to stone Jesus as well. And yet, in a matter of minutes, he had derailed their hopes and plans. How? Had they experienced a spiritual awakening or conversion, from a bloodthirsty mob to repentant saints? Not really, for this same group continued to plot how they might have Jesus killed, right up to the moment he was sentenced to death by Pilate. And yet, in the square, they dropped their stones and walked away. Why?

My former pastor, Dr. James Borror, was a scholar in the dialect of Greek in which the New Testament was written. Years ago he told me that he believed he knew what caused those callous men to drop their stones and walk away. He believed that the "words" that Jesus wrote on the ground were *names*—the names of women with whom each of these men had committed adultery. As each one saw the name of his particular mistress, he dropped his stone and walked away.

Not because each one had an awakening, but because each one was afraid that Jesus might *expose* his own secret to the crowd. Not one of them wanted to risk that humiliation and its potential consequences. Remember, these were the most "religious" men in Jerusalem. These were the men who judged the behavior of others and publicly condemned them for even the slightest infraction. Can you imagine the humiliation they would have faced if the entire community knew they had committed adultery? They would have lost everything. Their very reason for living would have been eliminated in an instant. As Dr. Borror told me, the Greek text could have been accurately translated, "He who is without *this* sin among you, let him throw a stone at her first."

As astonishing as Jesus's response to these religious hypocrites was, his response to the adulterous woman was even more surprising. She had been caught in the act of adultery with a married man. She was humiliated, terrified, and suffering an unbearable weight of guilt and shame. As she sat alone, "spiritually naked" and exposed before Jesus, she had to wonder what he would say. Jesus couldn't tell a lie—he couldn't in any way imply that her behavior was acceptable. After all, she had contributed to a married man's betrayal of his wife's sacred trust. She had broken one of the Ten Commandments. Jesus, more than anyone else, knew the full measure of her guilt and the requirement of the Mosaic Law. And yet he looked at her and asked, "Woman, where are your accusers? Has no one condemned you?" She replied, "No one, Lord." He then said, "Neither do I condemn you; go and sin no more." He was the one person in the world who could have condemned her and been perfectly right and just to do so—for, unlike the religious hypocrites, Jesus had *not* committed adultery, or any other sin for that matter. But instead, he extended love and mercy where justice was due. He *forgave* her for her sin. But he didn't ignore or excuse it. He told her to change her ways and forsake the behavior for which she had just been pardoned. He neither excused her nor judged her. He had lovingly fulfilled the Law of Moses, and the Law of Love. He not only lovingly corrected her but gently yet firmly set her on a new path. Think what kind of a world we would live in if all of us acted in this manner.

❀❀ Applying the Manner of Jesus to Our Own Behavior

Although we will never have the wisdom, insight, or knowledge of men's motives that Jesus did, we can still discover powerful, life-changing lessons by observing Jesus's manner of responding to a given situation. In the instance above, he didn't *react* emotionally to the question or to the insidious intentions of his detractors. He didn't "shoot from the hip." Instead, he took time to listen to them and formulate a thoughtful response. And instead of attacking them in kind, he asked a question that made them stop and think.

More often than not, when we react too quickly and emotionally to the questions or accusations of another person, we add fuel to the fire they have started. When we do, what we say or do often makes matters worse. Instead of shooting from the hip, we should pause, as Jesus did, and take our time to offer a well-thought-out response. Like Jesus, we should work to put out the fire, rather than fuel it. When someone hurls an incendiary comment or question at me, I will often wait for a time. I may reply, "Your question is too important for me to give a thoughtless answer. Give me a moment to give you the thoughtful answer you deserve." I've never had anyone say, "No! I want an answer right now." If I have said or done something that is hurtful to the other person, I will apologize and tell them, "There's no way that I can undo the hurt that I've caused. Can you give me any idea what I might do or say to make things better?" And I make it clear that I mean it. And if they say, "No, that's OK," I refuse to let them off the hook. I want them to know that I am genuinely sincere in my request. So I follow up. "There must be something that I could do. . . . I really need your help to figure it out, because I'm at a loss as to what I can do." Usually, they'll come up with one or two things I can do to help address the problem that I've created. By following Christ's manner, each of us can respond to even the most negative situations in a way that encourages others and helps them to hear what we say, rather than reject it outright. How can we follow Jesus's manner? Start by studying his words, responses, and behavior in the various stories of his life that are found in the New Testament. At the same time, think of why Jesus reacted the way he did, and look for ways that you can apply that kind of thinking and behavior to your own daily situations.

◉◉ Our "Manner Checklist"

If thinking of and applying the manner of Jesus to our own lives and careers is a journey, we need a kind of road map. First, we need to determine our current "location." The checklist below will help you determine your present behavior and manner.

1. Do you *react* to negative situations, getting caught up in the emotion and turmoil, or do you *respond* to them calmly, with wisdom, insight, and objectivity?

2. Do you wait for others to approach you, or do you approach others first?

3. Are you quick to speak and slow to listen, or do you listen carefully before speaking?

4. Do you see and approach others from your own frame of reference, or do you first consider theirs?

5. Are you disinterested in those around you, or are you empathetic?

6. Are you insensitive to the needs of others, or do you tend to be compassionate?

7. Do you prefer to receive from others, or are you someone who looks always to give?

8. Is your life colored by resentment (grumbling, complaints, envy), or do you feel grateful for the many gifts in your life?

9. Do you *calm* others when there is dissension, or in the heat of the moment do you tend to add fuel to it?

10. Do you criticize others and work to point out their faults, or do you build them up?
11. Are you critical or judgmental of others, or encouraging and tolerant?
12. Do you respond to others with gentleness, or do you react harshly?
13. Are you slow to serve and quick to expect others to serve you, or do you always look first to the other person's comfort?

If you are unsure of your answers to any of these questions, ask people you know best how they think you fare in each. Once you recognize where you currently fall in terms of your day-to-day behavior, you'll have a sense of what areas you need to work on to act more in the manner of Jesus.

When one of my sons was in eighth grade, he decided to run for a ninth-grade class office at his junior high school. He worked hard on meeting all of the requirements to qualify for that office. He prepared a video in which Chuck Norris pointed toward the camera and said, "I'm voting for Ryan, and I hope you will too . . . or else!" before smiling with his winsome grin. Ryan also made posters with Chuck's arm around him and a big smile, with a similar slogan. Ryan went to school extremely excited about his campaign, his posters, and the video that he had prepared for the school assembly that day. But when he arrived at school, he was told that he was disqualified because his citizenship grade was slightly below the qualifying standard. When he asked how that could be, the principal pointed to the number of tardies he had during a previous school semester. What the principal of the school didn't realize was that those tardies were the result of the fact that Ryan had broken his foot and had to go from class to class on crutches. All of his tardies had taken place the first week he was on crutches, before he had adapted and was able to move more quickly.

When Ryan came home from school that afternoon, he was devastated. The next morning I went to the principal's office and argued my son's case to the assistant principal. But it was too late. The decision had been made; the assembly had taken place. Ryan would not be allowed back into the election. I was more angry than I had been in a long time. I offered a few harshly worded statements, expressing them loud enough for the entire office staff to hear. As I stormed out of the office, one of Ryan's classmates overheard one of the school secretaries mutter a descriptive word about me, one that is normally used to describe one's posterior! For the next few months, she never looked at me when I was in the office, and the other office workers, too, would barely acknowledge my presence.

The next year, as the new school year started, I decided to make an effort to act in a completely different manner toward everyone in the school office, including the woman who had made the comment. I decided to act more in the manner of Jesus. In his famous Sermon on the Mount, Jesus said, "Bless those who curse you" (Matt. 5:44). He was talking about blessing those who genuinely hate us . . . who would curse us to our faces and tear us down behind our backs. This secretary didn't hate me at all. She had simply reacted to *my* overreaction. So I decided to follow the manner and the admonition of Jesus, to try to bless her and the others in the office. Although I was only in the school office once or twice a month (usually to drop something off that one of my sons had forgotten to take to school), I made a conscious effort to talk to this woman and the other secretary, to smile at them and ask how they were doing. I would initiate a conversation with them nearly every time I visited. The change in their attitudes toward me and the blossoming of our relationship was wonderful. When I told them that one of Ryan's friends had overheard the expletive that had been muttered about me the previous year, they were shocked and began to laugh with me. They told me that the previous day they had talked about the change they had noticed in me—they said they couldn't believe the difference a year had made. Here's what's crazy— they've *always* been really nice! I strive to be nice to people in most situations. But that one time, I had become angry on behalf of my son and had acted in a harsh manner, and it had horribly colored the secretaries' impressions of me. And the one secretary's "posterior" comment had colored my perception of her. Now we were able to see each other for who we really were. What a difference manner can make. We both had misperceptions of each other, based upon our manner in reacting to a single occasion. But here's the important point I'll never forget, and I hope you won't either. When *my* manner of behavior toward them changed to one that was more in keeping with that exemplified by Jesus, our relationship instantly and permanently changed as well. Now every time I go into the office I look forward to seeing them, and we enjoy our interaction.

෨ The Power of a Manner That Reflects Our Meaning, Mission, and Message

One of the greatest obstacles to achievement in our lives is the disconnect between our manner of behavior and our messages, missions, and meanings. Our manner often contradicts or even undermines our meanings and intents. It can result in others ignoring our ideas and goals and can provide our adversaries or competitors with a tool to defeat us. Others may see us as hypocritical, unreliable, incompetent, or worse. Our manner of behavior too often is the weakest link in the chain between our intent and its accomplishment.

This was not true with Jesus. His manner was consistent with his meaning, mission, and message; in fact, it was the perfect expression and demonstration of them. Instead of being the weakest link, his manner of behavior was the strongest link and the *demonstration* of the truth and incredible power of his message.

One of his missions was to serve and save mankind, giving eternal life to those who would believe in him. To accomplish that mission, he needed to live a life that was *perfectly* righteous, in every thought, word, attitude, and deed. Anyone can say, "I want to serve," but to actually serve others self-lessly, in every action you take, is far more difficult. Nearly everyone who gets married makes a promise to their spouse to love and serve them "until death do us part." And yet more than half of all marriages end not with death but with divorce. Talk is easy—*doing* is not.

Jesus didn't just *say* he was going to voluntarily give his life as a ransom for ours but embarked on a mission to do it. Three years later, when guards came to arrest him, instead of hiding, he told them that he was the one they were looking for. When his disciple drew a sword to prevent his arrest and cut off the ear of the high priest's servant, Jesus told him to put his sword away. He said, "Do you think I cannot call on my Father, and he will at once put at my disposal more than twelve legions of angels? But how then would the Scriptures be fulfilled that say it must happen in this way?" (Matt. 26:52–54, NIV). He then healed the man's ear. But he didn't stop there. As we saw earlier, when the Roman governor who seemingly controlled Jesus's fate said, "Don't you know I have the power to either free you or crucify you?," Jesus didn't ask to have his life spared. He let the governor off the hook. Jesus would not do or say anything to undermine his mission. Moreover, his manner of behavior was a perfect demonstration of his life's message of unconditional love and infinite forgiveness.

When Jesus gave the Sermon on the Mount at the beginning of his public ministry, he said, "I tell you not to resist an evil person. But whoever slaps you on your right cheek, turn the other to him also." He went on, "Love your enemies, bless those who curse you, do good to those who hate you, and pray for those who spitefully use you and persecute you" (Matt. 5:44). On the night of his arrest, he behaved in a manner that was a perfect demonstration of what he had said. Even while he was hanging on the cross, struggling for each breath, he loved, comforted, and gave assurance to a repentant, murderous thief hanging on the cross next to him. He asked his most trusted follower to care for his grieving mother. He extended his love to his enemies, the very men who had mocked him, stripped him, humiliated him, and nailed him to the cross, praying, "Father, forgive them, for they know not what they do" (Lk. 23:34). From the beginning of his life through every recorded instance and event, his *manner* always underscored and demonstrated his meaning, mission, and message. And that is part of the reason his message has the incomparable power that it does, even twenty centuries of human history later.

When your manner becomes a reflection and demonstration of your message and your meaning, your mission will gain a power that is truly extraordinary.

Understanding Changes Minds— Action Changes Lives

ELEVATING YOUR MANNER

1. Write down a recent situation in which your *manner* of behavior or communication detracted from or sabotaged your message or mission in that situation—one in which you "shot from the hip" or in which your *reacted* rather than responded.

2. Looking back, describe a better manner in which you could have responded to the same situation, a manner that would have empowered your message or mission rather than sabotaging it or distracting from it.

3. Imagine a future situation in which you want to effectively communicate a message or accomplish a specific mission or outcome. Then, write down some ideas on the *manner* of behavior or communication you could use to empower your message or mission.

MANNER CHECKLIST

1. Respond calmly, with wisdom, insight, and objectivity to put fires out instead of fueling the fires with a *reaction*.

2. Listen first—don't interrupt, don't quickly change the subject when you speak.

3. Listen interactively by asking questions that focus on what the other person is saying.

4. Approach others from *their* frame of reference.

5. Make an effort to become more empathetic to the concerns and needs of others.

6. Make an effort to become more compassionate.

7. Begin to look at others from the perspective of what you can *give* in the relationship rather than what you can receive.

8. Begin to make an effort to continually reset your focus from the negatives of situations to those things for which you are grateful.

9. Begin to focus on how you can *calm* others when there's dissension instead of contributing to the dissension.

10. Make a daily effort to be more encouraging and tolerant rather than judgmental and critical.

11. Make an effort to respond to conflict with gentleness rather than reacting harshly.

12. Be quick to serve and slow to expect others to serve you.

CHAPTER 8

——— ༀ ———

METHODS That Work Miracles

"And Jesus, walking by the Sea of Galilee, saw two brothers,
Simon called Peter, and Andrew his brother, casting a net
into the sea; for they were fishermen. Then He said to them,
'Follow Me, and I will make you fishers of men.' They
immediately left their nets, and followed him."

—MATT. 4:18–20 (NKJV)

Jesus certainly possessed all of the love, power, wisdom, and knowledge he needed to achieve absolutely anything that he was determined to achieve. If there was anyone who didn't need the help of another person to achieve his goals and missions, it was Jesus. And yet he chose a handful of men to proclaim his message. His "partnership" *began* with only these select few. But in the centuries that followed, that same partnership was extended to millions of men and women.

In choosing to partner with others to proclaim his message, Jesus set the gold standard of leadership. His partnering and mentoring strategies and skills were unparalleled. Why is this so important? Because no one—apart from Jesus— accomplishes anything extraordinary on their own. Study the life of anyone who has ever achieved anything of significance and you will see that they partnered in their pursuit and accomplishment of their achievements. Unfortunately, our culture does not teach the strategies, skills, and techniques necessary for effective partnering. And without them, one can only produce mediocre results, at best. By carefully looking at the life of Jesus, we can see all of these strategies and skills clearly illustrated. In fact, I would argue that by imitating his example we can experience the *best* of what effective partnering has to offer.

Effective partnering transformed John D. Rockefeller from a four-dollar-a-week bookkeeper to the richest man in the world. It is what transformed Bill Gates and Paul Allen from unemployed geeks to Microsoft billionaires. It helped to transform a blind and deaf Helen Keller from an angry, frustrated child who couldn't communicate into one of the most inspirational writers and speakers of the twentieth century.

◎◎ How Effective Partnering Changed My Life

In 1970, I graduated from the Business College at Arizona State University with a degree in marketing. During the next six years, I failed over and over again, including at two businesses that I started from scratch. Then Bob Marsh recruited me and became my business partner and mentor. The company we ultimately started, the American Telecast Corporation, has been successful beyond my wildest dreams. During my thirty-two years at ATC, the companies we created and the products we marketed have generated billions of dollars in sales and produced personal fortunes for my partners and me. On that job, I began using fifteen critical strategies from the book of Proverbs. Over and over again, I've been asked, "Of your fifteen strategies, which one is the most important?" I would answer, "All fifteen are extremely important. However, the most *powerful* of all of the strategies is that of *effective partnering*."

What Is *Effective Partnering*?

There are three ways to pursue any endeavor or project we undertake. The first is to tackle it as an individual. This is what our educational system and the world in general teaches us—it's all about *you*. In my experience, however, such an approach produces only mediocrity at best. Because it's self-centered, it keeps us from achieving extraordinary success and prevents us from being truly happy and fulfilled. The other two ways to pursue an endeavor or project involve partnering. The most common way to partner is to do what comes naturally, and this usually results in *ineffective* partnering. Ineffective partnering can produce better results than a solo effort, but unfortunately it produces results that are often less than optimal and are sometimes disastrous.

When I teach on the subject of partnering, I always have a number of people in the audience tell me horror stories of their partnering experiences. Some have lost their savings, some have lost their friends and families, and some have even lost their freedom because they partnered with someone who took their business down an illegal path. I have a dear friend who wouldn't even *think* of doing anything unethical, much less illegal. But unbeknownst to him, his partner broke a federal law, and the judge threw the book at both of them.

When I talk about partnering, I'm not just referring to business partners or partners in a legal sense. A partner can be a mentor, an advisor, a counselor, a key employee, or simply a friend or relative—anyone who helps us to complete a task or activity that we cannot accomplish by ourselves in a timely or effective manner. A partner can be a long-term associate, from a spouse to a coach. One of my sons has a track coach, a high-jump coach, a football coach, a school tutor, and lots of teachers. I consider all of these people "partners" in helping me to guide my son and help him achieve his various goals. Another of my sons has two piano teachers whom I consider partners in helping him to become a better musician. In every business endeavor I undertake, I draw on the advice and counsel of various partners, from advisers to help me achieve a single critical task to long-term partners to move a business to extraordinary achievement. The point is to make the most out of each of these partnerships.

Partnering can either accelerate success or accelerate failure. Partnering that accelerates success is effective partnering. But effective partnering can *only* be accomplished by following four specific strategies. We see all four of these powerful strategies perfectly exemplified in the partnering approach taken by Jesus.

❧ The Four Strategies of Effective Partnering

1) Identify the Specific Need

To accomplish his missions on earth, Jesus chose an "inner circle" of partners—the twelve men that he called disciples. He told his disciples, "You did not choose me, but I chose you and appointed you that you should go and bear fruit, and that your fruit should remain" (Jn. 15:16). In other words, he didn't choose these men just to "hang" with him and be his buddies but to accomplish *specific* purposes. He later commissioned them to become his messengers and ambassadors to the world. He gave them specific instructions on what he wanted them to accomplish and *how* they were to accomplish it. He told them to train others to do the very things that he had trained them to do. Just as he had partnered with them, so they were to partner with others. Just as he had mentored them, so they were to mentor their partners. They followed both his instructions and his example for the rest of their lives. All but one were ultimately sentenced to death, and yet even at the point of their executions, they remained faithful to Jesus and the work he had commissioned them to do.

The first step to effectively partner with others is to identify the specific projects for which partners are needed. Next, you must identify the specific *needs* you want your partners to fulfill and the *tasks* you want them to accomplish. As basic as this may seem, too many people fail to take this first step. That's because most people go through life without a clear vision of what they want to achieve in an endeavor. And without such a vision, they can hardly define what they need from a partner. That's another reason why the vision-mapping process I discussed in chapter 5 is so important. It not only provides the basis to effectively pursue a mission but reveals the steps and tasks that you may not be best suited to achieve on your own—those for which a partner is needed.

To identify the type of partner you need, you must determine (1) the specific goals and tasks that you want to accomplish and (2) the specific strengths, talents, abilities, or personality traits that are required and that you can't supply yourself. This second factor can be best determined by conducting an "audit" of your talents and skills and taking a simple personality test that reveals your natural strengths and weaknesses. For years, I've used a very simple five-minute personality test to help hundreds of thousands of people discover their extraordinary uniqueness. When you discover your personality type, it enables you to play to your natural strengths, strengthen your weaknesses, and, most important, identify the kind of individual you should partner with to achieve any goal or attempt any endeavor in which you want to achieve an extraordinary outcome. You can print a free copy of this test and a breakdown of the traits of each personality type at my Web site, www.stevenkscott.com.

Don't be afraid to ask others who know you to help you identify your strengths and weaknesses. They will often see strengths and weaknesses that you may overlook or be entirely blind to.

2) Identify the Right Person to Fill Your Need

The second strategy in effective partnering is to identify the right person to fit your needs. Start by creating a list of potential partners. This takes work—there are no shortcuts. First, create a "long list"—all the individuals who could potentially fill the role of partner, advisor, counselor, or mentor. Compiling this list can take a few minutes or a few days, depending upon how critical the role is that you need to fill. Include anyone you might want on that list—regardless of how impossible it may be to recruit them. Don't limit your selection to people you already know, people you can afford, people who are available, or people you think are likely to be interested. In 1983, when Bob Marsh and I wanted to create a television campaign for one of our favorite magazines and I needed to recruit the best possible on-camera endorsers, I asked myself, if I could get ANYONE, who would it be? And I came up with these names: Tom Selleck, Charlton Heston, and President Reagan. All three were seemingly impossible prospects. I didn't know them, I couldn't afford them, and none of them were available. Selleck and Heston had both turned down multimillion-dollar commercial offers and had claimed they would never do television commercials. President Reagan was still in office, and no sitting president in history had ever appeared in a nonpolitical television commercial. And yet, because they were at the top of my list, they were the first ones I went after. As it turned out, all three said yes. Moreover, because they loved the magazine, they all appeared in the commercial for free! As it turned out, this campaign more than doubled the magazine's subscription base and was the most successful magazine subscription campaign in TV history. It even outperformed campaigns for *Time* and *Sports Illustrated* by more than five to one. My point: in creating your long list of potential partners, don't sell yourself short. Reach for the very best people you can imagine.

After you've completed your long list, the next step is to prioritize that list, putting your first choices at the top. Now you want to do your "due diligence," looking at each of your prospects in great detail. Look at their experience, the level of success they've achieved, and how applicable their past experience is to the role you want them to play. Most important, look at their integrity.

I believe, as Jesus did, that integrity is the single most important trait in any partner, advisor, or mentor. Unfortunately, most of us are so enamored of a person's smooth talk, impressive credentials, or track record that we often fail to consider a person's integrity. Yet a lack of integrity is the number-one cause of failures in partnerships. The few times I have failed to check out the integrity of a person or company I was partnering with, I have lost millions of dollars. In Proverbs, King Solomon gave us seven red flags to watch out for when choosing a partner. If you see any of these flags in a would-be partner, take that person off of your list.

1. A lack of integrity (Prov. 29:24)
2. A quick temper or deep-seated anger (Prov. 22:24)
3. A pattern of foolish behavior (Prov. 14:7)

4. Anyone who offers a lot for a little, or quick riches (Prov. 25:19; 28:22)

5. An excessive use of flattery (Prov. 29:5)

6. An inclination to gossip or exaggerate (Prov. 20:19)

7. A disregard for rules, regulations, laws, or personal boundaries (Prov. 28:7)

3) Wisely *Recruit the Right Partner*

Once you've completed your due diligence on your top choices and have eliminated any people who suffer any of the above faults, it's time to recruit. This is another area where too often people fail. Whether they're trying to recruit a business partner or key employee, a personal coach or business mentor, they fail to recruit the people they want. Why? (1) They approach the person from the wrong point of view; (2) they ineffectively present their vision; or (3) they make a weak offer.

When most people are trying to recruit a partner, they approach him or her from their own frame of reference, rather than from the frame of reference of the potential partner. In other words, we focus on what they can do for us, rather than on what we can do for them. Although it's important for them to know how they fit into your vision, that should not be the focus of your initial approach. Rather, you should focus on them—their dreams, desires, drives, and needs. Later, you can communicate your vision and how they fit into it. And at the close, you should return to their perspective and communicate how their partnering with you is going to enable them to achieve their dreams, desires, or needs more quickly or more fully than any other opportunity they are considering.

The first followers that Jesus recruited were two brothers, fishermen named Peter and Andrew. Until Jesus approached them, their lives and livelihoods had revolved around fishing. Jesus had been a carpenter. But he didn't approach them from the point of view of a carpenter or talk about how *they* could fit into *his* plan. Instead, he offered to make them "fishers of men," using an image they could relate to (Matt. 4:19). When you approach someone for his or her help, do you begin with *I* or *you*? Do you focus upon your desire or their need?

You might ask, "How am I supposed to know *their* perspective?" This is where you have to do your homework. You need to find out everything you can about the potential partner from others. If you have a relationship with the person already, ask him or her questions that will help you understand his or her frame of reference, desires, needs, and priorities.

Once you know the person's perspective, you can design your approach. I follow a very simple "sandwich" method. The first slice of bread (the opening) focuses on their perspective—their goals, desires, hopes, or loves. The meat of the presentation is a clear and precise expression of my vision. And the final slice of bread focuses on how their participation in that vision can help them achieve their goals or desires. I also lay out a clear vision of the role they will play and the contribution I believe they can make. Once this is done, I am ready to move to the third and final step of recruitment, my offer.

Like the first two steps, it is easier to fail at this step than it is to succeed. It's human nature to try to offer as little as possible. This was never the approach Jesus took. As he said, "The laborer is worthy of his hire" (Lk. 10:7). In other words, a person's reward should be commensurate with their contribution. A big contribution is worth significant pay. A small contribution means modest pay. If you are going to err, I would suggest that you err on the side of generosity rather than stinginess.

When Bob Marsh recruited me to partner with him on the start-up of a television marketing company, I gladly would have worked for a modest salary. But Bob was wiser than that. He offered me a reasonable salary, plus a large piece of ownership. My ownership percentage ultimately helped to produce tens of millions of dollars in personal income for me and even more for Bob and his family.

During my thirty-two years with American Telecast, every project and new business we launched utilized celebrity endorsers. Our endorsers included Cher, Jane Fonda, Charlton Heston, Michael Landon, John Ritter, Kenny Rogers, Chuck Norris, Kathie Lee Gifford, Dick Clark, and at least eighty others. Each of our endorsers received royalties as well, based on their project's sales. Over the years, we paid out over $100 million in royalties to our various celebrities. Investment bankers looking at our business were critical of how much we paid our endorsers, believing that we had over-paid. What they didn't realize was that without the credible endorsements of our celebrity partners, our $2 billion in sales never would have taken place. And one of the reasons we were able to get such a great pool of celebrity endorsers was our track record in terms of the money we offered and the royalties we paid.

The *value* of your offer isn't always represented by the amount of money you offer or the ownership stake you put up. Value can also be defined by intangible benefits—such as personal fulfillment, contribution to a truly worthy cause, or establishing relationships with new people. One of my compa-nies is a software company that engineered a software program that protects children from inappropriate—and even danger-ous—Internet sites. Chuck Norris partnered with us as both a spokesperson and a major investor, not because of the money he would make but because he shared our vision of protecting kids from those who stalk children on the Internet.

In our personal relationships (including marriage), our of-fer is often based on such intangibles as commitment, trust, friendship, emotional security, respect and admiration, and devotion and faithfulness. Marriages built on such values have the kind of foundation that will enable them to last a lifetime.

4) *Effectively Utilize Your Partners*

The best partner in the world is worthless if he or she is not effectively utilized. One of my favorite examples of this is the 1899 partnership between a start-up automotive company and a young engineer recruited to be its chief engineer and corporate officer. The company was the Detroit Automobile Company, and the engineer was Henry Ford. The company's ineffective utilization of Ford resulted in his being fired in 1901. The company went bankrupt shortly after that. In the two years Ford worked for the company, it failed to bring a single car to market. It had partnered with one of the greatest visionaries in industrial history, but it had failed to effectively utilize him. Two years later, Ford joined another group and created the Ford Automobile Company. Within a few years, one out of every two cars in the world had his name on it. This illustrates the incalculable difference between effectively utilizing partners and using them ineffectively.

Jesus was the ultimate master when it came to mentoring and partnering. Initially, he partnered with twelve disciples. Later, he partnered with many others. And his disciples took his message and mission out to the world and changed the course of human history.

◉◉ How to Use Your Partners Effectively

The Four Components of Effective Partnering

1. *Give your partners the opportunity, the authority, and the means to accomplish their assignments.*
   Jesus provided his partners and protégés with the greatest assignments and opportunities ever given to

mankind. But he also gave them the *authority* they
needed to seize those opportunities and successfully
complete their assignments (see Matt. 16:19 and
Lk. 9:1). And he provided the *means* by which they
could accomplish all he set before them (see Jn.
14–15 and Acts 1:8).

In business we often give assignments to people
without giving them the power they need to achieve
those assignments. We don't give them the necessary
authority, budget, staffing, support, or direction.

One of the most brilliant stock analysts in
America is a friend of mine named Tom. For
decades, Tom has successfully managed the
portfolios of a number of high-net-worth
individuals. A small company in Arizona successfully
recruited Tom a number of years ago. Tom's joining
the company gave its owners a wonderful
opportunity to share with their clients the
tremendous benefit of his expertise and skills. But,
like the board of the Detroit Automobile Company,
the owners sabotaged Tom's ability to perform the
role they had recruited him for. They micromanaged
Tom's recommendations and constantly overruled
his decisions. Not only did their clients' portfolios
fail to achieve the gains they could have, but the firm
lost Tom as a partner.

Too often, we make similar mistakes in marriage
and in parenting. We make demands of our spouses

and kids without empowering them with all that is necessary to fulfill those demands. We fail to give them the love, support, encouragement, or direction they need. Then we get frustrated when they fail to meet our expectations. Ask yourself if your partner has what he or she needs in terms of resources and support, and then supply them—before you look for results.

2. ***Provide them with the right environment.*** Jesus couldn't provide his disciples with a nice place to live or a comfortable workplace. Their lodging was the floors of the Judaean deserts and the beaches of the Galilean sea. They never knew where their next meal was going to come from. And yet Jesus provided them with the most incredible "work environment" anyone has ever experienced—his presence. In his presence, they experienced love and security, an inexpressible joy, and an unshakable contentment they had never known before. They were present to hear all of his teachings, see all of his miracles, and witness firsthand the extraordinary manner in which he did all that he had to do. Nothing on earth could have pried them away from Jesus. How could a man of no means, no material possessions, and no physical security offer the greatest work environment ever provided? The answer can be found in words like *love*, *honor*, *truth*, *integrity*, *wisdom*, *compassion*, *inspiration*, and *purpose* beyond compare.

When Bob Marsh invited me to start a new business with him, he knew that providing the right environment was critical to maximizing my creativity and productivity. More important, he knew that providing the right environment was more about creating a secure and caring relationship built on honor, respect, and commitment than it was about a physical workplace or lavish office. He knew I needed his availability for counsel, rather than his oversight or micromanagement. He knew I needed lots of freedom to create, discover, and even fail. Bob knew that when I had a major strikeout, I didn't need a lecture, but rather I needed time, a listening ear, and wise counsel. In any given situation, he seemed to know exactly what I needed. He knew that whenever I asked for his ear, his time, or his direction, it was critical that I get it. He knew that love and honor would motivate me to do whatever it took to succeed. He knew that using fear, threats, or ultimatums would handcuff my creativity and crush my spirit. Bob knew that I could hit home runs only by being permitted to work at my pace and in my style. For example, he knew that I could never write a commercial or a show in my office—I needed the solitude and space of a hotel room. He knew that I couldn't write a script weeks ahead of a deadline but could write one only a few days or even a few hours before a production was to begin. As unnerving and unconventional as my work style was, he encouraged it rather than resisted it. While every other boss I had ever had was always upset that I would start three new projects before I finished one, Bob knew that if he *allowed* me to do that, I would finish the most important one in record time. He was the most incredible partner and mentor any man could ever have. His dealings with me were in many ways a mirror image of how Jesus dealt with his disciples.

Each partner has their own unique work style. Accommodating that style and their specific needs is often the key to empowering them to achieve the highest level of performance and success.

3. ***Offer generous incentives.*** I have never met anyone who did not *hope* to be significantly rewarded for his or her efforts and accomplishments. And yet I never cease to be amazed how many employers, husbands, wives, and parents seem to minimize or ignore this law of human nature. I've heard parents tell their kids that their reward for work is the sense of accomplishment they feel when they complete the work. And yet those same parents would be incensed if their employers gave them the same rationale for not giving them a raise or bonus for achieving something extraordinary at work. Likewise, husbands and wives take each other's efforts and contributions for granted and rarely reward each other for all of the effort and work they do to make the marriage, family, or home successful.

Jesus constantly provided incentives to his disciples and to others who followed him and "labored" in his "vineyard." Jesus made countless promises to those who followed him, from the security of God's love to the promise of eternal life. In other words, for those who fulfill the conditions he set forth, he promised incredible rewards. In Matthew 19:29–30, he promised that everyone who made major sacrifices to follow and serve him would receive a hundred times as much in return, as well as eternal life. When one of his disciples said, "We've left all and followed you," and asked what they would receive for doing so, Jesus didn't just give them a general idea, but rather made a very specific commitment to them. He told them that they would ultimately sit on thrones and rule the twelve tribes of the nation of Israel.

To effectively utilize a partner, we *must* provide incentives that will motivate our partner to go above and beyond their everyday efforts. Both Donald Trump and Warren Buffett have extolled the virtues of the business models of well-run multilevel marketing companies. One of the greatest driving forces behind the powerful growth that so many of these companies have enjoyed is the cash and material incentives these companies offer to their distributors. They offer everything from rank and award recognition to cash and travel bonuses to extraordinary new-car incentives.

A friend of mine who is a college professor offered her high school–aged son $100 for every A he got on his report card and $75 for every B. Moreover, she said that she would *deduct* $100 for every C and $150 for every D he received. Her son graduated from high school a year early with nearly a 4.0 GPA. He also received an academic scholarship to one of America's leading universities. Needless to say, her incentive program paid incredible dividends to her and her son. When it comes to incentives, be creative. The right incentives will pay you back a lot more in the long term than they will cost you. Don't ever fall victim to the illusion that your appreciation or love or the wage you pay is all the incentive people need.

4. ***Use the greatest long-term motivational strategy.*** When it comes to motivating others, we need to realize there are three great motivating factors that drive human behavior: the desire for gain, the fear of loss, and the desire to love and be loved. Incentives appeal to a person's desire for gain and thus provide strong short-term motivation. Fear of loss is also a very powerful motivating factor within one's life and can be easily played upon for short-term motivation.

But most of us are too quick to use fear as a motivational tool with our subordinates at work, our partners in business, and even our spouse and children. Why? Because it requires little effort on our part, no self-control or patience, and almost no explanation or instruction, and it usually brings about quick compliance. Unfortunately, although fear may bring about a quick fix, if used repeatedly it can easily demotivate the person and ultimately destroy the relationship. Love, on the other hand, may not bring about a *quick* fix, but instead of destroying a relationship it strengthens and builds it. The problem is, using love as a motivational tool requires patience, commitment, self-control, and instruction. It takes a lot more time and effort to use love than it does to use fear. Jesus occasionally used fear when there was no other way to get through the hardheadedness of those he was teaching. For example, he told those around him that anyone who caused a child to stumble in his or her relationship with God would be better off if a giant rock were tied around their neck and they were thrown into the sea (Matt. 18:6). He lashed out at hypocrites and rich people who didn't use their wealth to help others. But the strategy he used *most* of the time was based on love. He demonstrated an uncanny amount of patience with his disciples. He was quick to listen, and his dealings reflected compassion and kindness. And he demanded that his partners and protégés act in the same way with those they would teach.

When I talk about motivating with love, I'm referring to *honoring* the other person and motivating them in ways that build their self-esteem and value rather than tearing them down. Jesus was better at this than anyone in history. It is the essence of who he was. He said that he came to serve others rather than be served (Matt. 20:28). He not only gave his disciples the opportunity and authority to change the world, but he gave them a living example of how to do it. Motivating with love not only gets better long-term results, but it engenders long-term commitment.

Similarly, Bob Marsh almost never had to resort to fear with any of his partners—we were all driven by our desire to bless him the way he had so blessed us. Next time you find yourself reacting to someone at work or at home with demands, ultimatums, or threats, catch yourself midstream. Take a time-out. Think about Jesus, constantly encouraging his partners, building them up, forgiving them, and patiently leading and teaching them. Think of the many times he used phrases like "Be of good cheer" or "Fear not." Even on the eve of his execution, he focused upon the needs of his disciples. At the Last Supper, he comforted them with the words "Let not your heart be troubled." He gave them encouragement and instructions as to what to do in the hours and days ahead.

Remember, we can never achieve anything significant by ourselves. Extraordinary outcomes can be achieved only through effective partnering. And Jesus provided us with the perfect example and comprehensive instructions on how to emulate it in our work lives and in our personal lives.

Understanding Changes Minds— Action Changes Lives

UTILIZING THE METHOD THAT WORKS MIRACLES

1. Which of your personal or business endeavors, projects, or goals do you think would benefit significantly by re-cruiting a partner or mentor? Prioritize your list, beginning with the most important area first.

2. Identify the specific types of partners or mentors that you should try to recruit that would enable you to more quickly and effectively achieve your most important dreams and projects.

3. For each kind of partner or mentor that you have identified, make a list of specific individuals who could fulfill your need.

4. How do you currently motivate your peers, your loved ones, and those under your authority? Do you usually motivate with fear or with love and honor? Write down at least one instance in which you used fear as your motivational approach and one in which you used honor or love. How could you have replaced the "fear" motivation with one that reflected honor?

MISSION Accomplished

"'Master,' he said, 'you entrusted me with
five talents. See, I have gained five more.'
His master replied, 'Well done, good and faithful servant!
You have been faithful with a few things; I will put
you in charge of many things. Come and share
your master's happiness!'"

—JESUS (MATT. 25:20–21, NIV)

৩ Turning a Purpose-*Driven* Life into a "Purpose-*Accomplished*" Life

One of my favorite books of the past decade is *The Purpose Driven Life*. But according to Jesus, we gain no praise or reward for simply being purpose *driven*. Praise and rewards are reserved for those who *accomplish* the worthwhile purposes that drive them. At the end of the day, Jesus taught us to live purpose-*accomplished* lives.

Most people do *not* live "purpose-driven lives." As a result, they rarely achieve more than mediocrity in their lives and careers. It is only when a person is driven by a purpose that he or she has the *potential* to achieve extraordinary outcomes. And yet even people who live purpose-driven lives may not achieve what they set out to do. For more than fifty years, hundreds of scientists and engineers were driven by the "purpose" of inventing a practical electric light. But only Edison succeeded. Many were better educated, better qualified, and better funded than Edison. And yet they failed to accomplish the purpose that drove them day and night for years. Why? What kept hundreds of the world's best from accomplishing in fifty years what Edison accomplished in three? What are the obstacles that prevent even the most purpose-driven people from accomplishing their goals?

In my field, direct-response television marketing, the industry success rate is less than one half of one percent. Since we started our company thirty-three years ago, our career success rate in this field has been 62 percent, or about 124 times greater than the industry average. Michael Landon, one of my dearest friends in Hollywood, had a hit rate that was even better. 100 percent of his television projects became prime-time hits. In high school I sat next to Steven Spielberg at nearly every football game—he was in the band, and I was in the color guard. Steve's hit rate for successful movie projects is nearly 80 percent. When Steve and I ran into each other eighteen years after we graduated from high school, we compared notes. We had both achieved our impossible dreams—we had both achieved the highest success rate of anyone in our respective industries, and we had both used the exact same strategies. I discovered that Michael Landon had used the same strategies. But to my dismay, none of these strategies are taught in school—not in high school, college, or even grad school. We had each learned them from our mentors.

Amazingly, Edison and every other superachiever I have

studied used the same strategies—strategies that powerfully enable people to overcome the obstacles to extraordinary achievement and accomplish the very purposes that drive them. Edison used these strategies on every project he undertook. All of these strategies are taught in the book of Proverbs, and each of them can be seen in the life and missions of Jesus. These strategies can enable anyone to turn a purpose-driven life into a purpose-accomplished life.

◎◎ The Seven *Surmountable* Obstacles That Prevent *Most* People from Accomplishing Significant Goals

There are seven obstacles that keep most people from accomplishing their greatest goals. The good news is that there are easily learned strategies to overcome all seven.

1. Lack of Clear and Precise Vision

The vast majority of adults go through each day of their lives *without* a clear vision of what they want to accomplish in the days, weeks, and months ahead. As I pointed out in chapter 5, this first obstacle to a purpose-accomplished life can be overcome by mapping out each important mission you wish to achieve. Once you've clearly defined your vision, you can convert it into specific goals and convert the goals into steps and the steps into specific tasks. Jesus always had a precise vision of what he wanted to accomplish *before* he set out to accomplish it. He was always in motion, moving toward the accomplishment of his missions. He never let his focus on his mission's destination prevent him from living in the moment, but he also never let his focus on the present stop or deter his progress toward accomplishing his goals. For example, at the very beginning of his ministry, Jesus was about to leave one crowd that was enthusiastically pursuing him to go on to the next village to preach his message. His disciples wanted him to continue with the crowd at hand. He told them, "Let us go into the next towns, that I may preach there also, because for this *purpose* I have come forth" (Mk. 1:38, NKJV).

2. Ineffective Goal Setting

There are two basic approaches to goal setting. The first is the conventional method of setting achievable, reachable goals. This is what we are taught in school and by well-meaning motivational speakers and self-help authors. While this approach is far better than no approach at all, there is a more *powerful* approach, one that has been used by every superachiever in history. It is the one that was used by Jesus and his disciples. I call this approach "shooting for the moon." Jesus told his disciples that if they would truly "believe," they would do the very things he did, and even *more* (Jn. 14:12). More often than not, they followed the path of least resistance, setting goals that were easily achieved. Over and over again, they failed to attempt the impossible and settled for mediocrity. Only later did they begin to shoot for the moon, attempting the impossible and achieving it over and over again.

In shooting for the moon, one sets goals that are so high they are virtually *impossible* to achieve. You might think, "Well, if they're impossible, then by definition, I can't achieve them. . . . Why set them so high?" The answer is, they are impossible for you to achieve *by yourself*! The key to "hitting the moon" when you shoot for it is to reach outside yourself and effectively partner with others. No significant or extraordinary success in history has ever been achieved alone. Charles Lindbergh became famous for the first solo flight across the Atlantic. But Lindbergh's accomplishment was far from a solo effort. It represented the culmination of months of painstaking efforts by Lindberg, his partners at Ryan Aircraft in San Diego, and his investment partners in Saint Louis. As a result of their partnership, they shot for the moon and hit it. And their accomplishment ultimately changed the course of commercial aviation forever.

In chapter 8, I wrote about pursuing Tom Selleck, Charlton Heston, and President Reagan to endorse a magazine my partners and I had decided to help out. That is an example of shooting for the moon. Had I simply set achievable, reachable goals, I would have ended up with a minor celebrity endorsing the publication, and the project certainly would have failed. Instead, we *hit* the moon. The shooting-for-the-moon approach always starts with the question, "If I could achieve *anything* I want in this situation, what would it be?" This approach is so powerful and life-changing I've dedicated entire chapters to it and its execution in three of my previous books. It is an approach that can be used in any important

MISSION Accomplished   167

area of your life. I've used it in business, in my marriage, in my writing and television projects, and with my children. It has helped my fifteen-year-old son to become one of the top three high jumpers and long jumpers in the nation and my thirteen-year-old son to play piano pieces, like Gershwin's *Rhapsody in Blue*, that challenge even concert pianists.

Over the past thirty years, I have shot for the moon on *every one* of the hundreds of projects I have pursued in business. It has been key to every extraordinary success my partners and I have ever experienced.

3. Ineffective Partnering

A third obstacle that stands between us and significant and extraordinary accomplishment is our failure to partner effectively. Effective partnering is *critical* to turning a purpose-driven life into a purpose-*accomplished* life. In the previous chapter, I discussed what it takes to effectively partner. Jesus was a *master* of the art of effective partnering. When you learn how to effectively partner, you'll be able to hit the moon more times than you'll miss it.

4. Lack of Resources

The number-one reason people give for their failure to achieve the success they deserve is a lack of resources. So often I hear people say, "I just don't have the time." Or they claim they don't have the talent, education, experience, or money necessary to achieve their dreams. This may be a valid reason for failure for the person who doesn't effectively partner. But effective partnering easily eliminates the seemingly insurmountable obstacle of insufficient resources. The truth is, there are only a handful of things any one person does well; but there are *millions* of things we *don't* do well or *can't* do at all. Without effective partnering, we cannot overcome this obstacle to accomplishment. But with effective partnering, it is the *easiest* obstacle of all to surmount. Everyone who has ever achieved their impossible dreams, from Edison to Bill Gates, lacked *most* of the resources that were required to achieve their dreams. But unlike most people, they quickly realized that partnering with others who possessed those crucial resources was the key to achieving their dreams.

5. Failure to Plan for Failure

I never cease to be amazed at how surprised people are when one of their efforts, endeavors, or projects fails . . . or when they experience a major setback. Jesus said, "In this world, you *will* have trouble" (Jn. 16:33). No one succeeds without failing along the way. But those who ultimately succeed learn the best way to deal with those failures—a way that will strengthen the foundation upon which they will build a more substantial and significant success. Three out of every four new businesses fail within the first year. Three out of four! And yet almost no new businesses include in their plans a contingency for failing. If failing is so common, why does it take most people and most businesses by surprise? Perhaps the most successful businessman in history was Thomas Edison. He not only expected failure but *planned* on it. And because he expected it and planned on it, he created a plan for dealing with it.

Jesus is the only person in history who never failed. Yet he knew his partners would fail over and over again. So he told them what to *do* when they encountered failure. He warned them of the incredible adversities they would face, so they wouldn't be surprised or defeated by those problems. He told them that they would be hated by the world, thrown into prison, and tortured by their enemies. "In this world you will have trouble," he told them. "But take heart! I have overcome the world" (Jn. 16:33). He then explained *precisely* how to deal with all of the trouble they would encounter, so that *they* would ultimately be the winners.

I've had more failures in my business and personal life than anyone I know. But because I learned the *right* way to deal with failure, it has rarely stopped me from achieving my goals and dreams. While there are thousands of ways to deal with failure incorrectly, there is only one right way to deal with it.

The first thing we must do to effectively deal with failure is to change our attitude about it. Failure, instead of being the enemy of success, is a critical *component* of success. Instead of viewing it with dread, we need to begin to view it as a valued teacher. We never need to intentionally pursue failure, because it will pursue us. And on those occasions when failure overtakes us, it is how we react or respond to it that will determine whether it takes the role of an enemy or a teacher. If we react to it by turning our back to it and running away from the lessons it offers, it will remain a dreaded foe for life. It will chain us to ignorance when wisdom is needed and keep us from taking risks in the future. And without taking significant risks, we can never achieve extraordinary success.

On the other hand, if we respond to our failures by studying them and learning the lessons they have to offer, they will provide us with knowledge and insights that no other teacher can. In 1977, three out of every four television commercials I wrote and produced failed. I was devastated each time. But my mentor and partner made me study each failure to try to figure out what I had missed. With each failure, I discovered the mistakes that had contributed to that failure. In my next production, I would eliminate those mistakes. The next year, my failure rate dropped from 75 percent to 50 percent. That year, I did the same thing. I studied each failure and asked other people involved in the projects what *they* thought had gone wrong. Then, once again, I began to apply those insights to my future productions. The next year, my failure rate dropped from 50 percent to 25 percent. I was hitting home runs three out of every four trips to the plate in an industry where the hit rate was less than 1 percent.

My perseverance wasn't the result of genius, stubbornness, or an innate character trait. Rather, it was the result of effectively dealing with failure. I did that by using Thomas Edison's ingenious method for *creative persistence*. Edison never articulated or taught this method—I discovered it as I read his biography. But the fact is, he used this method to achieve more extraordinary, significant successes than any person or business in history. His method involves five strategies, which he used on every important project he undertook.

◎◎ Edison's "Creative Persistence" in the Face of Failure

Create a Vision ID

As I discussed in chapter 4, before Edison started a project he would always identify his "vision" for the project with a one- or two-page entry in his journal, creating a very simple drawing of what the idea might look like. I call this a vision ID. This is the first step in the vision-mapping process I laid out in chapter 5 and have illustrated in the appendices. When you vision-map a project, idea, or endeavor, you've taken Edison's first step in creative persistence.

List the Broad Ramifications of Succeeding and of Failing

Identifying the broad ramifications of succeeding and the ultimate consequences of failing can be an unimaginable source of power, strength, determination, and creativity in helping you to accomplish a goal. (See pages 61–62.)

Inspire Others with Your Vision

Edison wouldn't just communicate a need or an idea. He would use the broad ramifications of the project to create an infectious enthusiasm and commitment among his partners and staff, his investors and bankers, and his vendors and suppliers. And he would do it so well that the people he inspired found it hard to think about much else.

For more than three decades, whenever I have had a new project, I have shared my thoughts with all of the key people around me—my wife, my friends, and my business partners. I watch their reactions, seek their input, and try to build their enthusiasm. If people do *not* become enthusiastic supporters, it's either because I didn't effectively communicate my vision or because the person I'm talking to is not the right partner or because there is something wrong about my vision that is preventing others from being enthusiastic about it. I usually don't communicate a vision until I have really done my homework and have created an effective and persuasive way to communicate it. And sure enough, my partners usually enthusiastically embrace it and push me to keep going whenever I hit a snag, get discouraged, or feel like giving up.

Let Your Failures Help Guide Any Midcourse Corrections

Edison realized that failures were merely directional signs along the highway to success. As a result, he never resented them but welcomed them, analyzing them for insights that could take him ever closer to his goal. When I was first learning to fly a sailplane (glider), I quickly discovered that winds change often and quickly. And when they change, they always alter your heading. As a result, a pilot usually makes a number of midcourse corrections to stay on course and reach his destination. The more significant or extraordinary a project is, the more obstacles and failures a person will encounter along the way. The only way to complete a challenging project is to study your failures and discover the reasons for those failures. Then we must factor what we have learned into correcting our current course. If we do that diligently, we are far more likely to reach our destination.

Retire Any Three-Legged Horses

It's hard to look at a field full of young horses and figure out which one will win the race. Similarly, when we first begin our pursuit of a challenge, it's hard to tell which projects will succeed and which ones will not. Occasionally, we encounter obstacles that cannot be overcome no matter what resources we obtain to meet them. This happened to Edison a number of times. My mentor called such a pursuit a "three-legged horse." No matter how tall, strong, or good-looking it may be, if it has only three healthy legs, it can*not* win the race. And yet in business people throw good money after bad, desperately trying to keep a three-legged horse in the race.

I invested a great deal of money in a company that created prototypes of a product line that was truly revolutionary. They could replace paper and polystyrene (Styrofoam) products with products made of an all-natural, inexpensive, biodegradable composition. The prototypes and worldwide patents impressed investors at all levels. The company started up in 1992 and burned through a couple of million dollars. Then they raised $25 million and burned through that. They were finding it hard to achieve production runs that reflected the same quality of product they were able to make in smaller batches in the lab. Then they raised another $200 million in a public offering in 1998. A lot of us were sure that with $200 million they could commercialize the product. But year after year, problem after problem, they discovered why Edison said inventing took little genius but *commercialization* required genius and a whole lot more. After burning through more than $300 million, the company finally declared bankruptcy. While their prototype was a true breakthrough, commercializing it was akin to trying to race a three-legged horse. It never made it to the finish line.

6. A Lack of Sustained Passion

People have described me as a passionate person. A lot of people I meet tell me, "Oh, how I *wish* I had your passion." They think I was born with a higher level of passion than other people. In reality, I was born lazy. My nature is to do as little physical and mental labor as is necessary to get the job done. THAT is my *nature*! However, as Jesus said, the truth will set us free. . . . The night I first met this homeless carpenter, my life began to change in many ways, and my passion was one of those ways. Every extraordinary success that I have *ever* achieved has been fueled by an incredibly high level of passion. But I wasn't born with it. *None* of us are born with the passion we need to effectively pursue and achieve extraordinary success. The good news is that *any* of us *can* acquire all the passion we need—once we know where to get it. With it we can fuel even our most difficult goals—all the way to the moon and back. Without it, we'll run out of gas in the *early* stages.

There are two ways to acquire passion for something. I call the first way "catching a passion." We catch a passion the way a forest catches on fire—it begins with a spark that smolders into a small flame and, left unchecked, grows into a consuming blaze. Instead of being controlled by us, it takes hold of our will and desires and ultimately spreads out of control. It can rob us of our focus, our time, and our money and undermine our relationships. I've known men who for years, weekend after weekend, pursued their business or their hobby rather than spend the time with their wives and children. Now, there's nothing inherently wrong with golf or work, but, if unchecked, such pursuits can burn up too much of our most precious asset—time—and leave a path of destruction.

The second way to acquire passion is through what I call "*developing* a passion," and that way can be incredibly constructive and beneficial. Passion is the *only* fuel that can effectively power our drive for excellence and accomplishment. *Developing* a passion puts you in control of your passion instead of letting your passion control you. The difference between the two is like the difference between the destructive power of an atomic bomb and the nuclear fission that drives a nuclear reactor, which is controlled and directed. One can destroy a city; the other one can light it.

So how do you develop passion?

I've had lots of people tell me that it is impossible for them to be passionate about their jobs. I've had men and women tell me, "There's no longer any passion in my marriage." The problem is that they think passion is a product of circumstances and that it is defined by a feeling. But passion isn't a feeling; it's a choice we make. It starts with clear and precise vision—knowing where you are now and where you ultimately want to be, and then creating a map to get there.

The second ingredient behind passion is hope. Unfortunately, *hope* is one of the most misunderstood words in the English language. For most people, *hope* is synonymous with a wish or desire. But that is like equating the word *hurricane* with the word *breeze*. True hope is better defined as a well-founded, confident belief that what has been promised or committed to will be accomplished within a reasonable amount of time. Wishes and desires come and go as fast as a dry leaf blows across our path on a windy day. True hope, on the other hand, has a rock-solid foundation that will stay in place until the goal is accomplished. Each time we complete a task, a step, and a goal defined in our vision map that brings us closer to our destination, our hope is reconfirmed and strengthened. When I was a child, my family used to drive from Phoenix to the Los Angeles area for summer vacation. Back then, it was an eight-hour drive. Usually, about two hours into the drive, I'd start asking my parents, "How much longer?" When they replied, "Six hours," my heart would sink—it seemed like forever. But then, once we crossed the Colorado River into California, it was as if new energy filled every part of my body. Even though we were still four hours away, we were *in* California. And each time I asked the dreaded question, my parents' answer would reflect our progress—"three hours," "two hours," "one hour"! And with each new answer, my hope and excitement grew. Progress toward our defined destinations always deepens our hope.

The third ingredient behind passion is fulfillment. As you complete each step along the way, you gain a greater sense of fulfillment.

And it is this last ingredient that *ignites* the fuel of passion.

Bringing passion into your career or life isn't dependent upon the project, the job, or the other person. . . . It's dependent upon you! You alone can make the choice to act. And the only *obstacle* to our passion to achieve our goal is a *lack* of true diligence.

7. A Lack of Diligence

Most people think of diligence as simply working hard. In a job, we think being diligent means working overtime or working weekends. To some, it means eating, drinking, sleeping, and breathing a project. But none of this reflects *true* diligence. True diligence is so rare that the richest man who ever lived, King Solomon, said, "Do you see a man diligent in his business? He will stand before kings." Because the fact is, the vast majority of people are *not* diligent. And because of that, we experience the consequences of not being diligent: efforts that produce little profit, a loss of wealth and security, and our days spent under the control and direction of others.

True diligence is rare because it runs counter to human nature. Our nature is to be lazy and to pursue instant gratification. By nature, we want as much as we can get for as little effort as we have to spend to get it. By nature, we'd rather play than work. By nature, we'd rather follow the path of least resistance than turn our boat upstream and row like crazy. Diligence, on the other hand, follows a completely different course.

Based on Solomon's wisdom, I would define true diligence as "a learnable skill that starts with a clear vision that creates an intelligent and sustained effort, well planned and performed in a timely, efficient, and effective manner, to attain an exceptional result."

Jesus is certainly the most diligent person who has ever walked the earth. No wonder he accomplished all the missions he set out to accomplish in such a short time. For thirty years, I have tried to bring diligence into each of my business projects. And the results have been phenomenal. We've set response records in every field we've entered, and even our low-budget start-up companies have produced hundreds of millions in sales. Diligence can bring about extraordinary results in every area of our lives.

◎◎ Applying True Diligence to Your Pursuits

Jesus told his followers that their inclination was to procrastinate and focus on the future, to the point that they were missing the moment-by-moment realities that surrounded them. In two thousand years, human nature hasn't changed. Diligence starts by waking up and smelling the Starbucks. It is important to see where we are right now in relation to our goal and to have a clear vision of where we want to go.

The next step in being diligent is to undertake an intelligent, sustained effort. Many people work hard. But how many of us work smart? Diligence demands that we make the *most* of the time we have. If you and I are assigned the task of cutting down two trees, and you use a hammer and I use a chain saw, you may work a hundred times harder than me, but I'm going to successfully cut down the tree in minutes, while you may take months.

The best-planned and best-executed efforts will run into obstacles along the way. And if you do not know how to persist creatively, you will ultimately fail. When we were first launching our new company, Max International, we hired an outside consulting company to design our compensation or commission plan for our sales associates. The plan cost a quarter of a million dollars. Shortly after it was completed, we recruited two master distributors who had been very successful with other companies. As soon as they saw our compensation plan, they told us that there were various aspects of the plan that would raise big red flags to other potential sales leaders. They informed us that these people would walk away because of the structure of the plan. As much as I hated to do it, if we wanted to attract the best leaders in the country, we would need to change our plans. So we trashed the plan and started all over. This time, we created a plan that has been regarded as the best compensation plan in the industry. Instead of repulsing industry leaders, it has attracted them like a giant magnet. That is the power of creative persistence.

Finally, true diligence focuses on the end result, on achieving it efficiently and with excellence.

Now, diligence is not required in *everything* we do. We'd burn out in our twenties if that were the case. I enjoy skiing, but I have no interest in improving my skill level—and applying diligence to my skiing would force me to take significant time away from that which I value most in favor of a hobby for which I have no aspirations. But we do need to apply diligence to those endeavors, projects, or efforts that we consider important.

We were all created to accomplish extraordinary things. When we settle for less than our best—in our marriage, parenting, business projects, and the management of our time and resources—we are failing to live up to our potential. Jesus defined success by what one accomplishes, *not* by what one attempts to accomplish. Following his example, we too can live purpose-accomplished lives.

Understanding Changes Minds– Action Changes Lives

ACCOMPLISHING MISSIONS THAT MATTER

1. List any projects, endeavors, or goals in which you did *not* "accomplish your mission."

2. Using the list of surmountable roadblocks below, determine which roadblocks *prevented* you from accomplishing the missions you listed above.

    a.   Lack of clear and precise vision

    b.   Ineffective goal setting

    c.   Ineffective partnering

    d.   Lack of resources

    e.   Failure to plan for failure

    f.   A lack of sustained passion

    g.   A lack of diligence

3. Take one of your missions "not accomplished" and write out how you could have overcome any of the seven surmountable roadblocks that stood in your way.

4. Write down one of your current projects, endeavors, goals, or missions and how you can overcome whichever of the roadblocks are likely to stand in your way.

—— ∽∾ ——

CHAPTER 10

The Miracle of the Moment: Moving from Failure to Success—Right NOW!

"Do you not say, 'There are still four months and
then comes the harvest'? Behold, I say to you, lift up your
eyes and look at the fields, for they are already
white for harvest!"

—JESUS (JOHN 4:35, NKJV)

A grieving man worked his way through a crowd to approach Jesus. When he finally reached him, he fell on his knees and pleaded, "My daughter has just died. But come and put your hand on her, and she will live." Jesus followed the man to his house, told the mourners to leave, and then, with a touch of his hand and a word from his lips, he brought the man's dead daughter back to life. When Jesus left the house, two blind men in the crowd outside shouted out to him, saying, "Have mercy on us, Son of David." He didn't answer them immediately, but they followed him into another building. He then asked, "Do you believe that I am able to do this?" They replied, "Yes, Lord." He then touched their eyes and said, "According to your faith, will it be done unto you," and they received their sight (see Matt. 9:18–30).

I share this story not to focus on the miracles themselves,

but on the *timing* of the miracles. Imagine if the grieving man had simply thought, "If only Jesus had been around a few hours earlier, my daughter might not have died. Now that she's dead, it's too late to do anything about it." Had he acted as if it were too late, his life, the life of his daughter, and the lives of everyone they later influenced would have been robbed of the wonder and joy that followed the miracle. But instead of focusing on his daughter's death, he focused on the opportunity at hand—the opportunity to recruit the help of a miracle worker—someone who could perhaps bring his daughter back to life.

The same was true with the two blind men. Imagine if they had thought, "He's too far away and the crowd is too big. Maybe we'll be able to get closer tomorrow or another day." Or if they had decided they wanted to wait until they could ask him quietly to heal them, so they wouldn't make fools of themselves in front of the crowd by shouting for help. Had they not seized the opportunity of the *moment*, they could have missed the opportunity of a lifetime. They realized that if they didn't act now, the opportunity would be gone . . . and might never return. So they seized the moment.

Today, too often we focus on anything and everything *except* the present moment. Whether our thoughts are distracted by things around us or focused on the past or future, we fail to live in the moment at hand. I don't think a month passes where I don't hear my wife say, "Earth to Steve," as she tries to bring me out of the clouds and into the moment. In chapter 2, I told how my son Devin grew to hate my cell phone because he felt that I was more focused on the people I was talking to than I was on him. I was not only showing a preference to them, I was missing my "moments" with him. I was missing the chance to listen to him and show him how important he was to me and how wonderful he was. All of that for the sake of taking a call instead of waiting until a better time, when I was alone and not robbing my son of my presence.

෨ Before You Can *Seize* an Opportunity, You Must *See* It!

In business, seeing and seizing an opportunity is just as important as any other skill. One of the greatest strengths of American Telecast was our ability to see an opportunity in front of us and *immediately* act on it. Our competitors were often like giant ships on the oceans. As an opportunity came into view, it took so long for their bureaucracy to see it and respond to it that by the time they were able to "turn the ship," the opportunity had been missed. We were more like a small, high-speed jet boat. When we saw a potential opportunity, we could turn on a dime, race into position, and snag the opportunity before anyone else had a chance to respond.

In October of 1985, my partners and I received a terrible shock. We had been in an exclusive marketing partnership with a major life insurance company for six years. Our deal was simple: Each quarter, we would spend millions of dollars running television campaigns to generate leads and sell their health and life insurance policies. They would then reimburse us for the money that we had spent with the television stations that were airing the campaign. Then, at some designated point in the future, they would pay us 50 percent of the profits generated from the hundreds of thousands of policies we had sold.

That October, they owed us millions of dollars for the previous quarter's television campaign, and many millions more as our share of the profits that had been generated from six years of sales. Unfortunately for us, they had recently been purchased by a foreign company, and when we asked them to pay the media dollars they owed us and our share of the profits that had accumulated over the years, the new owners refused. They simply gave us a choice: "You can sue us, and we'll tie you up in court for years, *or* you can give us a release from our obligations and we will release you from your obligation to market exclusively for us, so you can be free to market for other insurance companies—your choice."

We were devastated! If we weren't paid what we were owed, we would almost surely be bankrupt before long. At the same time, if they tied us up in court, we would *definitely* go broke, and perhaps even more quickly. Our *only* hope was to accept their outrageous offer of a mutual release and to try to cut a deal with another insurance company to create a successful television marketing campaign. So we accepted, even though it appeared to be business suicide. We had only enough cash to stay in business for a few months, and we owed television stations $4 million for the last campaign we had run on the insurance company's behalf.

Our business seemed doomed. Then two dear friends

loaned us the money we needed to stay afloat for the next few months. Their loans, however, would not create any new sales to keep us in business beyond that, nor pay the television stations the $4 million we owed. We needed a marketing grand-slam home run, and we needed it quick.

Jesus told his disciples that they (like so many of us) had a habit of procrastinating. Moreover, they were so focused on the future that they were missing the incredible opportunities of the moment right in front of their eyes. He commanded them to lift up their eyes and look at the fields in front of them—for they were already ripe for harvest.

More often than not, we miss the opportunities that are right in front of us and all around us. All we have to do is open our eyes and look for them. Ben Weaver, our newest partner, went into overdrive and within a couple of weeks found another direct-response insurance company with whom he cut a deal. They agreed to pay us twelve dollars for every insurance lead we could generate. Now came the hard part—creating a campaign that would generate hundreds of thousands of leads quickly enough to save our business. Normally it takes twelve to eighteen months to sign a celebrity spokesperson, write and produce the television commercials, run the commercials in test markets, evaluate them, make adjustments to the commercials, and finally roll them out into a national campaign. Then it can take another year or two to generate enough leads to make the $4 million we needed to pay the TV bills we had incurred on behalf of the *previous* insurance company. But we didn't have three years, or two years, or even six months. We needed to generate that money in sixteen *weeks!*

On the first day of November, a couple of days after Ben made the deal with the new insurance company, I was having dinner with Harry Morgan, who had played the role of Colonel Potter on the TV series *M*A*S*H*. Harry was one of my closest friends and had been our spokesperson in previous insurance campaigns. He asked how things were going, and I told him of our plight. I told him we had just signed with a new insurance company and needed a new spokesperson for a campaign I was going to produce. He suggested that I use him. It was a generous offer, but I told him that I didn't think that would work because we had overexposed him in our previous campaigns. Then he said, "I think I could do something that would really work for you." A couple of years earlier, his wife of forty-seven years had unexpectedly collapsed and died of a heart attack. In the two years that followed, Harry had nearly died of a broken heart. But he had come through it and said he would be willing to talk about his ordeal in the commercial. I said, "Harry . . . I could NEVER ask you to do that." He replied, "Steve, you don't understand. I made it through it, and now I understand the terrible pain a person goes through when he or she loses a spouse. And I didn't have any *financial* struggles. Can you imagine what people go through when they have *both* the emotional loss that I experienced *and* a financial calamity at the same time? *That* is what I would like to talk about, and I know you could write it in a sensitive way."

I had been looking all over Hollywood for a new celebrity, for a "field to harvest," and God had put that white field right in front of my eyes. I told Harry I'd like to give it a shot. I wrote and produced the commercials two weeks later. We tested them two weeks after that and then rolled out the national campaign on December 18, 1985, just six weeks after Harry had first made the suggestion. The result was the grand-slam home run we had been hoping for, an ad that resulted in one of the biggest responses in television history. Within three months, we had generated over one *million* leads, making enough money to pay off the $4 million debt we owed to the television stations and the loans we had received from our two friends. And all because Harry Morgan saw that the field right in front of us was already white for harvest. All we had to do was seize the moment. Had we not done so, we would have been out of business in a few short months.

How many opportunities do we miss in business and in our personal lives because we are distracted by issues that aren't important, are looking back over our shoulders at the past, or are looking forward into the future? The principle Jesus revealed is, simply, don't waste time focusing on distractions or gazing back or ahead. Look up and focus on the opportunity that's right before your eyes. And then seize it. Jesus knew that most opportunities are lost because people are too caught up in other things to see them.

Opportunities to achieve extraordinary outcomes are around us . . . right now. But most people miss the harvest in front of them because they are focused elsewhere. Thinking about something that is going to happen in a few minutes or hours is as much "living in the future" as thinking of something that is a year or two down the road. Your thoughts of the past or future are blocking your view of the present. For example, let's say your spouse is trying to talk to you about his or her day, and you're thinking about dinner or a call you need to make after dinner. So you hear only half of what he or she says. Or imagine your kids are trying to have a conversation with you about school or a social activity, and you fail to respond because you're thinking about something your boss said earlier that afternoon.

Whenever you are thinking about something that will happen in the future, or that happened in the past, you are a million miles away. Jesus taught us that either was a misuse of our time. He taught "living in the now" more than two thousand years before Eckhart Tolle wrote his popular book. Of those who live in the past, Jesus said, "No one who puts his hand to the plow and looks back is fit for service in the kingdom of God" (Lk. 9:62, NIV). Similarly, he said of the future, "Therefore do not worry about tomorrow, for tomorrow will worry about itself. Each day has enough trouble of its own" (Matt. 6:34, NIV). The good news is, we don't have to wait a single moment to begin our journey toward extraordinary success. Whether at home or at work—we can start right now!

ᴄᴏ The Things That Prevent Us from Seizing an Opportunity

A couple of months ago, I was invited to speak at a church in Frisco, Texas. The pastor told the congregation the night before that I would be speaking the next night to tell of a new company I had started and the opportunity it offered people to earn income from a home-based business. About 150 people from his church showed up the next night. Among the folks who showed up were two young men who seemed to hang on every word I said. They saw the opportunity in front of them that night and joined our company as independent associates. More than anyone else in the room that night, they seized the opportunity with their whole heart. Within two months, they had become our company's top two recruiters, surpassing the efforts of our fifty thousand other associates. I believe they'll be earning seven-figure incomes within the next twelve to eighteen months. And both of these men are part-time in the business. One is a homebuilder, and the other is in the medical-equipment business.

On the other hand, I have presented this *same* opportunity to thousands of other people, in meetings and one on one, and yet most never seize it. I offer them an opportunity to be mentored in a business where they could make ten times the income they're currently making—and yet many let the opportunity pass by. Why? There are several obstacles that prevent most people from seizing the opportunities they see.

The Obstacles to Seizing Opportunities

1. *Inadequate Vision.* It may be the most important opportunity of your life, but if you don't recognize its importance and the short-term and long-term ramifications of succeeding or failing, you may not be willing to do what is necessary to pursue and seize the opportunity.

2. *Disbelief.* You simply do not believe that the opportunity is real or that you have the time, talent, ability, education, knowledge, or money needed to exploit the opportunity. Whether that disbelief is founded or unfounded, it can rule the day and ruin your future.

3. *A Lone Ranger Mentality.* You understand the opportunity and its short-term and long-term importance. But as you look at yourself, you decide that you don't have *all* of the resources that would be needed to successfully seize the opportunity. You're only one person, and you can only do so much! Even if you wanted to partner with someone, you wouldn't know where to start.

4. *Fear.* You may believe the opportunity is real and realize you have all of the resources you need, but you're afraid of failing or afraid of the consequences of failing.

5. *Lack of Motivation.* You may believe the opportunity is real and that you have the resources you need, but you're just not motivated to act. The

value of the opportunity in your mind just doesn't warrant the commitment of time, effort, and energy that you would have to expend to take advantage of it. You'd rather be doing something else.

6. *Procrastination.* You really want to seize the opportunity—and will do so, later! Now's not a good time. . . . You're too busy, too inexperienced, too financially strapped. Surely it will be no less an opportunity tomorrow. . . .

◎◎ Every Obstacle Can Be Climbed Over, Dug Under, Moved Aside, or Gotten Around

Expanding Your Vision

Solomon said that without a vision, people die. Jesus, taking that wisdom one step further, said that people see and yet do not perceive. I can present the same opportunity to thousands of people, in exactly the same way, and yet only a few will see it for what it is. And those few will usually achieve outcomes far beyond what others can even dream. By using the vision-mapping process, effective partnering, and Edison's techniques for identifying the broad ramifications of a vision, anyone can see and seize an opportunity they are truly interested in.

Transforming Disbelief into Belief

The second obstacle that prevents most people from seizing opportunities is that we do not believe an opportunity is real or significant. How can you transform your disbelief into be-lief? The answer is *not* to simply change your feelings. The ONLY foundation upon which a belief can be securely built is *evidence*. No one believed in Jesus simply because it made them feel good. Rather, he gave them undeniable, irrefutable, tangible, and visible evidence that he *was* who he claimed to be. If we are to change our disbelief concerning an opportunity, we must first gather evidence that convinces us that the opportunity is real.

Solomon wrote in Proverbs that the simple believe everything, but a wise man looks deeply into a matter. The stronger the evidence, the greater your belief will become. If you can't find enough evidence, the opportunity may not be as real or as great as you thought. This is not the case, however, when it comes to genuinely breakthrough opportunities. Early on, the most brilliant business minds in the world would not have been able to find much evidence to support the claim that there would be an unimaginable market for personal computers or for the Internet in the near future. The few who bet on that opportunity—before there was adequate evidence—became billionaires. I've spent my business life looking for breakthrough opportunities and, upon finding them, seizing them with every ounce of my being. In those breakthrough cases, there was little evidence to support the opportunity they offered. There happened to be just enough for me to believe in the opportunity, but not enough that many others would believe in it. So I swung for the fence. And I missed nearly 40 percent of the time. But

60 percent of the time, my partners and I hit home runs, making us a pioneer and the undisputed leader in our industry during our first two decades in television direct marketing.

Trading in Your Lone Ranger Mentality

If you are not good at gathering the evidence, you need to convince yourself of the opportunity at hand and partner with someone who is good at it. I have NEVER had the time, talent, ability, education, knowledge, or money to seize even ONE of the opportunities that have made me millions or affected millions of lives. Yet I've always believed that I could seize the opportunities. For every resource that I personally lack, someone else has it in abundance. All I've needed to do is to effectively partner with them.

We have been taught from our childhood to go it alone, to always "look out for number one." The reality is, life is about *us*. And the only way we can achieve anything significant or extraordinary is to partner with others. As we saw in chapter 8, no one, other than Jesus himself, accomplishes anything significant or extraordinary on his or her own. When it came to taking his message to the world, even Jesus relied on the partners he had mentored.

Replacing Fear with Confidence

For many people, fear is a barrier as high as Mount Everest. They routinely watch opportunities in their relationships, projects, jobs, and careers pass by, because they are afraid of failing or of the criticism and rejection of others. Such fear can paralyze us in our tracks.

Jesus's disciples were fearful about so much during their three and a half years at his side. They were afraid of what others thought. They were afraid of being injured and killed. They were afraid of criticism and failure. They were afraid of not receiving everything they had hoped to receive from their mentor. They were worried about who would get to sit beside him when he ushered in the kingdom of heaven. Over and over and over again, we find them fearful, and sometimes even terrified. And yet they were walking with a man who had healed the sick, given sight to the blind, and raised the dead. Over and over again, we find Jesus telling them, "Don't be afraid," "Fear not," and "Don't let your hearts be troubled." But fear they did.

So how are *we* supposed to confront and overcome fears that stand between us and an opportunity? The first step is always to confront the *root* cause of your fear.

The disciple who had the closest personal relationship with Jesus was the Apostle John. John wrote, "Perfect love drives out fear" (1 Jn. 4:18, NIV). *Perfect* in the sense John used it doesn't mean flawless. It means "mature" or "complete" or "whole." John is saying that when we have a mature or whole love for someone, our fear in that relationship will be driven out by the presence of a vastly superior force: mature love. If you struggle with fear in your relationships, it is likely because you are more concerned about what you can *get* from that relationship than about what you can *give*. When we focus on ourselves, fear can grow in our hearts and minds. Focusing upon the needs of others produces an environment that fosters confidence, courage, and love.

Many women fear being criticized. For men, our core fear is failure. The key to overcoming one's fear of criticism is to learn to embrace criticism rather than avoid it or run away from it. By learning to "mine" every criticism for gold, looking for any hint of something we can learn from, criticism becomes an opportunity for self-improvement rather than a school report card.

Our fear of failure, too, is easily dealt with when we know the right techniques. First, remember that failure is one of the world's greatest teachers. By revisiting past failures, whether in business or in your personal life, you can learn great lessons. As you do this, you'll also begin to lose your fear of failing. Not that you *want* to fail, but you won't be slowed down or paralyzed by your fear of it. Fear becomes a minor hurdle to jump over rather than a paralyzing roadblock.

Lay out a chart where you write down your worst-case scenario of failing at an opportunity, your best-case scenario of succeeding, and what you believe may be the most likely scenario. As you do this, you'll usually see that the benefits of your potential success far outweigh the potential downside of failing, even in the worst-case scenario. When you lay it out on paper, your fears can be managed and tamed.

Overcoming a Lack of Motivation

A lack of motivation is extremely easy to overcome. That's because one's lack of motivation is never the root problem.

No one is motivated to pursue or seize an opportunity that they don't believe is significant or one they don't believe they will be *able* to achieve.

If I offer you a million dollars to find my best friend's home in the next twenty-four hours but don't tell you his name or address, you won't be motivated to pursue that million-dollar opportunity, because you don't have a crystal ball and have no way to undertake a search. On the other hand, if I put the money in an escrow account with your name on it and give you instructions that provide you with clues to discover his name and address, then you'll begin to see the opportunity as real. When you believe the opportunity is worthwhile and real, you will find that you have all the motivation you need.

Breaking the Procrastination Barrier

What may seem to be the smallest and easiest barrier to overcome—procrastination—is in reality one of the deadliest. Procrastination is difficult to overcome because we rarely take it seriously. And the most successful enemy in any battle is the one we don't take seriously enough to address. We so often live in the illusion that time is our least important commodity and that there will always be more of it later to do what we need or want to do. So we simply put off our pursuit of many opportunities until later. It's not that we plan to *not* pursue them. We just don't want to pursue them right now. I see this nearly every week in business and in people's careers.

Jesus spoke very harshly to those who procrastinated.

One man who wanted to follow Jesus said, "Lord, let me first go and bury my father." Now, his father hadn't yet died. This was a common expression at the time that meant "Let me tend our family business until my father dies and his estate is settled." Jesus replied curtly, "Follow me, and let the dead bury the dead" (Matt. 8:21–22). He was literally telling him to not wait a single minute, to stop what he was doing and follow him now! As Jesus knew, if the man didn't follow him now, he wouldn't follow him later when it was a more convenient time. There will always be one more thing that needs to be settled. And if you wait until it's settled, you will miss the opportunity.

Procrastination is such a formidable enemy because it seduces us with an easy-to-believe lie. "You don't have to do it now—there'll be a better time to do it later." I believe procrastination has robbed more people of more opportunities than any other obstacle we face. People who achieve their impossible dreams *never* procrastinate in their pursuit of those dreams. They have learned to act, and act now! Vision-mapping and effective partnering are the two best methods I've found to avoid procrastination when it comes to important projects, whether at home or at work.

◎◎ Life's Most Rewarding Opportunities Often Appear in Little Packages

When I talk about missing opportunities in the moment, I'm not just talking about opportunities that appear to be major or significant. Nearly every night I'm home, when it's time for bed, my seven-year-old daughter asks me if we can snuggle and sing together. Because I've come to recognize that she's more important to me than any mere business opportunity, saying yes has become easy. And our snuggling and singing time is often the best part of my busy day. Someday when I'm gone, my daughter may not remember a single business opportunity I ever seized, but she'll always remember our snuggling and singing at bedtime.

A year and a half ago, my wife and I were on a vacation in Hawaii. As we were walking along an outdoor mall, we noticed a cute couple with their two young sons. The dad took his boys into one of the stores, and the mom sat down on a little brick wall to take a moment's rest. Shannon and I easily could have walked by without saying a word. But oftentimes, when we see young parents, we love to seize the moment to encourage them. So we stopped and said hi to this cute young mom and asked where she was visiting from. She told us that her husband was in the army and stationed in Hawaii. We then learned that she had grown up in our home state. One thing led to another, and we exchanged e-mail addresses. In the year and a half that have followed, Tammy and Roger have become two of our dearest friends. What a rich and rewarding lifetime relationship would have been missed had we simply failed to seize the moment.

As Jesus said, "Behold, I say to you, lift up your eyes and look at the fields, for they are already white for harvest!"

Understanding Changes Minds–
Action Changes Lives

OVERCOMING THE OBSTACLES TO SEIZING OPPORTUNITIES

1. List any opportunities that you saw but failed to seize.

2. Using the list below, which of the obstacles kept you from seizing the opportunities you listed above?

   a. Inadequate vision

   b. Disbelief

   c. A Lone Ranger mentality

   d. Fear

   e. Lack of motivation

   f. Procrastination

3. Are you currently looking at any opportunity that you *want* to seize? Which of the six obstacles are likely to keep you from seizing each opportunity you've listed?

4. How can you overcome the obstacles preventing you from seizing the opportunities you listed above?

—— ⊚⊚ ——

CHAPTER 11

Overcoming Adversity: Turning Roadblocks into Launching Pads

"In this world, you will have trouble. But take heart!
I have overcome the world."

—JESUS (JOHN 16:33B, NIV)

"Everything seemed to be going great, and then all of a sudden, WHAM! From out of nowhere I was blindsided! I never saw it coming." We've all heard comments like this from those who have encountered disappointments, heartaches, and outright tragedies. Their "whams" run the gamut from unexpected problems with a spouse, a child, a friend, or a relative to difficulties with a coworker, a boss, or a company. Many times adversity comes in the form of an unexpected illness or life-altering disease or the death of a loved one. But what surprises me is not that people encounter adversity in life but the fact that they are so surprised that it happens to them. They seem to act as if adversity were a rare event in human history, as if it were somehow a unique and abnormal event. In reality, adversity is as much a part of life as eating, sleeping, and breathing. While none of us *wants* to experience difficult challenges in life, I would wager that no one makes it through life without their share of adversity. What too many people don't realize is that adversity is very much a *normal* part of life.

Why do we experience adversity? How do we best deal with it? Jesus had profound insights and answers to both of these questions in his teachings and in the example of his life. And it's important to recognize this, for if we deal with adversity the wrong way, it can leave us confused, cynical, angry, and bitter. Unfortunately, that is our natural inclination. But if we deal with adversity the right way, it will make us stronger and better. Handling adversity at work and in our personal lives in the ways Jesus taught and demonstrated will produce a kind of compassion, empathy, wisdom, and love that nothing else can. It will lead us to spiritual fulfillment and personal success.

∞ "*Why* Is This Happening to *Me*?"

When we encounter adversity, the first question we usually ask is "Why is this happening to me?" It's a natural question. According to Jesus, there is always a reason for any adversity we face.

∞ Two Types of Adversity

There are really two types of adversity that we encounter in life: adversity that *we* cause or contribute to and adversity that has nothing to do with our actions or behavior. When we experience adversity we cause or contribute to, asking "why" can help us to discover our errors and gain the wisdom we need to avoid similar adversity in the future. It can also equip us to better help others to avoid or correct such problems. My father smoked and drank. His smoking resulted in two heart attacks, three heart surgeries, and ultimately, lung cancer. His drinking drastically limited his career success and deeply hurt his relationship with my mom. But he used the painful adversity he experienced to help *me* understand at a very early age that smoking and alcohol were dreadful addictions that could sabotage my life if I fell prey to them.

Many of the unfortunate things we experience in our lives we either cause or contribute to through our inattention, our behavior, our impulses, and our unchecked desires. If our actions are responsible for only 5 percent of an adverse situation, we *must* take full responsibility for *that* 5 percent. Several years ago, the brother of a friend of mine killed his ex-wife and then turned the gun upon himself. Now, he was obviously 100 percent responsible for that terrible act. *Nothing* his ex-wife did justified homicide. However, through years of arguing and fighting, they had both learned each other's "hot buttons" and how to incite each other by pushing them. There was *one* button that always drove him into panic and desperation. The night before she was murdered, she called him and deliberately pushed that button. The next morning, she was robbed of her life and their children were robbed of their mother and father. Did she deserve his response? Absolutely not! But had she not chosen to push that button, I wonder to this day if the two of them would still be alive.

Jesus said, "Love your enemies, do good to those who hate you, bless those who curse you, pray for those who mistreat you" (Lk. 6:27–28, NIV). More powerful wisdom has never been spoken. Most of the adversity we face in our lives results from actions we cause or contribute to. They would be avoided altogether if we simply followed the wisdom of Jesus's teachings, practicing love instead of hate, generosity instead of greed, serving others instead of controlling or manipulating them. Think how many concerns and problems at work, with colleagues, employees, and clients, would be avoided if we acted with compassion and a generosity of spirit; how many disputes at home would disappear, or never even occur; how many marriages would be not only saved but strengthened.

And then there's the second kind of adversity. Even if we follow his teachings to the letter, we are sure to encounter adversity sometimes that we do not cause or contribute to. People working in the World Trade Center on the morning of September 11, 2001, did nothing to cause or contribute to the tragedy that befell them. All of us have experienced problems and adversities that we did nothing to contribute to. For example, my best friend was recently in a car wreck that left him with permanent injuries. He was broadsided by a driver who ran a red light. Many people contract fatal diseases or illnesses when they've done nothing whatsoever to cause their conditions.

When that happens to us or to those we love, it is completely natural to ask why. In the end, what matters is how we deal with the answers we find or don't find.

We don't have the benefit of having Jesus here to explain to each of us the specific reasons why we encounter a particular adversity or challenge. However, if we approach problems with an open mind and heart, I believe we often come to discover the reasons that adversity has entered our lives. In 2001, I lost millions of dollars as a result of several bad investment decisions. When I asked myself why, I turned to the book of Proverbs for answers. Proverbs revealed to me that the losses in all three investments had been the result of my own naïveté and greed. My greed had made me vulnerable to the overhyped pitches of those who approached me about the investments, and my naïveté caused me to make the investments without doing due diligence on the individuals or the companies I was investing in. Discovering these specific answers from the book of Proverbs has helped me to avoid similar mistakes in the years that have followed.

◎◎ Problem: Incomplete Answers Can Lead to Wrong Conclusions

Sometimes we don't get a complete answer to the question "Why me?" In fact, some "whys" may not be answered in our lifetime. The dilemma can be compounded when we try to fill in the blanks with speculation or our best guesses. I've heard so many people try to answer the "whys" behind tragedies such as the Holocaust, September 11, the tsunami that killed a quarter million people in Thailand and Indonesia, or the devastation wrought by hurricanes such as Ike or Katrina. While there is nothing wrong with asking why, we have the potential to do tremendous damage by trying to answer with our own guesses or assumptions when the real answers are not apparent.

Whether a catastrophe is a personal one, such as the death of a child, or a universal one, such as a tsunami or the Holocaust, the biggest mistake we make is trying to understand it solely from our own limited, finite perspective. Human life is brief; sometimes there *is* no rational explanation to such tragedies. But when human life on earth is seen as only the first page of a trillion-page book, then even the greatest tragedies in this life are, relatively speaking, but a grain of sand on the beach. Jesus told us God is infinite; He is loving and merciful. He has all of eternity to mete out perfect justice. How can any human being, limited by a finite life span, begin to answer questions that can be answered only in light of eternity?

When someone asks me, "How could God allow_____?"— filling in the blank with every conceivable tragedy—I remind them, "You and I see this only in our very narrow, time-locked, human perspective. This tragedy is *not* found on the last page of God's book of life, but merely on the first page. Trying to explain God's purposes is like an ant trying to understand a human life and a human perspective—except a human brain is a lot closer to the brain of an ant than it is to the mind of God."

Jesus may not have revealed all of the mysteries relating

to the breadth of human tragedies. But he has given us every-thing we need to know to successfully navigate our way through any adversity that we will ever face.

∞ Breaking the Chains of Adversity

"Steve, you are the single greatest disappointment in my en-tire career. You will never succeed in marketing."

"Guys, it's hopeless. We're not going to make it. We're going to lose everything."

"Steve, this is Austin. I have some bad news about your son. . . ."

"I no longer love you—I want a divorce."

Each of these heartbreaking statements completely over-turned my life. In each case, I felt as if I had been thrown over the side of a ship into a dark, cold sea, with a thousand-pound weight chained to my feet. I felt a sense of panic and despair. My chest became as tight as if I had been wrapped in a straitjacket. My heart pounded so hard against my chest that it felt as if it were about to explode. I tell you this to let you know that I have an intimate understanding of what it feels like to experience a devastating loss or tragedy.

But here is the *great* news. As paralyzing as each of these events was, they did *not* ruin my life. And even though they created terrible heartache and despair at the time, their nega-tive impact was not permanent. In fact, they ultimately be-came launching pads to a renewed sense of gratefulness, joy, love, and success. Through it all, I've discovered that no adversity, no matter how great, has the power to destroy us or permanently derail us, *if* we follow the example and the wisdom of Jesus. In fact, it can make us stronger, and ultimately lead to greater success. But getting through such situations is *not* simply a matter of positive thinking. Surviving adversity requires specific tools. A person can tread water for only so long. I want to give you the specific tools that have helped me when I've encountered adversity, and in fact have ultimately taken me to incredible heights I otherwise would have never attained.

ᖰᖱ The *Thing* Is Never about the Thing . . . Every Thing Is about Everything!

Keith Craft is one of America's leading teachers on leadership. He is also the pastor of a wonderful church in Frisco, Texas. While attending one of his recent services, I heard him say, "The *thing* is never about the thing . . . but every thing is about everything." In other words, when we experience an event of any kind, the event is about much more than just the event itself.

During my first six years after college, every time I started a job, I thought, "This is the company I will work at for the rest of my life." Yet none of those first nine jobs lasted more than nine months, and most of them lasted for less than six. Each time I lost a job, I was extremely upset, because I thought my career and ultimate success had been permanently derailed. But the truth is, none of my jobs were about the job, and *none* were the basis of my career. Each time I was fired, my career and ultimate success were *not* derailed at all! In fact, if I *had* succeeded in job number one, I never would have taken job number two. If I hadn't taken number two, I never would have gained the entrepreneurial spirit, drive, and understanding that became a critical part of my future. Had I not failed at job number two, I never would have taken number three, where I learned all about direct-response (mail order) advertising. Had I not been fired from job number three, I never would have met Bob Marsh, on job number four, who ultimately became my mentor and partner. Had I not lost job number four, I never would have moved to Phoenix, where I met Gary Smalley, my mentor in communication and relationships. Nor would I have ever started job number nine, where I was introduced to direct-response *television* marketing. Had I experienced real success on any of my first eight jobs, I never would have made it to job number nine, which became my launching pad to job number ten. And it was on job number ten that my partners and I built our businesses that created billions of dollars in sales and tens of millions in personal income and, more important, allowed us to influence tens of millions of people in very positive ways.

I point all this out to show that the significance of each of those first nine jobs, their failures and their successes, was the role they were playing in my *unforeseeable* future. Even though I perceived each job loss as a tragedy, in reality, the jobs and the loss of those jobs were *necessary* steps to set the stage for the incredible lifelong success I've enjoyed as a result of my last job. Through the years, I have found that the following steps have enabled me—and countless others—to successfully navigate our adversity, emerging from our trials far stronger than we were before.

Step 1: Recognize that adversity produces benefits that can't be achieved any other way.

The first step in navigating adversity is realizing that it is only *temporary*. Moreover, if handled correctly, it will produce tremendous *benefits* in the future, benefits that never would have been achieved *without* that adversity. James, in writing to a group of first-century Jewish Christians who were being relentlessly persecuted (James himself would ultimately be martyred by these same persecutors), said: "Consider it pure joy, my brothers, whenever you face trials of many kinds, because you know that the testing of your faith develops perseverance. Perseverance must finish its work so that you may be mature and complete, not lacking anything" (Jas. 1:2–4, NIV).

Imagine being able to say that you have become totally fulfilled and contented, mature and complete in your character, that you do not lack for anything. That's what James said will happen when you respond to adversity the *right* way.

The Apostle Paul, writing to Christians who were

going through similar persecutions and trials at the hands of Caesar, said, "Though outwardly we are wasting away, yet inwardly we are being renewed day by day. For our light and momentary troubles are achieving for us an eternal glory that far outweighs them all. So we fix our eyes not on what is seen, but on what is unseen. For what is seen is temporary, but what is unseen is eternal" (2 Cor. 4:16–18).

Step 2: Treasure-hunt your adversity.

As I lost my jobs in those early years, I could not see any benefit whatsoever; all I could see were the problems—not being able to pay my bills, our ballooning debt, the tremendous stress my wife and I were experiencing. If I had known that it was all just setting the stage for what has become an extraordinarily successful and rewarding career, I might have viewed it quite differently. Many years ago, Gary Smalley taught me what Paul had taught others two thousand years earlier: that every trial we experience produces hidden treasures that we cannot see at first look. The only way they can be found is to dig beneath the surface.

As an adolescent, I had terrible acne. For four years, I went to the dermatologist every week and went through the pain of having him lance every pimple with a scalpel and then radiate my face with an ultraviolet lamp. It seemed like my worst pimples always flared up just hours before a date. The embarrassment was never ending. My sister, on the other hand, rarely had a visible pimple. Little did I know that the emotional and physical pain of my experience with acne would give me the background, emotions, and words I would need to write the first commercial that would launch our company years later. My opening words were "Acne is painful, both physically and emotionally. . . . I don't care if you're a teenager or an adult, acne causes embarrassment and anxiety." Little did I know that there was a two-billion-dollar treasure hidden in my experience. For that first simple commercial produced millions of dollars in sales that became the foundation upon which our television business was built.

But the business success that ultimately came from my acne problem wasn't the only benefit I received. More important, my acne gave me a sense of humility and empathy with others' pain. I gained a compassion for other kids who also had problems that made them "less attractive."

It was Gary Smalley who first taught me to treasure-hunt my trials. Since then, I've done it with every significant challenge I've faced. As world-renowned motivational guru Zig Ziglar says, trials and tribulations make you either bitter or better—the *choice* is yours! Treasure-hunting your adversity can be the single greatest step in transporting you from the "bitter" to the "better."

Step 3: Know that adversity can lead to spiritual fulfillment.

Many of my closest friends, even though they are devout Christians, have experienced considerable adversity. Some have lost their life savings, others their jobs and homes. Some have lost their health to cancer and heart disease, and a few have lost their children to death. But in every case, their adversity became a doorway to a closer, more meaningful and fulfilling spiritual relationship with Jesus. The same has been true for me and my family. While some might think adversity would diminish or undermine one's faith, for me, the opposite has been true. It has strengthened my faith.

As a youth, I encountered a number of difficult challenges. But my mom, dad, and sister were always there for me. They loved me, guided me, and encouraged me. Adversity drew us closer. The same is true, Jesus tells us, of our relationship with God. "Are not two sparrows sold for a penny? Yet not one of them will fall to the ground apart from the will of your Father. And even the very hairs of your head are all numbered. So don't be afraid; you are worth more than many sparrows" (Matt. 10:28–31, NIV).

In fact, in his Sermon on the Mount, Jesus promised that those who used their adversity to draw them closer to God would "inherit the earth." He also said, "Therefore whoever hears these sayings of Mine, and does them, I will liken him to a wise man who built his house on the rock: and the rain descended, the floods came, and the winds blew and beat on that house; and it did not fall, for it was founded on the rock" (Matt. 7:24–25, NKJV). In other words, by creating a strong foundation in our emotional and spiritual lives, one that is built on the wisdom and words of Jesus, we can survive the storms of adversity, no matter how hard they blow.

In times of adversity, we often find ourselves completely out of control of a situation, and even of our own life. It can reveal how powerless we really are. One of Jesus's disciples wrote, "God resists the proud, but gives grace to the humble" (1 Pet. 5:5, NKJV). Nothing humbles us more than adversity.

Step 4: Allow adversity to help you to replace worry and fear with trust.

"Your son Zach has been in an accident."

"Your son Devin has a malignant tumor in his abdomen; he is returning home this week for emergency medical treatment."

This past year, both of these statements were made to me. Each time, I was out of town. The situations were extremely serious and totally beyond my control. Both times, I prayed for strength for my boys and for wisdom and faith for my wife and myself. Though I was instantly gripped by fear, panic, and grief, I found that I had to make a choice: to act in fear or trust in God. In each case, after I garnered all of the information I could, I turned to Jesus and his wisdom for comfort, direction, and help. Here is what happened.

A Long-Awaited Getaway Cruise with My Wife

Because of my business commitments and the needs of our children, my wife and I rarely get away by ourselves. But in September of 2007, we set off on a long-planned four-day cruise from Vancouver, Canada, to Los Angeles. The cruise departed on Saturday night, and the first evening could not have been more wonderful. The next morning, we arrived in Victoria, Canada, and were awakened at seven in the morning by the room phone. Our friend Austin, who was caring for our children back home, was on the line. He told me that my twenty-six-year-old son, Zach, had been in an accident; my oldest son, Mark, and my best friend, Jim, had both called, asking Austin to reach me immediately and have me call them.

I was convinced that Zach had been killed in a car accident. I was in tears; I feared I would never see Zach's sweet smile or hear his voice again. My wife took my cell phone and dialed Mark's number. I kept thinking, "No, no, no . . . it can't be!" When Mark answered, he heard me crying; his first words reassured me. "Dad, Zach's going to be OK." At that moment, a profound sense of relief washed over me, and I was ready to hear what had happened.

Mark told me that Zach had been in an explosion; he had been admitted to the burn unit of a Philadelphia hospital. Zach was a culinary student in his last semester of school. He loves to cook and had decided to prepare a dinner for a friend at a home that he had moved into a few days earlier. He saw what he thought was a decorative candle that had been left on a shelf by the previous homeowner. As he lit it, he realized that it was not a candle—what looked like a wick was really a fuse. The "candle" was a quarter stick of dynamite. He took two steps toward a sink full of water and tossed the dynamite toward the sink. As it left his hand, it exploded, taking off his fingertips and fracturing his hand and fingers. Apparently, there was blood everywhere. Fortunately, his mother and the friend he was preparing dinner for bandaged his hand and called 911. Paramedics were there within minutes. He was in surgery at the time of the call.

My wife and I disembarked as quickly as we could and flew from Victoria to Philadelphia. During our hours in the air, I had a lot of time to reflect and to pray. Knowing my son's life was no longer at risk relieved my greatest fears. But I worried about Zach's disfigurement, the completion of his final semester of culinary school, his future as an aspiring chef. Jesus's reassurance in John 14 resounded in my mind: "Let not your heart be troubled, neither let it be afraid" and "Trust in God; trust also in me." My wife and I arrived at the hospital shortly after midnight. As we walked into Zach's room, I saw that both his hands were bandaged. His left arm was bandaged and in a sling, and I could see shrapnel marks and burns over his face, neck, and right arm. To my amazement, his first words to me expressed his gratitude. "Dad . . . Shannon . . . am I glad to see you! Am I blessed, or what! If I had released the dynamite even a half second later, I would have lost my whole hand. I might have died. Instead, I've only lost my fingertips on my 'holding hand.' My cutting hand is fine. . . . I'll still be able to cut an onion!" I was so proud of him. Rather than acting like a victim, he was filled with profound gratitude.

Although Zach missed that semester of school, he started back the following semester and graduated four months later. His courage, commitment, and endurance became the talk of the school, and he was nominated by his professors for an award from L'Academie Brillat-Savarin, the oldest culinary society in the world, established in France in the thirteenth century. The society awarded him one of only one hundred gold medals it grants worldwide each year, "for dedication and excellence in the culinary arts."

A short eight months later, I was minutes away from speaking to a room of 140 people in the Dallas area who had come to hear me talk about my newest company. Suddenly, I received an alarming e-mail on my cell phone. When I opened it up, I was shocked by the message. My twenty-year-old son, Devin, who was living in Uruguay, had been diagnosed with a malignant tumor. He would be returning home for treatment at the end of the week. My wife was on a flight home from Ohio and had no idea of the terrible news awaiting her when she landed. My first impulse was to cancel the talk. Yet 140 people had turned out to hear my presentation. I told my host, Pastor Keith Craft, of my e-mail, and, after a hug, went up to speak. Most of the attendees were from Keith's church. So at the end of my talk, I told them what had happened and asked them to pray for Devin and my wife, Shannon, as they went through their week. To my surprise, Keith came up and said, "We're not going to wait to pray, we're going to pray right now."

He then called a few of his church leaders up to circle around me to pray. He offered a fairly short prayer that included the following words: "Father, we know that *you* are the 'Great Physician,' and right now, in the name of Jesus Christ, I ask that you would vaporize Devin's tumor . . . just make it disappear. And when the surgeon opens him up, I pray that he would tell Steve, 'I'm confused. . . . I don't understand. . . . I couldn't find the cancer. . . . I've never seen anything like this.' Then we'll know that you performed the miracle, and you will receive all of the glory. And I ask for all of this in the name of Jesus Christ. . . . Amen."

With tears in my eyes, I hugged Keith and the others who had come up to pray. Then Keith said, "Brother,

God answered our prayer. Your son is fine. . . . You have absolutely nothing to worry about!"

As much as I wanted to believe him . . . I didn't. As I later told Keith, "I had ten dollars' worth of hope, but not a penny's worth of faith." I arrived home two days later to find my wife distraught. After holding each other for several minutes, I suggested that we read what Jesus said on the subject of anxiety, worry, and fear. He made about forty statements on the subject, and it took us about five or ten minutes to read them. But in that short period of time, an amazing thing happened. An incredible and inexplicable peace came over us. Here are a few comments Jesus made to help calm anxious hearts:

"Do not let your hearts be troubled and do not be afraid" (Jn. 14:27).

"In this world you will have trouble. But take heart! I have overcome the world" (Jn. 16:33).

"Blessed are they that mourn, for they shall be comforted" (Matt. 5:4).

"Why are you troubled, and why do doubts rise in your minds?" (Lk. 24:38).

"Don't be afraid; just believe" (Mk. 5:35–36).

In fact, he repeated his admonition, "Don't be afraid," over and over again.

The overriding message was clear. Jesus was commanding us to not be afraid, and to simply trust in him. He wasn't demanding that we magically erase our feelings of fear and heartache; rather, he was telling us to take charge of our behavior and to begin to act with faith and courage.

Two days later, Devin arrived at the airport, and we rushed him to the hospital to meet with the surgeon. After an exam and a review of the six ultrasounds that had been taken four days earlier, the doctor gave us the bad news. "We know the tumor is cancerous from its size (three-quarters of an inch by three-eighths of an inch) and its irregular shape, and from my physical exam. . . . I've scheduled surgery for Monday morning. While he's on the table, we'll do a biopsy to determine which type of cancer it is. We'll also do CAT scans of his abdomen, chest, and brain to see if it's spread. Then we'll decide if we need chemotherapy in addition to the surgery and radiation treatments."

At 12:30 in the afternoon on Monday, Shannon and I were told that the surgery was under way. At 2:20, the waiting room receptionist called us to her desk. "The doctor is still in the operating room, but he wants to talk with one of you." My wife grabbed the phone and listened. He told her that the cancer had killed the nearby vessel, which was now pitch-black. And then he shocked my wife. "But Shannon," he said, "I'm confused! I don't understand this. When I opened him up, I couldn't find the tumor. . . . It was gone. I sent over a frozen section of the surrounding tissue, and it came back cancer-free. I just don't understand this. I'll be out in a little while to talk with you."

I hadn't told Shannon about Keith's prayer a week earlier, because I simply had not believed it. But now I told her. She had just heard the doctor repeat three of the four statements that Keith had prayed he would say. Then the doctor came out. As he sat down across from us, he said, "I've never seen anything like this!" (just as Keith had prayed). My wife leaned toward him in disbelief. "You mean you've almost never seen anything like it?" "No, Shannon . . . I have NEVER seen anything like this! I was so baffled, I called every urologist in the hospital to come in and look at it. They were just as baffled as I was." He then told us he was sending out all of the tissue for a full pathology and we would have those results within a week. He said that sometimes a full pathology will turn up a cancerous finding that was missed in the biopsy.

Four days later, I got a call from his nurse. "Steve, the pathology is back. But before I give you the results, I just want to tell you that Devin is the talk of the urology department. The only word that is being used is *miracle*! He is cancer-free!"

As it turned out, tens of thousands of people had been praying for Devin that week. Motivational speaker Zig Ziglar had alerted his "prayer chain." I was told that in less than twenty-four hours, twenty-five thousand people had been praying for a boy they had never heard of before.

The lesson? Our adversity can be a bridge to our faith, if we but replace our fears with trust in the wisdom and words of Jesus.

Step 5: Use your adversity to act as Jesus would have acted.

On several occasions, people I had become extremely close friends with, whom I had helped when they were experiencing heartbreak, stabbed me in the back, inflicting unimaginable wounds on me and my family. In each case, I was tremendously angry initially. I had done absolutely nothing to offend these individuals—in fact, to this day, each would tell you I had shown them more love and thoughtfulness than any other friend. And yet they had hurt me and my family terribly.

But in each case, I found the key to *overcoming* my anger, hurt, and pain was to offer a forgiving heart. As I reflected on how Jesus had reacted to those who had condemned him to death, and had so mercifully forgiven me for all of my personal wrongs, it became easy for me to forgive those in my life who had wronged me. And as I forgave them, the emotional pain and anger that had tied me in knots disappeared.

The more I act the way Jesus would have acted, the more generous and close I feel to everyone around me. I not only feel better for it, but I find it easy to treat others so much better as well.

Step 6: Face adversity with boldness.

When we experience adversity, our natural inclination is to either withdraw into our shell or strike out in anger at whomever or whatever we can blame. Jesus did the opposite. There is not a single instance where he withdrew into a shell or attacked or blamed others for the adversity he encountered. He occasionally withdrew from the crowds to redirect his attention to more pressing matters. The night of Judas's betrayal, he withdrew from his disciples, not to shrink away from adversity but to enter into prayer.

In his teachings, he repeatedly tells his disciples to proactively face their adversity with courage. But while Jesus exhorts us to "Take courage! . . . Don't be afraid," he doesn't expect or demand that we magically shed our feelings of fear or distress. Rather, he desires that we do what he did—find answers in hope, courage, and faith. Whenever we feel tied up in knots, discouraged, or in despair, he promises that if we follow him and live according to his words, we "shall know the truth," and that the truth shall set us free! (Jn. 8:31–32)

Understanding Changes Minds—
Action Changes Lives

BREAKING THE CHAINS OF ADVERSITY

1. List a current or recent adversity that you have dealt with or are dealing with.

2. Is this adversity something that you helped create, or did you have nothing to do with its cause?

3. If you have contributed to the adversity you listed, what do you think you can do to correct your behavior in that situation?

4. Treasure-hunt the adversity you've listed. Write down any benefits that you have experienced or could experience as a direct result of this adversity. (For example, positive changes in your character or behavior, shoring up a weakness, or a new ability to empathize with or help others who are going through similar adversities.)

5. From what you now know about Jesus, how might he have acted or behaved if he had gone through this same adversity?

6. How can you "attack" this adversity with boldness?

—— ◎◎ ——

CHAPTER 12

A Whole Different Kind of Love

"Greater love has no one than this, that he lay down
his life for his friends."

—JESUS (JOHN 15:13, NIV)

More songs are written about love than about any other subject. More romance novels are sold in America every year than any other genre of books. Women long for love, and men will sacrifice nearly anything to gain it. When I fell in love with my wife, I fell about as hard as a person can. I was living in Malibu at the time, writing and producing a number of television campaigns for our company's various product lines. For the first time in my career, I was having a very hard time concentrating on my work. Before I met Shannon, I'd wake up to the sound of the surf, put on a large pot of coffee, and start writing around eight in the morning. I'd normally finish my work between midnight and one in the morning. Shannon lived over the mountain range in Calabasas. Every day from about a month into our relationship until we were married a year later, I would end my work day at 5:00 p.m. and drive as fast as I could through Topanga Canyon to arrive at her house by about 5:26. The terrible thing was, I'd start looking at the clock around 3:30, longing for the minute hand to move faster.

Yes, romantic love *is* grand! And yet men and women fall *out* of love almost as fast as they fall *in* love. Nearly every engaged couple would describe themselves as madly in love and tell you they couldn't even imagine their life without their future spouse. And yet at least 52 percent of those couples will ultimately divorce. Why does love seem so strong in the beginning of a relationship and become so weak as the relationship goes on?

The answer is fairly simple. Culturally, we equate love with the emotional feelings that are the substance and drive of "romantic" love. And because emotions are as up and down as a roller coaster and as temporary and unpredictable as the wind, anything based on emotions can be unstable and short-lived. The exhilaration stage of love usually passes rather quickly, and once that stage passes, everything else that competes for our time and attention can chip away at our feelings. At the same time, we become much more aware of our spouse's faults and weaknesses, which we were blind to or tolerant of during the exhilaration stage.

We use the word *love* to describe or justify any number of behaviors or actions, some of which have little to do with what we commonly associate with love. For example, an infamous sports celebrity, tried for the double murder of his ex-wife and a young man, explained his behavior by writing, "I loved her too much." Countless men and women have done terrible things in the name of love. They've left their spouses and their innocent, dependent children when they've "fallen out of love" with their spouse and "fallen *in* love" with someone else.

But romantic love isn't the only kind of love that has devastated the lives of so many. How many families have been emotionally starved by a parent who "loves" their work or a hobby so much that they steal time away from their family and spend it on far less deserving pursuits and activities? At times, I have been as guilty of this as anyone else. As I mentioned in chapter 9, when a person is swept away by any kind of passion, they can ultimately become a slave to that passion. And those kinds of infatuations are often described with the word *love*—whether a love for a person, a job, a hobby, or a game.

◎◎ A Whole *Different* Kind of Love—One That Is Infinitely Better

Jesus introduced a whole *different* kind of love to the world, a love that is *not* based upon human feelings or in any way dependent upon our changeable nature, our hormones, or even the person who is the object of our love. It's a kind of love that is infinitely more stable, reliable, and powerful than the *feelings* we normally define as love. This kind of love enables you to forgive someone who is undeserving of your forgiveness. It is so powerful it can enable you to be kind and help others who don't like you, or may even hate you! It is a love that can give you the vision, creativity, and power to bless the lives of others, even when you are physically or emotionally drained. A relationship that is based upon the kind of love Jesus talked about will truly endure "till death do us part." It can be used *anywhere* in any circumstances. Unlike romantic love, it is a love I can use with my employees, partners, or business clients. It is just as applicable and powerful in the workplace as it is in intimate, personal relationships.

Unfortunately, we do not have an adequate word to define this unique kind of love. But the New Testament was written in a dialect of Greek that was the spoken and written language in Israel at the time of Christ, and it *does* have a unique word for this particular kind of love. That word became the word that Jesus used to describe this kind of love. The word was *agape* ("ah-GAH-pay"). Although *agape* can result in emotional feelings, emotional feelings themselves are not *agape*'s source, its substance, or its foundation. In fact, *agape* can be experienced, and its power can be harnessed, even when one has absolutely no emotional, romantic feelings of love whatsoever.

If you are wondering, "How could such a love make that much of a difference with me?," let me tell you. When you bring *agape* into your workplace and personal life, it has the power to make a greater change in your life and the lives of those with whom you interact than any other trait or attitude you could ever develop or utilize. It will empower you to make positive differences in the lives of others that are unimaginable. You will be able to add worth, esteem, creativity, loyalty, productivity, and joy to others in a way that you have never done before.

In addition to creating stronger and more fulfilling and secure relationships, this kind of love will also create a higher level of fulfillment and joy in your own life, as you actively express it and personally witness how it liberates and empowers its recipients. In my case, it has not only enabled me to be the kind of husband and father I've always wanted to be but has created hundreds of fulfilling relationships and rich friendships in my business life.

What Makes Agape So Different?

To best understand *agape*, we need to compare it with conventional love, the kind of love most of us think of when we use the word *love*.

1. ***They Come from Different Sources.*** The source of conventional love is usually the *object* of that love. In other words, we love the other person because of *who* they are, what they do, or how they look. If they have an attractive personality or treat us wonderfully or look great, we consider them lovable, and thus we love them. The problem is, when they become less lovable, we tend to love them less. The traits we thought were endearing at the beginning of the relationship can become annoying or even offensive as the relationship goes on. As their behavior toward

us changes, our love for them usually changes with it. Many people find their spouse less attractive as he or she ages or gains weight, and their feelings about the spouse may change as well.

On the other hand, the source of *agape* is God Himself. As Jesus taught us, God doesn't love us because we've done something to merit or engender that love, or because we are particularly attractive to Him. To the contrary, our self-centeredness and failure to truly value Him and all that He values makes us very unattractive to Him. But as Jesus taught us, God loves us because of who *He* is, not because of who we are! *Agape* does not fade with time and is not changed by circumstances. Remember, we are not talking about an emotional, warm-and-fuzzy, Santa Claus type of love. It is truly a *value-centered* love and results in right behavior. It stands firm in its defiance of wrong behavior, even though it extends extraordinary care to the person engaged in such behavior.

2. ***They Are Expressed Differently.*** Conventional love is usually expressed through our emotions and is directly tied to the behavior of the object of our love and to how we *feel* about that person at any given moment. For example, we are less likely to express our love to someone who is misbehaving toward us than we are to someone who is pleasing us. And if we are physically or emotionally drained or

distracted, we are likely to feel less love than we might express if we were emotionally and physically energized.

Agape, however, is expressed through tangible actions and does not depend upon the behavior of the object of our love or our own physical or emotional state. If we open up our hearts and minds to follow Jesus's example and instructions on *how* to love others *his* way, we become a *channel* through which his love touches all those who cross our path.

3. **They Are Different in Their Reliability.** While conventional love is whimsical and as subject to change as our emotions are, such is not the case with *agape*. When we love someone this way, that person will be able to count on it. *Agape* always acts in the best interest of *others*, even when it's contrary to our self-interest. This kind of love creates honor, self-esteem, integrity, trustworthiness, commitment, and loyalty in any relationship in which it is introduced— whether at home or at work.

4. **They Are Different in Their Power.** Because conventional love is so dependent upon the object of our love and our own physical and emotional state, its power to effect permanent change and lasting improvement is limited. On the other hand, *agape* is empowering; it can permanently change the lives of others as we consistently apply it to our relationships.

Saul of Tarsus hated Christians and felt justified in having them arrested and executed. All that changed when he was confronted by Jesus while traveling on the road to Damascus. Years later, he wrote a letter to Christians in the city of Corinth, in which he gave a wonderful definition of *agape*. He described it by listing some of its characteristics:

> *Love is patient,*
> *love is kind.*
> *It does not envy,*
> *it does not boast,*
> *it is not proud.*
> *It is not rude,*
> *it is not self-seeking,*
> *it is not easily angered,*
> *it keeps no record of wrongs.*
> *Love does not think evil*
> *does not rejoice in wrong-doing*
> *but rejoices with the truth.*
> *It can handle anything,*
> *always trusts,*
> *always hopes,*
> *always perseveres.*
> *Love never fails.* (1 Cor. 13:4–7)

How different our marriages and families and our workplace would be if such love became the dominating force in our lives! No one can force this kind of love on others. But we can take responsibility for ourselves and become an agent of this kind of love, wherever we go. Paul decreed that this kind of love should be the driving, motivating, and guiding force in our lives.

My mentors, Bob Marsh, Gary Smalley, and Jim Shaughnessy, have each loved me with this kind of love. So has my wife. Their love not only changed my life, but it made me love them more than I can express. More important, it made me want to love others in the same way that they loved me.

◎◎ *Agape* in the Workplace

When I've taught on this subject, people have asked me how they can possibly employ it in the workplace. After all, most of us live in a backbiting, dog-eat-dog, take-no-prisoners corporate environment. We don't just struggle against our competitors for markets, we compete against our coworkers for promotions, popularity, and even job survival. When I worked in major corporations during my first years out of college, I was taken aback by the way so many of my coworkers, superiors, and subordinates behaved toward one another. They were all smiles one minute, and yet secretly backstabbing one another the next.

After thirty-nine years in business, I have learned a very important, tried-and-proven truth. No matter how terrible others in the workplace may act, what is far more important is how *I* act. When I first started out in business, I was told by one astute officer of a company, "If you don't stop being so nice and start watching out for yourself, you're going to be eaten alive." He was half right and half wrong. If I was nice and *foolish*, I would be eaten alive. But Jesus said, "Behold, I send you out as sheep in the midst of wolves. Therefore be wise as serpents and harmless as doves" (Matt. 10:16, NKJV). And that became the model I strove to follow. I studied Proverbs and continually asked God for wisdom in my dealings. Sometimes, I did get eaten alive. But even in my career disasters, my career and success advanced beyond anything I had ever dreamed possible. I can honestly say that I have never intentionally hurt anyone in my business pursuits, because I have tried to practice *agape*. Yes, I have hurt people in business without intending to. As those mistakes have been pointed out, I've done what I could to make matters right—sometimes successfully and sometimes not. The overall result of thirty-nine years of trying to bring this kind of proactive, practical love into the workplace is that I have developed many wonderful and enduring friendships and have made but a few enemies (and even those I regret).

How can you bring *this* kind of love into your workplace? Since a picture is worth a thousand words, let me try to give you an example. Many years ago, I took a test to determine my personality type. This particular test categorizes you as a lion, beaver, otter, or golden retriever. I am a lion. A lion is the most aggressive, least patient, most project oriented, and least people oriented of the personality types. My nature is to enter every business day with my focus on what needs to be done and getting it done as fast and as effectively as I can. By nature, I hate committee meetings, long discussions, and fluff! I like to get straight to the point and then get it done. Needless to say, this kind of behavior in the workplace can be quite offensive. But people with a lion personality typically put projects above people. In other words, my personality—my natural inclination—runs completely contrary to expressing *agape* in the workplace. And yet, because I met that homeless carpenter six years before I entered the workplace, I had already discovered the incredible benefits and joy of expressing this proactive love to anyone who crossed my path. So applying it to the workplace has been a natural adaptation for me.

First, I pay attention to others. Whenever I walk into a company's office, I pay attention to whomever I talk with. I look into their eyes, smile, and ask at least one or two questions about them. Second, whenever anyone talks with me, I focus on what they are saying, not on how I'm going to answer or respond. I often ask them to explain or illustrate a point—not because I necessarily need the explanation or illustration, but to show a level of interest that *honors* them by honoring their opinion or idea. Third, I look for opportunities to encourage others and express my heartfelt appreciation and gratefulness. I praise them for specific actions rather than just flatter them with generalities. My goal is to infuse them with honor and worth.

When conflict breaks out (as it often does in any business), I try to keep my temper in check, make peace between people with opposing opinions, answer anger with soft words, and maintain the attitude of a learner rather than a know-it-all. I almost never bring up people's past mistakes. I try to keep everyone feeling like they're a valuable part of the team.

One of my companies is owned by the three of us who founded the company and a group that purchased a piece of the company during our first year of operation. They are *awesome* partners. But creating the purchase contract was a hundred times harder than making the deal. The deal was done on an e-mail and a handshake, and the funds were instantly wired to our account—simple! But then came the attorneys. Our attorneys and their attorneys took eighteen months to create the agreement. Our attorneys kept inserting things that were in our interest but that were not part of the original deal, and their attorneys did the same. Our attorneys would tell us we were foolish if we didn't insist on these things, and their attorneys would tell them the same from their point of view. Finally, we received an e-mail that expressed the frustration, disappointment, and outrage that they were feeling. It felt like they were drawing a line in the sand, saying, "Do it, or else." What's crazy is that this was so unlike how these men are in "real life." Rather than following the nature and inclination of a "lion," which is to attack when backed into a corner, I prayed. I asked for wisdom about how I could defuse the situation and show these men how truly grateful I was for their partnership. Instead of responding with a poison-pen e-mail, I wrote a detailed answer, beginning by expressing my gratefulness. Throughout my e-mail, I attributed the highest esteem to them, their motives, and their words. I did not say one negative word, but framed everything with encouragement and hope. I then called the founder of their group and expressed my appreciation and openness to do whatever they decided was truly fair and right.

The founder wisely suggested that their CEO and our CEO get together for a face-to-face meeting *without* any attorneys or other representatives—their only goal would be to agree to get the deal done in a way that reflected everyone's original intentions. They did, and all issues were happily resolved, with fairness and generosity on both sides, in a single afternoon.

Jim Shaughnessy is one of my partners at American Telecast and for twenty-six years has worked with our manufacturers in Hong Kong, Taiwan, and China. For twenty-six years, he has expressed *agape* with every person he works with, every single day. He learns about their family members, their passions, their joys, and their sorrows. At least a thousand people around the world would tell you that one of their best friends in life is Jim Shaughnessy. He has so loved and honored them that they have treated him as if he were one of them. They work hard to deliver the highest quality and the lowest prices . . . not because they couldn't charge a lot more, but because they want to honor Jim the way he honors them.

Bringing Paul's list of *agape*'s attributes into the workplace means being more patient and kind. It means not acting arrogantly or bragging. It means not being rude, self-serving, or easily angered. It means not "keeping score" on the wrong actions of others. It means embracing integrity and being careful to avoid wrong behaviors. And it means doing all of this for the long haul, not just in the short run. *That* is how we bring *agape* into our workplaces.

◎◎ How Can We *Acquire* This Life-Changing Kind of Love?

Unfortunately, acquiring this kind of love is not as easy as driving to your nearest convenience store and picking up a carton of milk. In reality, there are only two ways to try to experience this kind of love. One way is to study its qualities, to review *agape*'s attributes every day and try to apply them as best as you can. Equally important is to follow Jesus's instructions about divine *agape* and follow his example. The problem is, this kind of love is *contrary* to our nature. Like it or not, human nature is extremely self-centered and self-serving. So applying such love through study and effort is a worthwhile endeavor, but it can be incredibly hard, if not impossible, to apply consistently. That's the bad news. The good news is that through the teachings of Jesus and a relationship with him, *agape* can *become* part of our character, part of our nature.

◎◎ How Jesus Described, Prescribed, and Exemplified *Agape*

In his Sermon on the Mount, Jesus taught his disciples about *agape* and told them how they were to apply it to the situations they would encounter. He was not offering a "love model" for governments or businesses to follow, even though many pacifists have mistakenly applied it to government actions. He gave a specific set of instructions for those he was mentoring and sending into the world to carry forth his message and effectively represent him. Theologians have argued for centuries about which of these instructions applied only to his disciples and which ones should be applied to everyone. I will not try to resolve that debate. Rather than split hairs, let's focus on the overriding principles Jesus revealed.

- Love your enemies.
- Do good to those who hate you.
- Bless those who curse you.
- Pray for those who mistreat you.
- If someone strikes you on one cheek, turn to him the other also.
- If someone takes your cloak, do not stop him from taking your tunic.
- Give to everyone who asks you.
- If anyone takes what belongs to you, do not demand it back.

- Do to others as you would have them do to you.
- If you love those who love you, what credit is that to you? Even the least among us love those who love them.
- If you do good to those who are good to you, what credit is that to you? Even "sinners" do that.
- If you lend to those from whom you expect repayment, what credit is that to you? No one is afraid to lend when they are expecting to be repaid in full.
- Love your enemies, do good to them, and lend to them without expecting to get anything back (Lk. 6:27–35, NKJV).

Notice that everything Jesus relates to *agape* involves tangible action. It has absolutely nothing to do with emotions or feelings. *Agape* is all about doing and giving. That's why *agape* is so powerful—because it generates specific, beneficial action to others, even when they do nothing to merit it.

Jesus gave us examples of what this love looks like in every recorded event in his life, from his ministry through his arrest and all the way through his execution. In his dying minutes, he asked his Heavenly Father to forgive those who were executing him. He forgave a thief and murderer who was nailed to the cross next to him and assured him that they would be together in paradise that very day.

Among the final instructions Jesus gave to his disciples on the night of his arrest were the following words: "My command is this: Love each other as I have loved you. Greater love has no one than this, that he lay down his life for his friends" (Jn. 15:12–13, NIV).

This is the kind of powerful, lasting love that can change any life it touches—at home and at work. Most important, this is the kind of love that I want to daily express in my own life, to my wife and to each of my children, in my business, and to the world. This is the joy and liberating power of this amazing love.

Understanding Changes Minds— Action Changes Lives

Experiencing and Expressing a New Kind of Love

1. Make a *short* list of the people you would really want to love with a more perfect love.

2. Using your list from above, think of how you have been with each of those people during the past week. Did your love demonstrate the following list of *agape* love's attributes?

    a. Patience

    b. Kindness

    c. Does not envy

    d. Does not boast

    e. Is not proud

    f. Is not rude

    g. Is not self-seeking

    h. Is not easily angered

     i.   Doesn't keep a record of wrongs

     j.   Does not think evil

     k. Does not rejoice in wrong-doing

     l.   Rejoices with the truth

     m. Can handle anything

     n.   Always trusts

     o.   Always hopes

     p.   Always perseveres

     q.   Never fails

3. During the past week, how could you have expressed or demonstrated *agape*'s attributes in a relationship at home or at work?

_____

CHAPTER 13

— ෧෯ —

Your Incredible Worth

"Look at the birds of the air; they do not sow or reap or store away in barns, and yet your heavenly Father feeds them. Are you not much more valuable than they?"

—JESUS (MATT. 6:26, NIV)

In 1987, I was filming Gary Smalley's seminar, which we named "Hidden Keys to Loving Relationships." In the first session, Gary said something that has stayed with me ever since. He was teaching about the differences between men and women and how, as married couples, we needed to value those differences rather than criticize them. He explained that he had discovered the single most important trait needed to create a fulfilling and loving marriage that would last a lifetime. It was a trait that is absent from too many marriages, and that was why so many marriages either fell short of creating lasting fulfillment or failed altogether. He said it was the same reason most personal relationships and most business relationships ultimately fail. The single most important trait needed to have a great relationship with another person is *honor*. He said that if we want to love others, we need to *choose* to honor them in ways that are meaningful to them. Most important, he said that honoring someone should not depend upon whether they deserve that honor. It should depend only upon our *choosing* to honor them. In other words, it is a *choice* we make.

To illustrate his point, he picked up an old violin with a very worn finish and a broken bridge hanging on the strings. He held it by the neck and dangled it so you could see the broken bridge swinging back and forth. He asked the audience, "How much do you think this beat-up violin is worth?" Everyone laughed. I'm sure they, like me, thought it was worthless.

Gary then said, "This was loaned to me for this filming by an antique dealer . . . and I can't even believe I'm holding it. Let me read you the inscription inside of it." He then drew it closer to him. Staring into the violin, he read, "1723 . . . Antonius Stradivarius." The audience instantly gasped, and the gasp was so loud it was heard on film.

"Listen to all of you," Gary said. "Your reaction was one of startled amazement. At first glance, when I held it up, you all laughed at it. But when I read the inscription, you gave an expression of awe. . . . What changed? It was the same piece of wood both before and after I read the inscription. The violin did not change; it was still broken and tarnished. *You* changed—you changed your mind about that old violin. You *chose* to honor it. From this point on, I want you to see your spouse as a 'Stradivarius.' Just write that name on your husband's or wife's forehead."

Everyone laughed, but Gary had made his point. We need to honor those around us—our spouse, our friends, our clients and colleagues—because the value we place on them is often driven by *our* perceptions, not by their intrinsic worth. And when we see our spouse or colleague or friend as valuable as a Stradivarius, they become more valuable in our eyes.

In the next few pages, *I* want to honor *you*! I want to show why you are so valuable. And I want to show how you can begin to honor those whom you love and those who cross your path on any given day.

◉◉ What *Really* Makes Us Valuable?

From about seventh grade on, I looked at myself as an unattractive, nonathletic, skinny kid with a mouth full of braces and a face full of acne. I was so embarrassed by how skinny I was that I would never swim in a coed pool. When I graduated from high school, I was five feet eleven inches tall and weighed 118 pounds and still had problems with acne. During my first three years of college, every girl I "went with" broke up with me after a few months. Girls wanted me to be their confidant and friend, but no one seemed romantically attracted to me. There was one girl I dated on whom I had a huge crush; when I went to kiss her, she just slugged me in the arm and laughed. Even after I was married, I continued to feel unattractive and undesirable.

Things weren't much better for me in business. As you

know, in my first five years, I went through eight jobs; my income was less than half that of the average wage earner in America. My self-esteem was in the basement in both my personal and business life. And yet, surprisingly, I was happy and fulfilled most of the time. From the night that I met that homeless carpenter shortly before my sixteenth birthday, I *knew* that I was dearly loved by God. So neither my unattractiveness nor my failings in my career had the power to erase all my feelings of self-worth. In fact, the tougher things got in both of those arenas, the more intimate my relationship with God became.

What undermines *your* self-esteem? Your looks? Your lack of success at work? How others feel about you or what they say about you? Your lack of income, the age and condition of your car, or the size of your house or apartment? Is it your title (or lack of a title) at work? The truth is that nearly everyone feels devalued at times. Those who are wealthy sometimes convince themselves that their success and wealth make them more valuable. They don't realize how shaky a foundation that is until their health is fading or their wealth disappears or their relationships dissolve. As Jesus said, "For what profit is it to a man if he gains the whole world, and is himself destroyed or lost?" (Lk. 9:25, NKJV). The fact is, *real* worth doesn't result from wealth, good looks, a new car, a big house, popularity, or a job title. All of these can be taken away or lost in a moment. If these are what bring you a sense of self-worth, your estimation of yourself will disappear when they do. True worth is based on that which can*not* be lost or taken away.

✆ Life-Changing Worth from an Unexpected Source

After three months of hard work, the day had finally arrived. It was a summer day in 1976. Bob Marsh, my mentor and partner, was betting his entire business and the careers of all of his employees on one roll of the dice—the market-test performance of my first commercial for our company's first product. As I've mentioned earlier, I had produced a two-minute commercial featuring Pat and Debby Boone talking about our new acne product. A test spot had been scheduled to air on a Detroit television station, WXON, at 4:58 in the afternoon. If enough people called an 800 number and ordered the product, we would have a winner and we would be able to get financing to roll it into a national television campaign. If we *didn't* have enough people call, the entire company would lose . . . big-time! We would all lose our jobs. Bob would likely lose the business and possibly his home.

Around four o'clock, Bob knocked on my door and stepped into my office. He walked up to me and put his hand on my shoulder. "I just want you to know that if the spot bombs, and I have to let everyone go, you and I will stick together," he said. "As long as I have a dollar in my pocket, you can have fifty cents." He then smiled and gave me a hug, and our eyes teared up. With those few words, he had added more worth, more value to me, and had given me more honor, than I had ever felt in my life. In fact, in those few seconds he changed my life forever! A little over an hour later, we received a report from the answering service that was taking the orders. We had a winner . . . a giant winner! We had hit a bases-loaded home run in the bottom of the ninth. Our company was successfully launched. I would go on to have the joy of Bob's mentorship and partnership for the rest of his business life and the partnership of his wonderful sons for the next thirty-two years. But as thrilling as that first triumph was, it was Bob's comments that truly changed my self-worth and the course of my business life.

I later wondered what it was about Bob's comments that meant so much to me as a twenty-seven-year-old. I realized that Bob's comments affected me so powerfully because (1) they came from a man that I held in highest esteem; (2) they were expressions of the highest form of affection and love; (3) they reflected a deep and lasting commitment to me that I knew would not change with circumstances; (4) they were delivered with warmth and sincerity; and (5) they came from a person who had the integrity and *power* to *deliver* on the commitment he had made.

That is why Jesus and the promises and commitments he made were—and continue to be—so powerful. But we first have to be aware of *what* he said. If I put a million dollars in your checking account, but you didn't know it was there, you would not get even a penny's worth of benefit from my deposit. The same is true with the words and comments of Jesus—you need to know what he has said before you can bank on it.

The supersonic Concorde was built to fly people across the Atlantic Ocean at twice the speed of sound. When I flew my film crew to Paris in 1995, it took us only three hours to fly from New York to Paris. But here's a fact. No matter how powerful and fast the Concorde was, it *could not* take you from New York to Paris in three hours if you didn't climb on board. It took countless people across the ocean quickly, and it did so every day for twenty years. But that doesn't mean a thing to you *if* you never climbed on board! The Concorde could deliver, but you had to put yourself into a seat to benefit from that delivery. The same is true of the wisdom of Jesus. The only way to receive the benefits of his messages and the wisdom from his life is to read or hear his words and then act upon them. Jesus made more than 1,900 statements that were recorded in the New Testament. Reading them and following their guidance will give you a level of self-worth that no person and no circumstance can ever take away.

◎◎ True Worth That Cannot Be Lost or Taken Away

This past year, Bob Marsh passed away. But the legacy of his love, commitment, partnership, and mentoring of his sons and me will be with us for the rest of our lives. As wonderful as that is, for me there has been an even greater source of true worth, one which can never be lost, taken away, or even diminished in the slightest. It is the worth that comes from knowing that God knows me intimately and loves me more than any human being ever has or ever will.

Jesus said, "Look at the birds of the air; they do not sow or reap or store away [a harvest] in barns, and yet your heavenly Father feeds them. Are you not much more valuable than they?" He went on to say, "Are not two sparrows sold for a penny? Yet not one of them falls to the ground apart from the will of your heavenly Father. And even the very hairs of your head are numbered. So don't be afraid, you are worth more than many sparrows" (Matt. 6:26–27; Matt. 10:29–31, NIV). These are only two of the many statements that Jesus made about the value God places on each of us and the unconditional love that God holds for each of us, a love that will never be lost or taken away. If Jesus sees that much worth in each of us, how can we not see the same worth in ourselves and in one another? Think how much better our world would be today if we valued ourselves and those we work with, meet, and interact with in the manner of Jesus.

☜☞ *How YOU Can Create Worth in Others*

The question now becomes, what can *you* do to create worth in others? The one thing that *doesn't* create self-esteem is to praise others when they haven't done anything to merit sincere praise. When I was in Little League baseball, only the members of the team that won the league championships were awarded trophies. The players of every team in the league practiced every day of the spring and summer in the desert heat of Phoenix, because we *all* wanted to win those coveted trophies. School wasn't any different. The only kids who got stars on their homework and tests were the kids who turned in perfect papers. The kids who worked hard for the most part got good grades and occasional gold or silver stars.

The kids who didn't, didn't. And at home, things weren't much different. My parents were quick to compliment me when I did something that was truly deserving of praise. But they didn't compliment me for just "showing up."

Today, every member of every kid's team in every sport seems to get a trophy. For what? For showing up and playing and having fun. My two sons played football and each got trophies their first year . . . when their teams won only *one* game in the entire season. While I do not believe that one should deride kids for poor performance, neither should we praise them for doing anything less than their best. I'm for end-of-season parties to celebrate a team's hard work and efforts, regardless of the season's results. I'm for snow cones after a game and praise for kids who try hard. But I believe in honesty, as opposed to false flattery. You don't genuinely build a child's self-esteem by telling them they're good at something when they are not. To the contrary, you set them up for a major fall later in life, when the world tells them otherwise. We laugh at the horrible singers who show up for the *American Idol* television auditions. But what is so telling is how shocked and upset some of these young people are when they hear the truth. Chances are they've had a lifetime of parents and others telling them how good they were, only to be humiliated when the *Idol* judges and audiences tell them the truth. Excessive and misplaced flattery cannot build genuine self-esteem. But there *is* a way that we can build self-esteem in our children, our spouses, our coworkers, and even complete strangers who cross our paths. Jesus did it with those who followed him. Here's what he told his disciples: "I have set you an example that you should do as I have done for you. I tell you the truth, no servant is greater than his master, nor is a messenger greater than the one who sent him. Now that you know these things, you will be blessed if you do them" (Jn. 13:15–17, NIV). Jesus tells us that we can value the lives of others by simply following his example and loving one another both in words and in deeds, just as he loved us.

How Can We Build Self-Esteem in Others?

1. *Proactively Listen.* Today, more than ever, we are quick to speak and slow to listen. Jesus, on the other hand, listened intently *before* he spoke. One of the greatest needs of every man, woman, boy, and girl is to be heard. Most people speak first and listen later. And when they do listen, they listen inattentively. When we listen proactively, we honor the other person and can drive their self-esteem right through the roof. Proactive listening involves simple choices. First, be attentive while they speak. FOCUS on what they're saying, not on what *you* are going to say in response. Don't rush them, interrupt them, or change the subject after they've finished speaking. When you immediately change the subject after they have finished speaking, you are telling them that what they just said meant absolutely nothing to you. After they have said what they intended to say, acknowledge their comments before you change

course. The second step in proactive listening is to use the "drive-thru" communication technique I discussed in chapter 6, restating what they said to you, to show that you are really trying to understand their comments. When you're listening, *don't* try to solve their problems—just listen and clarify your understanding of what they are saying.

2. ***Understand Their Frame of Reference and* Value *Their Opinions.*** One of the strongest ways in which we *devalue* or undermine others is by *not* valuing their opinions. We are quick to view their words and opinions from our own frame of reference and then debate, correct, criticize, or even ridicule their opinions. Sometimes we devalue their opinions without saying a word—just by rolling our eyes, shaking our head, or giving a sigh of disapproval. On the other hand, when we try to understand their perspective and draw out their opinions, we are telling them that they are worthwhile. Even when they say something that is blatantly wrong, *don't* jump in to correct them. Ask questions that may help them to see their error. Then *later* approach them and let them know you've been thinking about what they said and ask if they have ever "thought of it this way." As Solomon said, "The tongue of the wise makes knowledge acceptable" (Prov. 15:2, NASB).

3. ***Use Words Wisely.*** The words we use have incredible power. They can infuse the other person with

tremendous self-worth or devastate them. Jesus tells us to love our neighbor as we love ourselves. The words that we use to demean others we would never think of using on ourselves. Jesus asks us to use the gift of communication to build others up rather than to tear them down. As the Apostle Paul said: "Don't let any evil talk come out of your mouths. Say only what will help to build others up and meet their needs. Then what you say will help those who listen" (Eph. 4:29). What should you do when the other person is wrong? You can offer to correct them—later—in a patient and kind manner. But never attack or demean the other person or their character. Instead, focus on correcting any facts they may have gotten wrong or any behavior that seemed out of place.

4. *Replace Flattery with Genuine Praise.* There is nothing wrong with using a little token flattery to bring a smile to another person's face. But in our day and age, flattery is overused, and others see through it pretty quickly. Genuine praise, however, can make a lasting impact on the other person's self-worth. What's the difference between flattery and praise? Flattery focuses upon something that is untrue or over which the person has little or no control. Praise focuses on something in which they make an effort and contribute. For example, you might flatter a person's hairstyle or clothing. But you would praise

an accomplishment for which they made a worthy effort. When you praise someone, offer specifics, so the praise will be remembered and taken at face value. Flattery may bring a momentary smile, but praise can help to permanently raise others' self-esteem.

5. ***Speak the Truth Kindly.*** Even when the truth is potentially hurtful, it can be delivered in a way that builds up the other person rather than tears him or her down. There are a thousand ways to criticize others in a way that will hurt them but only one way to criticize and build up at the same time. You might try using Gary Smalley's "sandwich method," which I described earlier. First, call the person's attention to something they're doing or have done that is truly praiseworthy (the bottom slice of bread). Then gently transition to the meat of the criticism. It's always useful to use questions or word pictures to help the person better hear or receive the criticism. It's also good to include an instance from your own life of a similar failure on your part, so they can see that you are *not* talking down to them from a self-righteous or arrogant point of view. Finally, finish with the top slice of bread, another statement of specific praise. Remember, keep in proper perspective the behavior you are criticizing. Don't magnify it, and don't be condescending or demeaning. And use a soft tone of voice and words

that are not harsh or cutting. When I criticize someone, my goal is to help them clearly understand the problem, see a clear-cut solution, select a specific corrective action, and be motivated to embrace the correction. I want them to feel better about themselves, not worse. Remember Jesus's encounter with the woman caught in the act of adultery. He corrected her behavior without condemning her. The same was true with his encounter with the woman at the well. He used questions and salting statements, and as a result, changed her life forever.

6. ***Proactively Love.*** Last but not least, we need to love others—colleagues, clients, family, friends—the way Jesus loves us . . . not just emotionally, but with "practical action." We need to care about them and express that interest and care in our actions. Whether offering someone a smile or a helpful conversation or meeting a pressing need, nothing builds a person's self-esteem faster than an expression of love. And no one in human history was better at expressing that love for each and every one of us than Jesus. There is certainly no greater example to follow.

We live in a cynical and negative world. Zig Ziglar quotes experts who report that our children hear seventeen *no*s for every *yes*. Things are not much better for adults. Most people are quick to criticize and slow to encourage. Every person we encounter is criticized and demeaned by others, and likely has deep-seated feelings of inadequacy in various areas of their lives. We are all in need of encouragement and praise. Each time you and I interact with others, we can be a source of encouragement and worth or a cause of worry, concern, and doubt. The choice is ours. Let's choose to be part of the one instead of the seventeen. At the end of his earthly life, Jesus told his disciples that he had a new command for them to follow—that they love each other in the same manner as he had loved each of them. And he tells us to love our neighbor as we love ourselves. How much fuller and more rewarding our lives and careers would be if we heeded his words!

Understanding Changes Minds— Action Changes Lives

CREATING WORTH IN OTHERS

1. Think of a recent situation in which you lowered someone's self-worth.

2. Using the list below as a guide, how could you have *increased* that person's self-worth?

    a. Proactively listening

    b. Understanding their frame of reference and *valuing* their opinions

    c. Using words wisely

    d. Replacing flattery with genuine praise

    e. Speaking the truth kindly

    f. Proactively Loving

3. Make a list of the people whose worth you would like to build up in the week ahead.

4. Using the list from number 2 above, write out some ideas on specific things you can do this week to build their self-worth.

As the week progresses, continually review the list, to see if you are succeeding in your effort to build their worth.

—— ∅∅ ——

A Change of Heart: *Why* We Do What We Do

"The good man brings good things out of the good stored up in his heart, and the evil man brings evil things out of the evil stored up in his heart."

—JESUS (LUKE 6:45, NIV)

Have you ever said something that hurt someone's feelings and thought, "Where did *that* come from?" or "What was I thinking?" or "Why on earth did I say that?" How many times have words left your mouth that you instantly wished you could pull back?

Have you ever wondered why all of us are so quick to condemn others for their faults and yet are so tolerant of or even blind to our own?

Have you ever wondered how you—or someone else—could be so in love one day, and so out of love the next?

All of these are matters of the heart. We often say and do what we feel. When Jesus talks about our "heart," he's talking about the center of our emotional being—the very core of who we are. And Jesus teaches us that as hard as we may try to change what we say or our behavior, such change is usually short-lived. Our behaviors, whether negative or positive, are functions of our hearts—they flow naturally from our inner person. The only way to bring about significant, lasting, positive change is to bring about a change of heart—a change in *who* we are.

As Jesus said, "The good man brings good things out of the good stored up in his heart, and the evil man brings evil things out of the evil stored up in his heart" (Lk. 6:45, NIV).

How many times have you been blindsided by someone else's words or behavior? Have you ever wondered how someone can do something terrible to another person—lie, steal, cheat, or harm—and not seem to care? A day doesn't go by that we don't read or hear tragic stories in the news about men and women committing terrible crimes against others.

How can such things happen? Aren't people basically good? According to Jesus, we are not! In fact, one of the greatest mistakes we make is to assume that everyone is good. Jesus said the opposite is true. All of us are self-centered to one degree or another. And the more self-centered we are, the less important other people become to us. And the less im-portant others become, the easier it is to excuse our misconduct.

❧❧ Overcoming Self-Centeredness

Would you rather be liked or disliked? Would you rather be loved or hated? Would you rather be appreciated by others or seen as worthless by them? Would you rather have your spouse, children, coworkers, and friends be grateful for all that you are to them or ask why in heaven's name they have to put up with you?

Most of us would clearly prefer the former. The fact is, the more self-centered we become, the less we will be liked, loved, appreciated, and tolerated. And the less self-centered we are, the more we will be liked, loved, appreciated, and enjoyed. Moreover, when we are liked, loved, and appreciated by others, we are happier and more fulfilled. Our focus on ourselves is like cancer. If left untreated or unrestrained, it continues to grow until it cuts us off from those around us.

Let me tell you something—I love going to work. As enjoyable as being successful at work is, what I love most about my work is that I've been able to build some amazing and enduring relationships. I love coming home as well—not because I live in a beautiful home, but because five of my favorite people on earth are waiting for me each night. No matter how successful we are in business, or how big our homes are, if we live a life that is self-centered, if we don't nurture and build worthwhile relationships in our lives, we undermine our chances of long-term happiness and fulfillment.

⊚⊚ Changing the Built-In Bias of Our Hearts

Can you admit that you are a *little* selfish? I'm far more than just a little selfish. Every day, I find myself behaving selfishly, even when I work against it. In almost any given situation, the first thing I think about is how *I* am going to be affected, before I think of how the other person may be affected.

There is a game that men play in Great Britain called bowls. Two competing teams roll a giant ball around a field, trying to get the ball into their goal and to keep the other team from getting it into theirs. It would be fairly easy to do, except for one thing. There is a lead weight inside the ball; the ball never wants to move in a straight line. No matter which way you push it, the ball seems to have a mind of its own and wants to squirm off to the left or right. That weight is called a bias.

Like that giant ball, we too have a bias. It lies within our heart, right at the core of who we are: our self-centeredness. Left to their own devices, our hearts will naturally put our interests first and the interests of others second. Our *illusion* is that doing so is in our best interest. But most of the time, that isn't really true. The best things in life are rarely about *me*— they are nearly always about *we*. So putting myself first may get me what I want in the short term, but it won't give me what I really need, and it may undermine my ability to get what I really want over the long term. This bias toward self is always present and nearly always urges us in the wrong direction.

What can we do to overcome that bias? Obviously, we can't surgically remove it from our heart. In fact, it can be dealt with only one step or one choice at a time.

But doing so requires insight and wisdom. It requires that we know the difference between the good, the bad, and the best choice in each situation. And that often requires a reference point outside of ourselves. The reference point is found in the teachings of Jesus. His words are our "GPS," pointing out where we are, where we want to go, and how to get there.

The other day, I was searching for a parking place at a nearby college where my son trains in track and field. The school was in session, so every parking space within a block or two was taken. I went into another lot and finally found a space. Just before I turned in, a coed cut in front of me, blocking the space so she could back into it. I couldn't believe her audacity. My natural inclination was to argue with her over the spot. Although she was blocking it, she couldn't turn her vehicle into it if I didn't move. In my mind, I had a *right* to that spot. My inclination was to stand my ground and demand that she find another spot. But one of Jesus's statements from his Sermon on the Mount came into my mind. "Give to everyone who asks you, and if anyone takes what belongs to you, do not demand it back" (Lk. 6:30, NIV). The light went on, and I thought, "How dumb to argue over a parking space." So I gave her the space, but I got the blessing. In the end, I found a space at the other end of the parking lot and walked a little farther. Not only did I get the benefit of the extra exercise, but I felt good.

◉◉ The Difference between Our Minds and Our Hearts

Our mind is like a computer. It receives information, processes it, and stores it for later use. It also gives us the ability to analyze information so that we can use it effectively. It can turn information into visual images that can have a significant influence on our decision making. Most important, the mind is the *gateway* to the heart, which is the source of our emotions, the core of who we are. Our hearts are where we embrace or reject moral and ethical values. And the values we embrace ultimately become the true essence of who we are.

While our minds can drive a temporary adjustment or modification of our behavior, they lack the power to bring about long-term, consistent change. For that kind of change, we need a change or *exchange* of values. We literally need a change of heart.

No matter how sincerely a person may want to change their behavior, if their heart isn't changed, they will experience little progress. One of my friends has had a never-ending battle with his temper. He is a wonderful man in so many respects. And he's a successful business executive with extraordinary skills. And yet people dread doing business with him because of his quick and explosive temper. His bosses have told him to bring it into check, "or else." And he really *wants* to bring it under control. The problem is, he can't. Why? Because there is a lot of anger in his heart. Until he is able to resolve the reasons for his anger, he will not be able to consistently bring his temper under control. Like most angry people, he blames his anger on the behavior of others, and as long as he does, he will be unable to resolve the real sources of his anger.

৯৯ Changing Our Hearts

To create lasting change within us, we first need to recognize the built-in bias toward self-centeredness and self-gratification within us.

Second, we need to screen out the destructive influences that we willingly absorb into our lives. Like a dye that changes the color of every thread in a piece of fabric, destructive influences can seep into the fabric of our heart and permanently change its makeup.

The prophet Jeremiah, addressing our bias toward self-centeredness, said, "Can the Ethiopian change his skin or the leopard its spots? Neither can you do good who are accustomed to doing evil" (Jer. 13:23). Jesus, however, taught that faith makes everything possible, even a change in our heart. He said, "If you have faith as small as a mustard seed, you can say to this mountain, 'Move from here to there' and it will move. Nothing will be impossible for you" (Matt. 17:20). Jesus isn't talking about a religious faith. The faith he's talking about is more akin to believing what he says, to the point that we act upon it. If we believe and do what Jesus says, we can effect amazing changes in our heart. Our bias toward self-centered thinking will lessen its hold over our behavior, and the fruits of *agape* will begin to make themselves felt.

Which brings us to the second challenge in changing our heart: the outside influences that color our thoughts and shape our minds. Today, we have thrust upon us more negative images and information than at any other time in history. With television, movies, radio, and the Internet—we are constantly exposed to images of all sorts.

King Solomon wrote in Proverbs that we need to "guard our hearts" against negative outside influences. For, Solomon went on, "as a man thinks (or reasons) in his heart, so is he" (Prov. 4:23; 23:7). In other words, what we think and focus on we become. Most people do not take Solomon's admonition seriously enough. We don't always pay attention to the information we take in, the people we associate with, or the experiences we seek out. For example, we'll see movies that are filled with images that are contrary to our values—and yet those images, once in our minds, are not easily erased. We ignore or dismiss the power of these images, telling ourselves it's just entertainment. We subject ourselves to all sorts of experiences, thinking to ourselves, "It's no big deal—I can handle it." But most of the time, we *can't* handle it; it has a subtle effect on our hearts and, ultimately, our values and our behavior. How can we guard our hearts against such influences?

Jesus says it starts with our eyes, as our eyes are the gateway to our mind. As Jesus put it, "The eye is the lamp of the body. If your eyes are good, your whole body (or person) will be full of light. But if your eyes are bad, your whole body will be full of darkness" (Matt. 6:22, NIV). Jesus realized the immense power of negative and positive imaging two thousand years before modern social scientists made the same discoveries.

King Solomon told us to keep our eyes looking "straight

ahead" and not to glance to the left or right (Prov. 4:25). In other words, keep your focus on those things that are uplifting, and don't even glance toward those things that would pull you astray. The Apostle Paul, speaking to this issue, said, "Finally, brethren, whatever things are true, whatever things are noble, whatever things are just, whatever things are pure, whatever things are lovely, whatever things are of good report, if there is any virtue and if there is anything praiseworthy—meditate on these things" (Phil. 4:8, NKJV).

✹✹ Stopping the Birds

Martin Luther once said, "You can't stop a bird from landing on your head; but you *can* stop him from building a nest." Today, articles and images and ideas come at us so fast from so many sources that it is often impossible to screen out the negative ones. But we can keep them from "building a nest" by refusing to dwell on them and instead quickly refocusing our attention on more beneficial and positive material.

What do we do about the images, thoughts, and ideas that have *already* become a part of the fabric of our heart?

King David asked the same question: "How can a young man cleanse his way?" Then he gave us the answer. He said that he sought the Lord with his whole heart and "hid" God's word in his heart (Ps. 119:9–11). The single most powerful tool to change our hearts and keep changing them is to read and think through the teachings of Jesus. I have found that his words can lift me from the depths of despair and bring me to the heights of joy and fulfillment, sometimes in an instant. They can transform a hateful heart to a loving one, a bitter heart into a grateful heart, and a greedy heart into a generous heart. Jesus said that if we would study and apply his teachings, we would discover truth so powerful that it would set us free (Jn. 8:31–32). And the freedom Jesus was talking about was liberation from the self-centered bias of our heart.

Finally, to change our hearts over the long term, we need to change what we *treasure*. Jesus said, "For where your treasure is, there will your heart be also" (Matt. 6:21). What do *you* treasure? If you could have any ten things in life, what would they be? More money, a nicer home, a nicer car, a bigger boat, a better job or profession, a more prestigious job title, a fitter body or better-looking face? Would you want more respect, a more loving spouse, more physical intimacy or gratification? Make a list! Now, if you could have any three of the things on your list, which ones would you pick? What do you *really* treasure? Next, make a list of the things you already have in your life that you would most hate to lose. Which of those things would you do almost anything to keep?

Next, create a list of the *people* you treasure the most. Finally, create a list of what you treasure most other than people or things—such as your health, your freedom, your reputation, your job or career, the work you do, or your favorite hobbies.

Once you have created these "treasure lists," look them

over. Are the things you treasure most those things that are of greatest value to you? Do they reflect the meanings or "whys" in your life that you embraced in chapter 4? My point is, if you really want to change your heart, you need to change what you treasure. If you treasure your golf weekends more than you treasure your time with your spouse or children, your heart will reflect those priorities, and you and your family will likely pay a terrible price. Is that what you truly want?

Jesus urged us to consider the "ultimate" treasure checklist. In Matthew 6:19–21, he said, "Do not store up for yourselves treasures on earth, where moth and rust destroy, and where thieves break in and steal. But store up for yourselves treasures in heaven, where moth and rust do not destroy, and where thieves do not break in and steal. For where your treasure is, there your heart will be also" (Matt. 6:21, NKJV).

He was not telling us what to buy, but rather what to "store up" and what to treasure. We all need material possessions to live. However, most of us don't need nearly as much as we buy. And what we "store up" often has little *permanent* value. The things we "store up" can easily steer us away from what matters to us the most. And any treasure that turns our hearts away from the things that matter most can have devastating consequences to our relationships with our families, our friends, and our colleagues and to our spirit. Do *not* treasure those things, Jesus tells us—they will steal your heart away.

What are the things in your life that can't be stolen, worn

out, or destroyed by time? For me, it's my relationship with each member of my family. My relationships with friends and others who come into my daily path. My relationship with God and my ability to share His love and wisdom through the inspiration and revelation of His words.

In the four-plus decades of life I have experienced since meeting Jesus in 1964, the greatest changes in my heart have taken place as a result of the wisdom and words and example of Jesus. I am convinced that no force in the world can better make a bitter heart glad, an angry heart happy, a greedy heart generous, a fearful heart courageous, and a hateful heart more loving than his words. As he said, "My words are spirit and they are life" (Jn. 6:63, NIV). When I am hurting in any way, even if I am in the depths of depression and despair, what I need more than anything else is an infusion of his Spirit and life.

⊚⊚ The Heart of the Matter Isn't the Matter

When things get us down, we usually blame our depression or distressed feelings on outside circumstances or other people. People say things like, "If you knew how bad things were on my job (or at home, etc.), you'd understand why I'm so angry." But as Jesus says, our happiness isn't dependent on outside circumstances or other people. The heart of the matter isn't the *matter*—it's the *heart*.

Corrie ten Boom and her father, sister, and uncle were all

sentenced to Nazi concentration camps for helping more than 140 Jews escape from the Nazi-occupied Netherlands. She was the only member of her family to make it out of the camps alive. Although she could never change the terrible circumstances of her past, she became an example of love and forgiveness that has inspired millions. How? Her happiness and sense of spiritual fulfillment were not tethered to what had happened in the past to those she loved but were dependent upon her heart in the present. Her heart was focused upon eternal truths, such as her love of God, and those who crossed her daily path. She learned to treasure those things that couldn't be lost or frayed with time.

Jesus told us, "Love your enemies, bless those who curse you, do good to those who hate you, and pray for those who spitefully use you and persecute you" (Matt. 5:44). But Jesus not only talked the talk, he walked the walk. Even as he was suffering on the cross, Jesus interceded on behalf of the men who had nailed him to that cross, as well as those who had mocked him, spit on him, and gambled for his clothes.

Believing in the words and wisdom of Jesus means making the choice to trust in him, learn from his teachings, and follow his example. As we do this, he promises that we will discover a new source of life, joy, and blessing; they will flow from within our heart to those around us. He said, "If anyone thirsts, let him come to me and drink. He who believes in me, as the Scripture has said, out of his heart will flow rivers of living water" (Jn. 7:37–38, NKJV).

Understanding Changes Minds—
Action Changes Lives

CHANGING YOUR HEART

1. Write out at least two situations within the past week that demonstrated your own *self-centeredness*. (If you can't think of any, ask your spouse, your kids, or one of your peers at work.)

2. Why were you driven to behave in that manner?

3. What do YOU believe you can do to bring about a lasting change in your heart?

—◉◉—

CHAPTER 15

Unparalleled Success and Unshakable Happiness

> "I will show you what he is like who comes to me and hears my words and puts them into practice. He is like a man building a house, who dug down deep and laid the foundation on rock. When a flood came, the torrent struck that house but could not shake it, because it was well built."
>
> —JESUS (LUKE 6:47–48, NIV)

How do you define success? Do you define it in terms of a job title, an income or salary, an accumulation of assets or net worth? Do you define it by the number of employees who report to you, the annual budget of your division, or a dollar volume of sales or revenue?

How do you define happiness? Do you recognize it through feelings such as cheerfulness, giddiness, a physical or emotional high? Is it a state of pleasure, contentment, or fulfillment? Or does it inspire a sense of exhilaration, excitement, or ecstasy?

It is important that you understand what your definitions of success and happiness are. First, your definition of each of these words creates your current "tape measure" by which you measure your own degree or level of success and happiness; and second, if your measure isn't a *true* measure, you will discover its shortcomings as it is compared to a more accurate measure.

Each year, my son Ryan competes in our state track and field championships in various sprints and jumping events. Each year, he qualifies to compete at the National Outdoor Track and Field Championships, as both a high jumper and a long jumper. He recently jumped eight inches higher than any other fifteen- or sixteen-year-old high jumper in America. Now, imagine how he would feel if he arrived at the National Championships and discovered that the tape measure used at our state meet was radically different from the real measure used by everyone else in the nation. Imagine if the measure he had been using to gauge his progress contained only six inches to a foot, while the measure used by everyone else contained twelve inches per foot. Imagine his shock when he discovered that all of the other jumpers were, in fact, jumping twice as high as he was. Yes, you're right, this would never be the case, because our linear measurements, whether in centimeters or inches, have long been standardized.

Unfortunately, there are no such fixed standards of measurement when it comes to gauging our levels of success and happiness. Everyone has their own measuring tape, and everyone's measuring tape for each of these qualities is very *different* from everyone else's. And yet Jesus provides the ultimate standard of measure against which all levels of success and happiness can be gauged. His measurements are based upon reality instead of illusion, upon significance rather than superficiality.

∞ The True Measures of Success

In high school, we measured our success by three criteria: popularity, athletic success, and grades. But in reality, none of these were genuine measures of success. By these measures, my classmate Steven Spielberg and I were both unsuccessful and would have been voted by our teachers and our classmates as the two students least likely to succeed. By these standards, in their youth, Bill Gates, Thomas Edison, and Benjamin Franklin would all have been judged hopelessly unsuccessful.

In the business world, we tend to measure our success by our job title, salary, department budget size, and sales volume. In our personal lives, we often measure our success by the size of our house, the makes of cars in the garage, a country club membership, or our financial net worth. But these too fail to measure true success. By these measurements, Jesus and his disciples would have been deemed *complete* failures.

Have you ever heard of an American businessman named Robert Morris? In 1798, at the age of sixty-four, he was sent to debtor's prison, where he spent the next three years of his life. After his release in 1801, he lived in poverty under the care of his loving wife until he died in 1806. By many measures of success, Mr. Morris could be judged a failure. And yet, according to George Washington, the United States never could have waged the Revolutionary War, much less won it, *without* Robert Morris.

Robert Morris was one of the signers of the Declaration of Independence. As such, he and all the other signers pledged their fortunes and their lives to pursue, against all odds, the dream of democracy. But far more important, Morris was *the* financier of the Revolutionary War. He personally paid Washington's army when the government itself could not pay the troops. He paid for our navy. In fact, our navy's first ship was donated by Morris. It was the finest ship in his personal fleet. It was *his* money that paid for the horses, the boots, the rifles, the cannons, and nearly everything else it took to fight the war. Morris also created America's spy network, which gave Washington the intelligence reports he needed on the movements of the British fleet. Without that intelligence, Washington would have been defeated and the war would have been lost. But Morris didn't just write the checks from a comfortable office away from the front. He actively participated in moving Washington's troops from New York to Yorktown, Virginia, for the final battle of the war. He personally borrowed every dime he could muster to continue to pay for the war effort. When Benjamin Franklin asked France for the loans we desperately needed to continue the war, it agreed to make those loans on *one* condition— that Robert Morris *personally* guarantee their repayment. He agreed, the loans were made, and the war was won. Morris created and personally funded the first national bank to be chartered in America, to provide stability to America's failing economy. When the state of Pennsylvania ran out of money to pay its troops in the Revolutionary War, Morris stepped up and paid their wages. When Pennsylvania went bankrupt in 1780, Morris paid its debt and restored its economy. After the war, while Washington, D.C., was being built, Morris gave his home to be used as the president's residence for both President Washington and, later, President Adams. He was asked to be the secretary of the Treasury, but he didn't feel he could dedicate the necessary time, so he recommended his good friend Alexander Hamilton instead. A few years later, due to a failed business venture, he eventually lost everything and was sentenced to debtor's prison. It was the one offense even President Washington didn't have the power to pardon. President Washington visited Morris most weekends while he remained in prison. So, yes, Robert Morris died in poverty, a failure. And yet, by any true measure, he was one of the most successful and important American businessmen and American revolutionaries in our history.

So what *are* the true measures of success? Jesus revealed three measures of success, both at work and at home. They relate to the specific talents, abilities, and gifts we've been given, the contribution we make when we accomplish what we set out to do, and our success at accomplishing them in the *right* manner. Jesus made over 1,900 statements in the New Testament. Though success as we define it was not the subject of his teachings, every statement Jesus made was highly relevant to the subject of success. He told an extremely pointed and revealing story that dealt with business success.

✆ The First Measure of True Success: Significant Missions Effectively Accomplished

The first measure of our success has to do with the significance of the missions we undertake and how effectively we accomplish them. In Jesus's parable of the talents (Matt. 25:14–30), he tells of a business owner who has to take a long journey and must leave the management of his investment portfolio in the hands of three capable money managers. Some historians estimate that the eight "talents" of money that he divided among the three managers would be worth approximately $720,000 per talent in today's currency, or a total of $5,760,000. Here are the facts of the story:

1. He allocated the money according to the individual *ability* of each manager. He gave the manager with the greatest ability $3,600,000. He gave the manager with the second-greatest ability $1,440,000. He gave the manager with the least ability $720,000.

2. He gave them a specific, time-sensitive mission: *manage the money for the period of time that I will be away on my journey, and achieve the best results you are capable of achieving.*

3. When he returned, each manager was required to give a full accounting of his individual success in accomplishing his mission.

4. The manager of the $3,600,000 portfolio had doubled its size to $7,200,000. The manager of the

$1,440,000 portfolio had doubled its size to $2,880,000.

5. The third manager had buried the money in a safe place and gave the owner his money back when the owner returned. He took no risk, made no effort, and generated no return on the investment. He simply maintained the status quo.

6. The two managers who doubled their investments were generously rewarded, praised, and promoted, based upon their individual performance. Their most important reward was based not upon how they performed in relation to one another but upon how they performed in relation to their particular ability.

7. The manager who turned in the best performance of the three also received a *bonus* on top of his reward.

8. The third manager felt that he was *entitled* to a reward and praise as well, because he had safely protected the money that had been entrusted to his management. He hadn't *lost* a penny. But instead of being praised and rewarded, the owner called him lazy and evil, and he was fired. While preservation may have been an adequate short-term goal in a declining economy, it was *not* a praiseworthy goal here, because he had both the ability and the time to achieve a significant gain (as seen with the other two managers).

So what are the applicable lessons of Jesus's parable?

Let's start by looking at the failure of the third manager, since the consequences of his failure robbed him of everything he valued in life. He made a number of mistakes that resulted in the end of his career and ultimately robbed him of his happiness. Unfortunately, we make the same kind of mistakes today, and they produce the same kinds of consequences. The bad news is, they are so common that nearly all of us fall into this way of thinking to one degree or another. The good news is, when we are made aware of these mistakes, we can consciously work to avoid them.

The Five Critical Mistakes of the Third Manager

1. *A Mentality of Entitlement.* The third manager took his job for granted; he thought that "showing up" was all that was necessary. He didn't believe that his job and his future were dependent upon his performance. How often do we think the same way, assuming that our employers or the government or our spouse owes us something? It is an attitude that robs us of the motivation to achieve extraordinary success in virtually any area of our lives. It also eliminates the opportunity to be happy, because it creates false expectations.

2. *Minimal Effort and Lackluster Performance.* Unlike the managers who actively invested and traded for months, the third manager made no effort to increase the owner's stake. He hid the money away

and thought no more about it. He received room, board, and his daily wages for months, even though he did *nothing* to earn that salary. In a sense, he was stealing his wage, and that is probably why his master not only labeled him "lazy," but called him "evil" as well. When we "show up" in life and do only enough to "just get by," we are not much better. It is not enough to do what is necessary to *keep* our job—we need to make an effort to perform *beyond* the expectations of our boss or spouse or children.

3. ***He Squandered Time and Opportunity.*** Although we rarely live our lives this way, the fact is that *time* is our most important asset. The third manager squandered the time he had been given to produce a good rate of return on his employer's money. Had he at least deposited the money with a banker and merely earned a small interest rate, he would have done more to earn a return on his employer's investment. We too squander time every day. We live as if we have all the time in the world and waste it on frivolous pursuits that bring no significant or lasting benefits to others or ourselves. Those minutes, hours, or days can never be regained. Our time on earth cannot be extended by a single moment. The other two managers made the most of their time and achieved extraordinary returns. And as a result, they were praised and rewarded.

4. *He Abandoned the* **Purpose** *of His Employment.*
The reason this manager was given a portion of his
employer's portfolio to manage in the first place was
to *increase* the assets that had been entrusted to him.
His attitude and performance reflected the fact that
in *his* mind, his employer existed for *his* benefit. The
reality was, his relationship with his employer was
based on the degree to which he could benefit his
employer. Though he may have known this in his
mind, his behavior reflected an abandonment of the
purpose of his employment. In our professional
lives, we are hired for a purpose. That purpose must
be at the foundation of our attitudes and behavior.
At home, purpose should drive our marriage and our
parenting relationships. This is why discovering your
"whys" and mapping your missions are so important.
Doing so empowers your purpose and helps you
accomplish it.

5. *He Lost the* **Opportunity** *for Achievement Because
of His Complacency.* When his employer entrusted
$720,000 to him, he had both the time and the
opportunity to make a *significant* contribution to his
employer's success and well-being. Instead, he
avoided taking any risk or making any effort. He
stayed in his comfort zone. When we stay in our
comfort zone in life, turning our backs on new
opportunities for learning and growth, we stagnate
and become cut off from the greatest benefits of

life. It is impossible to achieve anything significant in life when we embrace complacency. Our drive to accomplish significant things helps to energize our thinking and fuel our behavior. By choosing to *act*, we are embracing life as it is meant to be embraced.

What the Two Successful Managers Teach Us

So how can we avoid making these same mistakes in our lives? For one thing, we can learn the lessons of the first two managers and follow their examples.

1. *Diligence Leads to Extraordinary Success.* To be successful, we must be diligent in pursuing success. Unfortunately, diligence is not a common commodity in life. King Solomon wrote, "Do you see a man diligent in his business? He will stand before kings" (Prov. 22:29, NASB). Solomon would define *diligence* as a learnable skill that combines *persistence, intelligence, planning,* and *performance* in a *timely, efficient,* and *effective* manner to attain a superlative result. Diligence means not merely working hard, but working intelligently, over time.

2. *Extraordinary Success Leads to Extraordinary Rewards.* When we just do the minimum necessary to perform a job, our reward is that we merely get to keep our job. On the other hand, if we achieve outcomes that are truly extraordinary, a good company will reward us proportionately—if not at

first, then eventually. And if it *doesn't*, someone else will!

3. ***Success Is Not Defined by Money Alone.*** There is nothing inherently wrong with money when it is made legitimately and ethically. Though money may be an indicator of material achievement, money alone is not a true measure of success. More important is achieving your *full potential* in the limited amount of time you are given. The better a steward you are of the talents you've been given, the more successful you will be.

My oldest son, Mark, is a high school English teacher in the inner city of Philadelphia. His administrators and the parents of the students he teaches have a right to demand Mark's diligence in making his students successful in the classroom. Mark is a wonderfully talented teacher, driven by his love and compassion for the kids he works with. Giving them only 80 percent of his efforts would be a waste of his talent and an abdication of his responsibility to them. But he doesn't give 80 percent—he works harder than anyone I know. His reward as a teacher is not an increased profit-sharing plan or a Christmas bonus. But in many ways, his reward is far greater. He helps kids who might otherwise fall to drugs, gangs, and incarceration. Many are transformed by his performance, care, and concern. His reward is seeing the students he works with gain a love for education and learning and then go on to graduate. What's the worth of a single changed life? More, perhaps, than a million-dollar bonus paid to a CEO of a Fortune 500 company.

◉◉ The Second Measure of True Success: Achieving Our Missions in the Right Manner

The financial meltdown of 2008 resulted from businesses and politicians trying to provide lower-income families with home ownership in the *wrong* manner. Politicians passed legislation allowing lending institutions to provide mortgages to people who were not creditworthy. And those institutions used those loans—and financial derivatives created by packaging those loans into investment vehicles—to increase their profits. What was in the worst *long-term* interest of the institutions was then in their *best* short-term interest. Greed took over, and everyone turned a blind eye to the long-term risk. Even when warned, congressional leaders refused to pay attention to the whistle-blowers. As a result, trillions of dollars of investments and the retirement accounts of millions of Americans evaporated.

Putting people who didn't have a lot of money or solid credit into houses may have seemed like a worthy mission. But the manner in which it was carried out created devastating consequences. If Congress really wanted to improve the living conditions of these people, a better way would have been to improve their educational and vocational opportunities. But *that* kind of responsible solution would take a lot of time and effort and would fail with those who weren't motivated. Greed, and the desire to take shortcuts to achieve the desired ends, proved disastrous.

As Jesus taught us with his example, as well as his words, it is critical that we accomplish our missions in the *right* manner.

The Right Manner in Pursuing Success

1. *Guard Against Greed.* Greed is a dangerous and seductive thief. According to King Solomon, it "steals the life" of the one who possesses it (Prov. 1:19). Jesus warned, "Watch out! Be on your guard against all kinds of greed; a man's life does not consist in the abundance of his possessions" (Lk. 12:15, NIV).

2. *Take the Initiative; Seize the Opportunity.* Every day, we are surrounded by opportunities in every important area of our lives. And yet they pass us by because our eyes are closed to them. We miss business opportunities that are all around us every day. We decide we're too old or too unskilled or too set in our ways to take action. But those limitations exist solely in our minds. There are those who see opportunity and seize it, and their whole life begins to change. I know of an eighty-nine-year-old blind woman in Toronto, Canada, who tried our nutritional product and saw such an improvement in

her energy level and quality of life that she decided to join our company as an independent distributor. At eighty-nine! She recruited so many of her elderly friends as customers and distributors that she achieved the rank of "gold," earning more than three thousand dollars her first month! Yes, she was blind. But she saw an opportunity and seized it, rather than letting her age or disability get in the way.

Jesus was never a passive observer in the world around him. Instead, he took the initiative in every recorded moment of his life. And he taught the men and women whom he mentored to do the same. He told them, "Ask, and it will be given to you." He said, "Seek, and you will find; knock, and it will be opened to you" (Matt. 7:7, NKJV).

Few of us are initiative takers. Too many of us "go with the flow." To be successful in accomplishing any important effort, project, or area of your life, you must take the initiative. It is not enough to simply sit on the sidelines or watch from the stands.

3. *Be Generous.* Jesus said, "Give, and it will be given to you. A good measure, pressed down, shaken together and running over, will be poured into your lap. For with the measure you use, it will be measured to you" (Lk. 6:38, NIV).

When it comes to giving, most of us hide behind the rationalization "I would be more generous if only I had more to be generous with." We think that because we can barely pay our mortgage and our bills, we can't afford to be generous. That is the kind of *passive* behavior that Jesus cautioned against. Perhaps you genuinely don't have any extra money. If so, then be generous with your time, care, and concern. Offer a listening ear, an encouraging word, or another set of hands in helping others accomplish a task. Some of the most generous people I have ever known have been those who have had the *least* money to give. But they generously gave what they had. There is no more sure way to gain an abundance of happiness—happiness that no one can steal away. We all have some talent, time, or ability we can share or contribute.

4. ***Choose Wisdom Rather Than Expediency.*** To accomplish your mission in the right manner, act in a manner that reflects both wisdom and kindness. Jesus knew that we live in a world surrounded by wolves; given the chance, they will take advantage of us. But he didn't tell us to fight fire with fire or to become wolves ourselves. As you'll remember, he said, "Behold, I send you out as sheep in the midst of wolves. Therefore be wise as serpents and harmless as doves" (Matt. 10:16, NKJV). To become wise as serpents, we need to avail ourselves of wise counselors, partners, and mentors—people who have already successfully navigated the minefields that lie ahead of us.

5. ***Love and Live in the Moment.*** To Jesus, the journey is as important as the destination. In his parable of the Good Samaritan, a man was robbed, beaten, and left naked and unconscious by a band of thieves. Two men encountered him lying on the road, but both were in a hurry to get to their destination and chose not to become involved. But the third man, a Samaritan, was moved by compassion. He disinfected and bandaged the wounds, set the man upon his own donkey, and brought him to an inn. He took care of him that day and night. The next morning, he gave the innkeeper money to continue to take care of him and told him, "Look after him, and when I return, I will reimburse you for any extra expense you may have."

   The first two men saved the time, money, and effort they would have spent had they cared for the man. But they shortchanged their lives and missed the blessing of their journey. The Samaritan, on the other hand, acted in a manner that exemplified a life well lived. The rewards he received from that single action remained with him for the rest of his life.

   The greatest joys of my life haven't been my successes but rather the incomparable experiences I've had with the people I have met and partnered with day in and day out. Although many of these people created unexpected detours from my daily path and scheduled destinations, I've never regretted a single detour. In fact, some of my greatest successes have come about from relationships that began as a *result* of a detour.

A Demonstration His Disciples Would Never Forget

The night before Jesus died on the cross, he gave instructions to his disciples that were among the most important instructions he ever gave. His disciples' world was about to be shaken to the core. They were about to lose the person whom they had relied upon for more than three years for everything they valued most—his love, his teaching, and his guidance. They had left everything they treasured—their jobs, their homes, and their families—to follow him. And now he was about to leave them. They had come to believe that he was the Messiah, the Son of God. They had witnessed his miracles. Now, in the hours ahead, they were to watch Jesus be arrested, beaten, nailed to a cross, and killed. If ever there was a time that they needed his advice, *now* was that time. What would he say? What would he do?

Immediately after they finished eating, Jesus got up from the table, poured water into an empty basin, and began to wash the feet of each of his disciples. What on earth was he doing? The man whom they had worshiped was washing *their* feet. He told them, "I have set you an example that you should do as I have done for you." Jesus was showing his disciples the *right manner* that should define their hearts, their attitudes, and their behavior. More than anything else, what should guide their behavior was a willingness and desire to *serve* one another and serve those whom they would lead.

We all know people whose personalities and lives are characterized by their determination to serve others. This was true of my mother. At my mother's funeral, one of her coworkers of many years said to me, "You know that everyone at the bank referred to your mom as 'the angel.' Whenever any of us had a problem, *she* was the one person we would run to. She always took time to listen, and then would set about finding a way for us to work through our problems." My mother was *driven* by her servant's heart.

Most of us do not have a servant's heart by nature. That's certainly true of me, and it was true of most of Jesus's disciples. But as Jesus showed his disciples through his actions, even though it may not be our *nature* to serve, we can all make the *choice* to serve. And we can make that choice every day. Here's an amazing reality: the more we choose to serve others, the more such actions become second nature to us. In the beginning, serving won't come naturally to most of us, because it runs contrary to our natural focus on ourselves. If we remember Jesus's example and follow it, however, we will not only bless the lives of those we serve, but *we* will be blessed as well.

◉◉ The Third Measure of True Success: Creating a Legacy That Endures

While most of us are concerned about just getting through our day, Jesus taught his followers that success that doesn't endure and create lasting benefit is *not* true success. After Jesus told two brothers who were fighting over their inheritance,

"Beware! Don't be greedy for what you don't have. Real life is not measured by how much we own," he went on to tell them this parable:

> A rich man had a fertile farm that produced fine crops. In fact, his barns were full to overflowing. So he said, "I know! I'll tear down my barns and build bigger ones. Then I'll have room enough to store everything. And I'll sit back and say to myself, My friend, you have enough stored away for years to come. Now take it easy! Eat, drink, and be merry!" But God said to him, "You fool! You will die this very night. Then who will get it all?" (Lk. 12:16–20, NLT)

How tragic. And yet how many people do we know who spend a lifetime accumulating their "stuff" for their own benefit *without* creating a legacy to bless the lives of others? What a waste of life. As Jesus said, "This is how it will be with anyone who stores up things for himself, but is not rich toward God" (Lk. 12:21, NIV).

Jesus had a *better* model to follow. Imagine if you could leave a rich legacy to future generations *and* act in a manner that would create *eternal* benefits for you as well. As Jesus told his followers, "Do not store up for yourselves treasures on earth, where moth and rust destroy, and where thieves break in and steal. But store up for yourselves treasures in heaven, where moth and rust do not destroy, and where thieves do not break in and steal" (Matt. 6:19–21, NIV). Regardless of our social or economic status, we can make choices *now* that will create an *eternal* legacy for us in heaven. Jesus instructs us to *shift* the focus of our hearts from storing up earthly treasures to storing up treasures that last beyond the grave.

Leaving a Legacy That Endures

One of my friends, who started with nothing in 1977, has amassed a personal fortune worth *billions*. And yet he *will* leave it all behind. How sad to have achieved so much for himself and given so little to others. How can we leave a legacy on earth that will continue from generation to generation and create treasures after our time on earth?

My father turned away from God during World War II. He died an atheist. Nonetheless, he left behind a wonderful legacy to his family, the community, and the world. His legacy to me was to give me an example of a loving and caring father who *always* had time for his son. He taught me how to think before I reacted. He gave me love and encouragement and support. He was always there when I needed him and always gave me freedom and independence when I needed it. He had a strong work ethic, born out of the Depression, and I am grateful for his example. He also saved countless lives that would have been lost to traffic accidents. He started the movement for the daytime use of headlights back in the early 1950s. He invented the blind-spot mirror and the "flashing headlights circuit" for emergency vehicles and persuaded fire departments all over America to change the color of their equipment from red to white and yellow so they could be more easily seen by other drivers. He taught tens of thousands of professional drivers his sixty-six accident-evasion techniques. He reduced the accident occurrence rates of thousands of car and truck fleets. And yet he never made a dime from any of his highway safety efforts.

We leave a legacy by serving the needs of others without the expectation of receiving anything in return. My dad spent a lot of nights coaching Little League baseball—not to win a championship, but to spend time with his son. We leave a legacy by providing an example to others of dealing with people and life's circumstances in a manner that builds others up rather than tearing them down. Bob Marsh's greatest legacy to me was not the gift of marketing strategies that work but rather the example of how to succeed in business with integrity, honor, and love. And, I hope, I'm passing that legacy on to those whom I am fortunate enough to influence.

Jesus taught that life is truly about "bearing fruit." He said that the "fruit" of a person's life is how we are to judge him or her. If a person produces good fruit, that person is a good man or woman. He who produces no fruit has lived a life without value. Jesus said, "I am the vine and you are the branches. He who abides in me, and I in him, will bear much fruit" (Jn. 15:5, NIV). The best way I know to produce a lot of fruit, to bless the lives of others in a permanent way, is to follow the example and teachings of Jesus. That fruit will endure from generation to generation and will create a legacy beyond calculation. In many ways, my father's behavior and manner toward me throughout my youth reflected Jesus's example with others. The fruit of my father's behavior continues to fill my heart with gratitude and love to this very day.

When you turn to Jesus for wisdom on loving, day-to-day living, and spiritual matters, you can expect to see powerful, miraculous changes take place in your heart, your life, and the lives of those people you serve and influence. Jesus said, "Therefore whoever hears these sayings of mine, and does them, I will liken him to a wise man who built his house on the rock" (Matt. 7:24–25, NKJV).

The more we embrace and follow the teachings of Jesus, the more we are able to set our self-interest aside and begin to serve others and the greater the *treasures* we are laying up. Of course, these are not material treasures—they're of much greater value. They are the treasures of *agape*, with a servant's heart toward others—a hunger and thirst for truth and that which is right. They are the treasure of a changed heart—a mean-spirited heart made generous, a hateful heart made loving, an angry heart made compassionate, and an arrogant heart made humble. Perhaps the greatest treasures we can lay up are the lives we have changed and influenced and nurtured.

◎◎ You Don't Need Riches on Earth to Become a Billionaire in Heaven

Some of the people I have known have laid up vast spiritual fortunes, despite the fact that they have had almost no *earthly* treasures. For example, I met one man when I worked on a janitorial crew at a bank building during my senior year in college. He cleaned all the bathrooms and toilets on all of the building's thirteen floors for more than twenty-five years. Because the last bus for downtown Phoenix left his neighborhood at 5:30 p.m. and his shift didn't start until midnight, he worked fourteen hours a night, even though he got paid for only eight. His shift would end at 8:00 a.m. After arriving home, he would take a brief morning nap, and then he would take care of his invalid wife until it was time to go to work again. And he held no resentment—he did his work with a joyful heart. His secret? He loved God, he loved his wife, and he enjoyed working for his employer. He didn't harbor a sense of entitlement, but rather possessed a heart full of gratitude for all the good things in his life. He told me he felt he had the best job in the world, because the bathrooms were like "echo chambers," where he could sing his hymns as loud as he wanted, and nobody minded.

For me, embracing Jesus on that Sunday night in 1964 has proven to be the single most important decision of my life. Everything I value has ultimately come my way as a result of that decision. Moreover, the *heavenly* treasures I've experienced on earth have been more gratifying and life changing than the material treasures I have received.

In the next two chapters, you will encounter the two greatest questions you will ever face: "Who is Jesus?" and "What must I do to receive eternal life and gain an unshakable assurance that I have truly received it?" If you come to know Jesus as he really is, your life will take on a level of purpose, joy, and fulfillment that your natural mind could never imagine. Most important, your eternal destiny will be forever changed and you will gain the opportunity to influence the eternal destiny of countless other people.

It is my hope that you will consider the content of the chapters that follow with an intellectually honest and open mind, and that God will give you a picture of his Son—and the eternal life he offers—that will change your life, *forever*!

Understanding Changes Minds— Action Changes Lives

Achieving *True* Success

1. Until now, how have *you* measured success—by what standards?

2. Are you currently a victim of the Five Critical Mistakes of the Third Manager?

   a. Do you have a mentality of entitlement?

   b. Do you make a minimal effort and achieve a lack-luster performance?

   c. Do you squander time and opportunity?

   d. Have you abandoned the *purpose* of your employment?

   e. Have you lost the *opportunity* for achievement because of your complacency?

3. Are you pursuing success in the *right* manner?

   a. Are you guarding against greed?

b. Are you taking the *initiative* and seizing the opportunity?

c. Are you being generous with your time, talent, and money?

d. Are you applying wisdom or simply doing that which is expedient?

e. Are you living "in the moment" and loving those who share the moments with you?

CHAPTER 16
— ◎◎ —

The Most Important Question You'll Ever Ask

"For God did not send his Son into the world to
condemn the world, but to save the world through him."

—JESUS (JOHN 3:17, NIV)

Who was Jesus? *If* Jesus was indeed who he claimed to be,
then this is the most important question you will ever ask. If
he was who he claimed he was, then discovering the *right* answer and its implications for your life would be the most important discoveries you will ever make.

On the other hand, if he was *not* who he claimed he was,
then not only is this question irrelevant to your life, but we
could conclude that Christianity is the greatest hoax ever per-
petrated. There is no middle ground. Either Jesus is the
greatest fraud in history or he is the centerpiece of history. If
he is who he claims to be, then his words and how we respond to them will determine whether we will spend eternity
in the presence of God or be forever separated from God in
a place of indescribable emptiness and loneliness.

I answered this question for myself one night in 1964

when I was first confronted by Jesus's claims. In the following decades, that answer has been confirmed and reconfirmed thousands of times. Jesus is the only way to God. But my answer can't be *your* answer—you are the only one who can discover, embrace, and act upon *your* answer to Jesus's claims.

In this chapter I will share the compelling evidence that persuaded me that Jesus was *indeed* who he claimed to be. In fact, one piece of this evidence was so compelling that it transformed one of the world's most brilliant and articulate atheists into one of the twentieth century's most passionate defenders of the Christian faith.

The Lord of the Rings Genius Versus The Chronicles of Narnia Genius

C. S. Lewis was chairman of the literature department at Oxford University. J. R. R. Tolkien was a tenured professor under Lewis and was Lewis's best friend. Both men were recognized as literary and philosophical geniuses. In fact, Lewis had also chaired the philosophy department at Cambridge University. He was one of England's most brilliant atheists. Tolkien was a devout Catholic whose love for Jesus Christ was known to his peers. According to one, Tolkien asked Lewis a simple question whose answer shook the foundation of Lewis's atheistic beliefs. The answer changed the course of his life.

The question and the conversation that followed are said to have gone something like this: Tolkien asked, "Who do *you* think Jesus was?" Lewis answered, "A good moral man, and perhaps the greatest teacher of morality the world has ever known." Tolkien replied, "That is impossible! He could not have been *just* a good moral man! Look at his claims."

Tolkien then recited a number of Jesus's claims of divinity. For example, he claimed to be the Messiah, the anointed one of God. He claimed to be the *only* begotten Son of God. He claimed to be able to give eternal life to anyone he chose to give it to. He claimed to be able to forgive the sins that people committed against each other and against God. He claimed that he was the Light of the World and the Bread of Life. He claimed that he came from heaven to save the world. He claimed to have power over life and death. He claimed that *all* authority and power had been granted to him by his Father, who he said was God. He claimed to be the one who would ultimately judge every human being who had ever lived. He claimed that the words he spoke on earth would be the standard of judgment by which all humanity would be judged. He claimed that he would be killed and buried, and that on the third day he would raise himself from the dead and revisit his followers who had watched him die. He said his death would be the source of humanity's redemption.

Tolkien then said that if Jesus was *not* who he claimed to be, there were only two alternatives: Jesus was either a liar or a lunatic. And not just an accidental liar or a mere eccentric. If a liar, then he would be the greatest liar who ever lived— for his lies would have deceived hundreds of millions of people who had placed their hopes for eternity on him, all because of his claims. And if a lunatic, then as Lewis later wrote, Jesus would be "a lunatic on the level of a man who thinks he's a poached egg."

As the conversation continued, the two men looked at the possibility that Jesus was the greatest deceiver who ever lived. They knew that a sane man lies for only two reasons: self-preservation or self-exaltation. A person wants to preserve himself and what he has, so he lies to ensure that preservation. Or he wants to *appear* to be more than he is. Lies are told to manipulate the minds and actions of others to fulfill the liar's self-interest.

Lewis realized that, in the case of Jesus, this eliminated the "liar alternative." Jesus never tried to preserve or protect himself. From the beginning of his public ministry he proclaimed that he had come to earth to die—to lay down his life. As we saw in an earlier chapter, he didn't even try to prevent his own execution, but rather told his disciples and his executioner that his death was part of God's plan.

Nor did Jesus want to exalt himself. When the crowds wanted to make him their leader and earthly king, he refused. Instead of exalting himself, he gave all the credit for everything he said and did to his heavenly Father, whom he continually exalted. When Jesus told the rich young ruler to sell everything he owned, he did *not* say, "and bring the money to me and we'll change the world." Even though Jesus had no home and no material possessions other than the clothes on his back, he didn't want a penny. He simply told the man, "Go and sell all you have and give the money to the poor, and you will have treasure in heaven." Over and over he told his listeners that he came to glorify his Father in heaven. Conclusion: Jesus was not motivated by self-preservation or self-exaltation, so he wasn't a liar!

With the liar alternative eliminated, only two possibilities were left: Jesus was either a lunatic or who he claimed to be—the Son of the Living God. A lunatic is defined by his preposterous claims or crazy behavior. For example, if I made all the claims Jesus made, I would quickly be committed to a mental institution. Likewise, if you and I were standing at the edge of the Grand Canyon and I told you I was going to jump to the other side, you would quickly call a park ranger. *But* if I stepped back fifty feet, started to run, and then jumped off the edge and miraculously flew to the other side, I'd no longer be a lunatic—I'd simply be the world's best long jumper! When someone makes preposterous claims and then *backs those claims with the appropriate action,* that person can no longer be considered a lunatic.

The same logic applies here. Jesus didn't just *claim* that he had "the power over life and death," he proved it by raising a corpse that had been dead and rotting for four days. And he did it in front of hundreds of witnesses who had been mourning the dead man. Jesus didn't just claim to be able to walk on water, turn water to wine, or be able to feed thousands of people with a few fish and loaves of bread, he *did* all of the above. He healed the sick, gave sight to the blind, and brought more than one dead person back to life. He didn't just claim that he would raise himself from the dead—he did it!

Jesus died in front of a huge crowd and was declared to be

dead by Roman soldiers who had seen death hundreds of times. He was wrapped in burial garments and placed in a tomb that was sealed with a stone that weighed hundreds if not thousands of pounds. A squad of Roman soldiers guarded the tomb against anyone who might attempt to steal the body. But the guards were mysteriously knocked out, the stone was moved, and Jesus appeared, alive and well, in front of hundreds of people in the days that followed. Jesus backed up his seemingly preposterous claims with the appropriate miraculous actions—actions witnessed by crowds ranging in size from hundreds to thousands.

C. S. Lewis conceded that Jesus could not be a lunatic.

Concluding that Jesus was neither a liar nor a lunatic, Lewis was left with only one alternative—the shocking alternative—Jesus was indeed the person he claimed he was, the Messiah, the eternal Son of the Living God. And that conclusion of course demands a second conclusion—that there *is* a God. Being an honest intellectual, Lewis not only conceded the existence of God, he spent the rest of his life doing all he could to get to know God more intimately and to serve God passionately. In his book *Mere Christianity,* Lewis concludes his "Shocking Alternative" chapter with the following statement:

I am trying here to prevent anyone saying the really foolish thing that people often say about Him: "I'm ready to accept Jesus as a great moral teacher, but I don't accept His claim to be God." That is the one thing we must not say. A man who was merely a man who said the sort of things Jesus said would not be a great moral teacher. He would either be a lunatic—on a level with the man who says he is a poached egg—or else he would be the Devil of Hell. You must make your choice. Either this man was, and is, the Son of God: or else a madman or something worse. You can shut Him up for a fool, you can spit at Him and kill Him as a demon; or you can fall at His feet and call Him Lord and God. But let us not start with any patronizing nonsense about His being a great human teacher. He has not left that open to us. He did not intend to.

ꜚꜙ Who on Earth Could Beat These Odds?

Who do *you* say Jesus is? Is he a liar, a lunatic, or the Son of God? If you're still figuring it out, let me give you another fact to think about. A mathematics professor once told me, "If something passes the 'math test' it doesn't need to pass any other test. If math proves something to be wrong—it's wrong! If it proves it to be right—it's right."

In his brief life, Jesus fulfilled hundreds of prophecies recorded in the Old Testament describing the birth, life, and death of the Jewish Messiah. Mathematics professors Peter W. Stoner and Robert C. Newman, PhD, calculated the statistical probability of one person during one lifetime fulfilling just forty-eight of these highly detailed prophecies. The odds turned out to be 1 chance in 10^{157}. That's a 1 in

10,000,000,000,000,000,000,000,000,000,000,000,000,000,
000,000,000,000,000,000,000,000,000,000,000,000,000,000,
000,000,000,000,000,000,000,000,000,000,000,000,000,000,
000,000,000,000,000,000,000, 000,000,000,000 chance.

To put it in perspective, let's say you built a wooden box so big that our solar system would fit inside it. And then you filled the box with silver BBs, and placed just one copper BB in the box. The chances of anyone reaching into the box and picking out the copper BB on his or her first try would be trillions of times *more likely* than the odds of one person fulfilling just forty-eight of the prophecies that Jesus fulfilled. There is no occurrence in history or physical science that beats these odds. In other words, nothing else has been verified with a higher degree of statistical certainty than the fact that Jesus is exactly who he claimed to be—the Messiah, the Son of the living God.

◎◎ The Miracle of First Century Multiplication

Imagine that you could step into a time machine and transport yourself twenty-one hundred years into the past, to an obscure place in the middle of nowhere—the desert of the Middle East. There is no Internet; there are no telephones, no radios, no television sets, and no newspapers or magazines. There are no printing presses and even paper as we know it doesn't exist. Copies of any written documents must be meticulously copied by hand on papyrus. There are no airplanes, trains, or cars. Most people travel by foot.

In this setting, a young peasant woman gives birth to a son in a stable. From an early age, the boy serves as apprentice in his stepfather's carpentry shop. The son works at that trade until he is thirty years old. Then, for three and a half years, he walks from village to village preaching unpopular messages to other peasants. He criticizes the rulers, the lawyers, the religious leaders, the educators, poor people, lazy people, and the wealthy. (His teachings offend just about everybody—not a great approach for a public speaker.) He never travels more than two hundred miles from his home. However, his teachings and the authority with which he teaches set him apart from *anyone* that these people have ever heard. On top of that, he performs incredible wonders that astound everyone who sees them. Crowds flock to him just to see what he's going to say and do next.

Then one night he is arrested, put through the mockery of a trial, and executed on a Roman cross between two criminals. As he's dying, crowds mock him, saying, "He saved others, but he can't even save himself." His closest followers, including all of his disciples except one, flee for their lives. After he dies, a Roman guard thrusts a spear into his side to make sure he is dead. His lifeless body is then wrapped in burial clothes and laid in a borrowed tomb.

All of these things took place in an obscure part of the world. And less than forty years after Jesus's death, Jerusalem was reduced to a pile of rubble by Roman legions, and the Jewish people were dispersed throughout the world.

If you were a gambler, what do you think the odds would

be that the story of this homeless carpenter would *ever* be heard beyond the Judean hills? A trillion to one? If ever there was a man who should have been overlooked by history it was Jesus. And yet, his story didn't die! Even though his followers had no easy way to spread his message, spread it they did. His story was written by those who witnessed his life and teachings firsthand, and *thousands* of copies were made by hand, letter for letter.

And could the Roman emperor stop the good news of this man's story from spreading? To the contrary, the greater the persecution of Jesus's followers, the more Jesus's message spread. Hundreds became thousands, thousands became tens of thousands, and hundreds of thousands became millions. Through the centuries, millions have become hundreds of millions. Once again, the infinite odds were beaten.

✑ Dying for a Lie?

Like most entrepreneurs, I've taken lots of business risks over the years. I've dug a lot of holes, hit a number of "gushers," and turned up a lot of dry holes. The cost of some of my failures has been financially devastating. But risking money for the chance of achieving extraordinary success has been a calculated risk I've been willing to take.

Still, I would never risk my *life* for a business opportunity. Even more certain, I would never risk the life of my wife or any of my children. If someone pointed a gun at my family and said, "Give me everything you own, or else," it wouldn't even require a thought. I would immediately give everything I own rather than risk the lives of my family. And yet, for nearly three hundred years, Jesus's followers were hunted down, imprisoned, and executed. Thousands were thrown into Roman arenas to be ripped apart by lions—whole families at a time. For what? For refusing to change their story or give up their faith in Jesus. At any time, each one could have ended their suffering and prevented their death simply by denying their faith. But they did not.

The chosen disciples who witnessed Jesus's life, teachings, and miracles—and then proclaimed what they had seen—were given similar choices at different times in different places. "Change your story or lose your life!" Not one of them changed their story. One was deported and the others suffered slow, tortuous executions. They could have stopped their torture and prolonged their lives. All they had to do was recant their testimonies. But they did not.

Would *you* be willing to die for something you knew to be a lie? I don't know anyone who would do that. Yet the disciples of Jesus did die, and *not* for a lie—for something they knew to be true.

◎◎ What Requires More Faith—to Believe or to Not Believe?

A few years ago, I was given a tour of a Volvo automobile factory in Sweden. I saw each of the stations at where workers added various components to the chassis of each car that

310 THE GREATEST MAN WHO EVER LIVED

moved down the line. It was impressive. Each part, from the most simple to the most complex (such as the engine), had been perfectly designed, tooled, and assembled to be added to each car at the appropriate assembly station. And yet, as wonderfully as these cars had been designed and built, not *one* of them was capable of manufacturing its own fuel. Not one of the cars could drive itself or maintain and repair itself.

Imagine if I told you that each part of each Volvo had spontaneously created itself, and then the thousands of parts came together on their own to perfectly assemble themselves into a smooth-running car. And that was just the beginning. Once it created itself, the car could drive itself. What's more, it could consume natural ingredients and then create its own fuel from those ingredients. Plus, for the next seventy to ninety years, the car will perform all of its own maintenance. And last but not least, these cars pair up and produce more cars.

Then imagine that I assured you that all of this takes place without the help of any designer or engineer, and without input or physical involvement from anyone on the assembly line. It just *happened.* I insist that self-producing automobiles started with one simple part—a piece of sheet metal that gradually became more complex over billions of years. It took on different shapes and forms, then joined with other changing pieces of metal and began to look more and more like a Volvo. Ultimately, the parts came together to become the wonderful cars we have today.

What would require more faith on your part—to believe

my story, or to believe that every car begins with a designer and requires the input and efforts of lots of other people to end up a fully functional car? Even then, these wonderful machines can't drive themselves, create their own fuel, or maintain themselves.

By comparison, the human body makes the automobile look like a primitive device from the Stone Age. We do create our own fuel, drive ourselves, and perform our own maintenance. The complexity of the human body dwarfs the complexity of even the highest-performance Formula One race car. There is no computer in the world that can even begin to approach what the human brain does. There is no pump in the world that can compare to the human heart; no electrical system that can perform like the human nervous system, and no camera that can begin to approach what the human eye can perform. And yet most scientists would try to convince you that the human body just "happened"—starting as a single-cell organism and, over billions of years, evolving into the most complex, self-sufficient machine ever known.

Which alternative requires more faith: to believe that you with all your senses, feelings, and reasoning simply evolved from a single cell, or that the greatest designer and manufacturer in the universe designed and created you?

If we evolved from a single cell that began mutating billions of years ago, there is no need for God. However, many of the most brilliant scientists of the twentieth and twenty-first centuries have taken the other position—that the *only* plausible explanation for life in general, and human life in particular, is the creative genius of God. Nuclear physicist Dr. Charles Payne held *eight* earned doctorates and was one of our nation's leading nuclear physicists. He was a devout atheist, and when a fellow scientist became a Christian, Payne set out to prove scientifically that Christianity was nothing more than a myth. He decided to read through the Bible eight times, and each time he would apply one of his eight areas of expertise. With each reading of the Bible, he planned to fill a notebook with biblical statements that contradicted scientific facts he knew to be true. After seven readings, he still had not discovered a contradiction to any scientific fact. On the other hand, he found many statements that revealed scientific discoveries two to three thousand years before those facts were discovered by modern science.

Payne's repeated readings of the Bible, along with his study of the life and teachings of Jesus Christ, gave him *more* evidence to believe that Jesus was who he claimed he was than existed to the contrary. Like C. S. Lewis, Payne went on to become an articulate defender of Christianity.

Dr. Payne's testimony was one of many from intellectual giants that influenced me to be intellectually honest as I considered the claims of Jesus. Another was that of Dr. Ralph Byron, chief of surgery of the City of Hope Medical Center. He was unique in that he was both a heart surgeon and a brain surgeon. As a new Christian, I sat spellbound one Sunday night as I heard Byron describe the scientific evidence that persuaded him to follow Jesus Christ.

Too many people are convinced that the only people who

believe in God are idiots and old ladies. I have observed just the opposite. I have met many of the world's leading experts in various scientific and medical fields, and the most brilliant have *not* been atheists. Most of the atheists I have known have not studied the wealth of evidence that shows that Jesus is exactly who he says he is. Like C. S. Lewis, they made their judgments without considering either the scientific evidence or the person and words of Jesus Christ. On the other hand, every atheist I have known who studied the person and words of Jesus ultimately became a Christian. But that's them, and we're now talking about you!

Like so many others, you can make your judgments based on feelings and personal biases or you can honestly consider the evidence. Lew Wallace was not only a great Civil War general, he was one of America's most respected historians. He was also one of Indiana's United States senators and later the first territorial governor of New Mexico. Wallace hated Christianity, so much so that he decided to write a historical novel with the hope of destroying the faith of Christians. The title of his book was to be *The Myth of Christianity.* While working on it, he began reading the words of Jesus and the accounts of Jesus's life, detailed in the four gospels of the New Testament.

To Wallace's amazement, as he was reading the account of the crucifixion he came upon Jesus's words from the cross. When he read Jesus's statement "Father, forgive them; for they know not what they do" (Luke 23:34, KJV), it was as if he heard Jesus saying, "Father forgive *him,* for he knows

not what he's doing." As the power of those words pene-
trated his hardened soul, Wallace found himself crying out to
Jesus, begging his forgiveness and asking him to be the Lord
of his life. He immediately felt God's love and forgiveness
and arose from his knees a brand-new man, with a sense of
peace and joy greater than anything he had known before. He
immediately returned to the manuscript of his novel and tore
it to shreds. That night he began a new novel, one that went
on to become the best-selling historical novel of all time: *Ben-
Hur: A Tale of the Christ.*

When my partners and I launched our nutritional company two years ago, we focused on the overwhelming scientific evidence that proved the efficacy of our product. We had
the first nutritional product whose effect at a cellular level
could be quantified and verified through blood tests. We were
quick to highlight that tests of lymphocytes demonstrated a
300 to 400 percent rise in glutathione levels in only ninety
days. But then something amazing began to happen. As more
and more people began to use the product, we heard countless stories of the remarkable improvements those people
were seeing. Although we never stopped talking about the scientific proofs, the personal testimonies of the product's users
were so amazing that sales skyrocketed. As impressive as the
science was, *nothing* was more convincing then a man or
woman's personal testimony.

J. R. R. Tolkien's simple argument of "liar, lunatic, or Son
of God" could not be denied, even by one of the world's
most articulate atheists. It is a logical proof that's hard to

break. The $1{:}10^{157}$ odds that Jesus beat when he fulfilled forty-eight messianic prophecies gives a mathematical proof that no intellectually honest mathematician could easily dismiss. But without a doubt, the most compelling proof for me that Jesus was and is the one he claims to be is what he has done in my life. He is real! He has been right by my side through every season and circumstance. In the darkest hours, those times when circumstances left me feeling alone and in despair, he was there. In my times of greatest joy he was there. We have talked to each other hundreds of times every day. I have not only seen him perform countless miracles, but his miracles have been as tangible as life-saving healings and interventions into my business and financial life that have spared me from bankruptcy more than once, and catapulted the successes I've experienced beyond anything I could have hoped or dreamed.

But these have not been the greatest miracles in my life. God has given me eternal life—not because I've done anything to deserve it, but because God sacrificed his only Son who was willingly crucified for *my* sins. He has filled me with his Holy Spirit and produced *agape* love in my heart—both for God and for those who cross my path. I've seen dozens of friends whose hearts and lives were as self-centered and godless as my life used to be experience miraculous transformations when they became followers of Jesus.

Remember, I'm not talking about religion. I'm talking about an intimate, living relationship with the God who created the universe. During the past forty-four years I've been asked one question in high school, in college, in the work-place, on airline flights, in restaurants, and just about every other place. Simply stated, people ask, "How can *I* have the kind of relationship with God that you have?" This is one of the greatest questions a person will ever ask, and Jesus is the only person who provides the answer, which is the focus of the following chapter.

ꙮ Jesus Alone Deserves the Title "The Greatest Man Who Ever Lived"

Bill Gates is one of the richest men in the world. He and his partners started with nothing and brilliantly built Microsoft and a financial fortune. Some time ago, Gates announced he was leaving 95 percent of his fortune to charity. The remaining two to three billion would remain in his family.

But imagine this scenario: We learn of a tribe of natives in the South American jungle that has contracted a terrible disease that could infect the entire human population. The disease seems harmless in its early stages, but in the end it brings about a slow, painful death. It kills every person who contracts it.

In an unexpected turn of events, doctors discover that Bill Gates is the one person whose blood contains an anti-body that will cure the terrible disease. Gates announces to the world that he is leaving his wealth, his accomplishments, and his family behind to embark on a critical mission—one that is both terrifying and wonderful. He is going to parachute into the most remote jungle in the Amazon basin. He will take nothing with him except the clothes on his back. Once on the ground, he'll spend years searching for the diseased tribe. If he fails to accomplish his mission, every man, woman, boy, and girl in that tribe will die a painful death. Meanwhile, migratory birds could spread that disease to the rest of the world. If Gates succeeds in his mission, he'll show a number of the tribe members (every one who is willing to trust him) how to receive an injection of his blood and be saved.

The only problem is, the tribe is highly superstitious and believes in human sacrifice. They have tortured and killed every outsider who has ever made contact with them. They think white men are devils. Gates is aware of their superstitions and the dangers inherent in his mission. But he is driven by his desire to save them from sure death and to keep the disease from killing others around the world.

He is told by his advisors that he doesn't have a prayer of surviving this mission. And even if he saves a few people, most will refuse an injection of his blood. In fact, they will believe they are serving their gods when they torture and kill him. And yet Gates boards the plane that will drop him into the jungle.

Once on the ground, he discovers a nearly impenetrable jungle. It takes him three decades just to make contact with the tribe. He then spends three and one half years telling them of their plight and explaining how they can be saved. A few believe him, trusting him so much they accept his cure.

But not so with the others. They finally have enough of his message and decide to kill him.

While he is dying, he urges them to trust in his blood so they can be saved. He tells them that he loves them and forgives them. And then…he dies.

Were this to happen, such a sacrificial effort would be considered one of the greatest acts of love of the twenty-first century and would warrant for Bill Gates the crown of Philanthropist of the Year.

As amazing as such a story would be, it can't begin to compare with the *real* story of what Jesus Christ did. He made the greatest series of sacrifices anyone has ever made. He left heaven, where he reigned as the King of kings. He humbled himself to become a mortal man. He faced all the physical needs and temptations that we all face, and yet he lived a perfectly righteous life. And then he subjected himself to the humiliation surrounding his execution.

Jesus experienced a level of suffering that none of us will ever be able to appreciate. The suffering was far greater than that of the skin being ripped off his back by thirty-nine lashes from a whip full of hooks and sharp stones. The suffering was far greater than having his hands and feet nailed to the cross. He took on all the sins of humanity—literally becoming our sin. In a single moment he was a murderer, an adulterer, a thief—every sin of every sinner who ever lived. And for the first time in eternity, Jesus's heavenly Father completely withdrew his presence, and an agonizing separation took place. It was an unbearable agony so great that Jesus let out his only scream throughout the entire ordeal of crucifixion. He cried out, "My God, my God, why hast thou forsaken me?" (Matt. 27:46, KJV).

Why did Jesus voluntarily put himself through all this? One word—love! He loved us that *that* much!

Our terminal disease is the spiritual disease called sin. Its power over us is never-ending. It enslaves us in this life, preventing us from experiencing an intimate relationship with God. And there is more: sin prevents us from experiencing eternal life with God when we die. Jesus came to earth to change that by opening the door for us to gain entrance into God's kingdom for eternity.

But how can we gain eternal life...and know beyond any shadow of a doubt that we have it? The prophet Isaiah answered this question with a direct quote from God. Isaiah wrote: "'Come now, and let us reason together,' says the LORD, 'though your sins are like scarlet, they shall be as white as snow; though they are red like crimson, they shall be as wool'" (Isa. 1:18, NKJV).

We *can* be delivered from the power and consequences of our sins, no matter how numerous they might be. We *can* have eternal life, and that life can start right now. That's what the next chapter is all about. Although it is the last chapter in this book, it can become the first chapter in *your* eternal life.

—— ✺✺ ——

CHAPTER 17

Wouldn't You Like to Live Forever?

"My sheep hear My voice, and I know them,
and they follow Me. And I give them eternal life,
and they shall never perish; neither shall anyone
snatch them out of My hand."

—JESUS (JOHN 10:27–28, NKJV)

✺✺ The Most Important Reality Check of Your Life!

When I was nineteen years old, the air force named me the ROTC Cadet of the Year at Arizona State University and offered me a full flight scholarship. All I had to do was agree to sign a contract to become an air force pilot upon graduation. As part of the inducement, they gave me a ninety-minute ride in a supersonic jet fighter. It was truly the ride of a lifetime.

We took off in formation with another fighter, and right after liftoff my instructor pilot ignited the afterburner and turned the jet's nose vertical. The aircraft became more like a rocket than a plane. In a matter of seconds we rocketed to eighteen thousand feet. After a few minutes, the pilot said, "Ya know, you get no concept of speed at this altitude," and he threw the jet into a six hundred miles per hour dive. He finally pulled out at treetop level over the forests of north-ern Arizona. Flying at the speed of three football fields per second, just seventy feet off the ground, you *do* get the con-cept of speed—big time!

After a few minutes, he pulled back the nose and we re-turned to our cruising altitude. We then dove into the Grand Canyon and flew in between the canyon walls, sometimes upside-down. We continued on to the Gila gunnery range at the other end of the state, where we did a full regimen of high-G aerobatics and combat maneuvers, pulling as many as seven G's in the tight loops.

During one of the maneuvers, I lost sight of the horizon and couldn't tell if we were flying straight up or straight down. This is similar to the condition referred to as vertigo. I finally decided we were flying straight up. I was so sure of it that I could have passed a lie-detector test, swearing the jet's nose was pointed toward the sky. Unfortunately, the plane's instru-ments indicated the opposite—that our nose was pointed straight down. I had received my private pilot's license two years earlier and had performed aerobatics a number of times. Had I been in control of this flight, I would have faced a life-and-death decision: "Do I trust my feelings or do I trust my instruments?" If the nose was pointed up, I would need to push forward on the stick to fly straight and level. But if the nose was pointed down, I would need to pull back on the stick to level the plane's attitude. The wrong decision would mean death.

I had learned long before my flight in the jet fighter that

the instruments never lie. They are carefully adjusted to conform to absolute standards. No matter how strong my feelings were that the jet was flying straight up, I had to trust my instruments. At that moment, with my hand resting lightly on the stick, I felt the instructor pull back on his stick (the two were connected), and the nose began to lift. The instruments were right, and my feelings were wrong. Had I been in control and acted on my feelings, we would have died.

The Fatal Flaw of Basing Decisions on Feelings

Nearly every decision we make starts with our feelings. We add in a little logic based on our frame of reference, which is built on past experiences and reasoning. While this approach may serve us well in some areas, in critical matters the results can be catastrophic, as was the case when John F. Kennedy Jr.'s plane went down in the Atlantic in 1999.

Most people rely far too heavily on their feelings or their limited reasoning power to make critical decisions. After a distinguished career as a sea captain, Edward John Smith agreed to postpone his retirement in order to make one last crossing of the Atlantic. He would pilot the maiden voyage of the largest, most luxurious passenger ship ever built. During the crossing he received numerous warnings from other vessels of icebergs along his route. His gut feeling told him there was nothing to worry about as he cruised at top speed through the calm waters of the North Atlantic. When the ship's lookout spotted an iceberg dead ahead, the ocean liner was cruising too fast to avoid a collision. Had the ship been sailing just one mile per hour slower, there would have been no collision. But Captain Smith's gut feeling that he was safe traveling at top speed was wrong, and the *Titanic* took Smith and more than fifteen hundred other men, women, and children to their deaths.

Are You Relying on Your Gut Feeling or on the Evidence?

Imagine that you were facing a life-or-death decision involving two unknown paths. One path would lead to a longer, happier life, and the other would lead to a painful death within twenty-four hours. If your most trusted advisor handed you a ten-million-dollar instrument that could identify the right choice—an instrument that had proven its accuracy 100 percent of the time—would you make your decision based on your feelings and reasoning, or would you follow the readings of the instrument? Remember, the right choice will result in a long, happy life, while the wrong choice will result in a painful death. A few stubborn people might follow their feelings…and die! But those who are wise would follow the guidance of the instrument, to the letter.

We have such an unerring guide available to us. *If* Jesus is who he claimed he was, then he is the *one* person who knows the absolute truth about life—both on earth and in eternity. And his statements would provide us with the only instrument that is based on absolute truth. His teachings would give us the perfect GPS directions from where we are now to the ultimate destination of eternal life.

By using Jesus's words as the standard of measure, we can determine whether the statements of all others—and whether our own feelings and logic—are accurate or misleading. Jesus said, "I have come into the world as a light, so that no one who believes in me should stay in darkness. As for the person who hears my words but does not keep them, I do not judge him. For I did not come to judge the world, but to save it. There *is* a judge for the one who rejects me and does not accept my words; that very word which I spoke will condemn him at the last day" (Jn. 12:46–48, NIV).

Based on the evidence we've already looked at, and volumes more that I have studied, I am fully persuaded that Jesus is exactly who he claimed to be—the Messiah, the only begotten Son of the one true God. Once you decide for yourself whether he is who he claimed to be, you should ask: "Did Jesus claim to *know* what it takes to gain eternal life in heaven?" The answer is yes. He did make that claim, as well as many others. Here are just a few of his statements on this subject:

- "No one has ever gone into heaven except the one who came from heaven—the Son of Man" (Jn. 3:13, NIV).
- "For I have come down from heaven not to do my will but to do the will of him who sent me" (Jn. 6:38, NIV).
- "For I did not speak of my own accord, but the Father who sent me commanded me what to say and

how to say it. I know that his command leads to eternal life. So whatever I say is just what the Father has told me to say" (Jn. 12:49–50, NIV).

- "For God did not send his Son into the world to condemn the world, but to save the world through him" (Jn. 3:17, NIV).

- "For God so loved the world that he gave his one and only Son, that whoever believes in him shall not perish but have eternal life" (Jn. 3:16, NIV).

- "I am the way and the truth and the life. No one comes to the Father except through me" (Jn. 14:6, NIV).

- "I am the light of the world. Whoever follows me will never walk in darkness, but will have the light of life" (Jn. 8:12, NIV).

- "I am the good shepherd; I know my sheep and my sheep know me…. My sheep listen to my voice; I know them, and they follow me. I give them eternal life, and they shall never perish; no one can snatch them out of my hand" (Jn. 10:14, 27–28, NIV).

- "You are from below; I am from above. You are of this world; I am not of this world. I told you that you would die in your sins; if you do not believe that I am the one I claim to be, you will indeed die in your sins" (Jn. 8:23–24, NIV).

In those statements Jesus made the following claims:

1. He's the *only* one who has come to earth from heaven, and he came to earth to do what God, his

Father, wanted him to do—lead people to eternal life.

2. He said only what his Father wanted him to say.

3. He was sent into the world to save the world, not to condemn it.

4. He was God's gift to the world, and whoever would believe in him would avoid eternal death and experience eternal life.

5. He alone is *the* way, *the* truth, and *the* life—and he is the *only* pathway to God the Father.

6. He is the *light* of the world, and if we follow him (obeying his teachings and following his example), we can avoid living in illusion and darkness. Instead, we can live in the light of absolute reality.

7. He is the Shepherd, which means he intimately knows his sheep (his followers) and they intimately know him. They listen to his voice and follow him, and he gives them eternal life. And that's not all: no one can steal the sheep from him, nor can anyone take eternal life from Jesus's followers.

Jesus does claim to know exactly how you and I can gain eternal life. He claims to not only be the one who can give it, but most important, he *wants* to give it to us. But he can give us eternal life only according to the guidelines that God the Father revealed. As we saw in an earlier chapter, Jesus told an old man named Nicodemus that to "enter the kingdom of God" a person *must* be born again by experiencing a second birth (see Jn. 3:3–7). The first birth, "of water," is a physical birth. The second is a *spiritual* birth, and the good news for Nicodemus was that his old age would not prevent him from experiencing this new birth.

This of course leads to the next question, "What must *I* do to have this spiritual birth?"

After Jesus told Nicodemus that he needed to be "born again" to enter God's kingdom, he clarified what was needed to gain eternal life. He said:

> For God so loved the world that he gave his one and only Son, that whoever believes in him shall not perish but have eternal life. For God did not send his Son into the world to condemn the world, but to save the world through him. Whoever believes in him is not condemned, but whoever does not believe stands condemned already because he has not believed in the name of God's one and only Son. (Jn. 3:16–18, NIV)

To understand what Jesus really meant in this passage, one question must be answered clearly: What does it mean to "believe in him"? This is one of the most important messages in the New Testament. Unfortunately, it is also one of the most misunderstood. In the English language, the word "believe" has lost a great deal of its meaning. It has come to mean "think, hope, or wish," or a mere mental acknowledgment or mental assent. We might say, "I believe it's going to be sunny tomorrow" or "I believe John really does love Judy" or "I believe I'm ready for my presentation."

In contrast, at the time the King James Version of the Bible was translated, the word *believe* meant to be "fully persuaded—to the point of total commitment and reliance." This is much closer to the meaning of the ancient Greek word that is translated as "believe" in John 3:16. The Greek word is *pisteo,* and can be accurately rendered as "to be so fully persuaded that you totally rely upon, rest upon, or act upon that which you are believing in." Consequently, your actions always reflect your true beliefs, and in reality they emanate from your beliefs.

Imagine I were with you right now, and the floor we were standing on began to shake. Imagine further that I told you I was the engineer who designed the building, and that even a mild earthquake would collapse the building. If you *believed* me, you would immediately run for your life. Our actions and behavior reflect what we believe.

If you have decided that you think Jesus is the Son of God, then you will thoughtfully consider his statements—but you may or may not choose to do what he says to do. On the other hand—if you truly believe he is the Son of God and that his words provide the ultimate GPS for your behavior, then you will do whatever he instructs you to do. I'm not saying you will always do *everything* he said. We all have a strong bias in our hearts that makes us want to serve our self-interests more than we want to serve God. But as our faith in Jesus grows, our behavior will begin to reflect our faith more and more, and our self-centeredness less and less.

◎◎ How Can You Enter into Eternal Life and Know That It Will Never Be Taken Away from You?

God the Father and Jesus Christ *want* to give you eternal life. How do I know? Jesus said so. In John 6:40 he said, "For my Father's will is that everyone who looks to the Son and believes in him shall have eternal life, and I will raise him up at the last day" (NIV). If we look to Jesus and believe that he is the Son of God, and if we put our trust in what he did on the cross, we will gain eternal life. Jesus promised this: "For God so loved the world that he gave his one and only Son, that whoever believes in him shall not perish but have eternal life. For God did not send his Son into the world to condemn the world, but to save the world through him. Whoever believes in him is not condemned, but whoever does not believe stands condemned already because he has not believed in the name of God's one and only Son" (Jn. 3:16–18, NIV).

Gaining eternal life is a simple matter—but not an *easy* one. It's simple, because we receive it once and for all, for all eternity, by believing that Jesus is the Son of God, and that the sacrifice of his life completely redeemed us from the consequences of our sinful nature. But it's not easy, because to "believe" the words of Jesus means to totally commit your life to him as your Lord, which involves a total commitment to follow him. We follow him by learning what he said and doing it.

I'm not talking about religion or a religious experience, I'm talking about a relationship—entering into a committed union with God through Jesus, God's Son. You commit to follow him, and he commits to be your God and your Shepherd. He commits to place you in his hand, so that nothing and no one will ever take you out of his hand. He commits to give you eternal life, and he makes more than 108 specific, incredible promises to you.

But the question at hand is, "What does a person have to do *specifically* to enter into this saving relationship that results in eternal life?" In Revelation 3:20, Jesus said, "Behold, I stand at the door and knock; if anyone hears My voice and opens the door, I will come in to him and dine with him, and he with Me" (NASB). Jesus is knocking on the door of your heart and mind. But how can you open that door?

The people Jesus was talking to about opening the door to their hearts thought they were rich and good and felt they had no material or spiritual needs. But Jesus said the opposite was true. In the light of God's righteousness and standards, they were "wretched, pitiful, poor, blind and naked" (Rev. 3:17, NIV). They had no means whatsoever to be what they needed to be to enter into a saving union with God.

That is the case with you and me as well. A lifetime of loving ourselves more than we love God has led us down a pathway of what the Bible calls "sin." It has left us with a debt to God that is impossible for us to repay. It has bankrupted us spiritually and blinded our eyes to who God is and what he desires. Being spiritually blind, naked, poor, and wretched means we have none of the resources that are required to enter into God's kingdom. That's the bad news.

The good news is that Jesus has *everything* we need to enter into a saving relationship with God. He has "spiritual gold" refined by fire that can make us spiritually rich; he has white garments of righteousness to cover our shameful spiritual nakedness, and he offers a spiritual eye ointment that enables our spiritually blind eyes to see. In short, he has *everything* we need to enter into an eternal relationship with God.

How can we receive these resources from him? His instruction in Revelation 3:19 is to "be zealous and repent" (NASB). The Greek word that is translated "zealous" means "to be heated" or "boil with passion." The word that is translated "repent" means to "change one's mind from one course of action to another." We must passionately change our minds about our self-centeredness and the selfish pursuits we have followed. Instead, we have to turn away from our self-centered habit of putting ourselves above God and turn *toward* him and embrace his words and teachings. We have to begin walking in a new direction. In turn, *he* will provide the GPS directions that reveal his paths that we are to follow. Repentance is *not* a religious decision—it's simply a choice and an action to turn away from the direction in which our biased nature has been driving us and to a new direction of passionately following him. It's a choice that makes *God* the boss of your life.

Jesus said, "My sheep hear My voice, and I know them, and they follow Me" (Jn. 10:27, NASB). But he doesn't stop there. His next statement is, "And I give eternal life to them, and they will never perish; and no one will snatch them out of My hand" (Jn. 10:28, NASB).

◎◎ Moving from Darkness into Light, Illusion into Reality, and Death into Life

Jesus taught that our nature is to walk in darkness. We follow pathways that are attractive to our self-centered human nature but are void of the light that reflects God's values. Without his light, we make decisions based on responses to temporary illusions that offer gratification, but no true and lasting fulfillment and significance. In chapter two of this book we saw how such illusions attract us to behaviors and choices that often are self-ish and foolish—and sometimes destructive. We miss wonderful opportunities to bless the lives of others while we pursue activities and actions that serve ourselves. We often accept good in place of the best, and bad in place of good. We make choices that fuel our greed, arrogance, and lust. Our hearts are left unhappy and unfulfilled.

Jesus said it this way: "Men [and women] loved darkness instead of light because their deeds were evil" (Jn. 3:19, NIV). He's not talking only about the Adolf Hitlers of the world; he's talking about all of us who choose to pursue the values of the world over the values of God—who choose to love ourselves more than we love the God who created us.

But Jesus can change everything—the desires of our hearts, the direction of our lives, and the benefit we can provide to others. He can make our lives truly significant—for eternity. He can throw so much light into our pathway that we begin to recognize the things that have real value and those that do not. He said, "I am the light of the world.

Whoever follows me will never walk in darkness, but will have the light of life" (Jn. 8:12, NIV).

We can begin to experience an intimate relationship with a God who loves us infinitely more than we could ever love ourselves. We talk to him through prayer, and he will talk to us through his teachings in the Bible. Jesus said, "If anyone loves me, he will obey my teaching. My Father will love him, and we will come to him and make our home with him" (Jn. 14:23, NIV). He makes it possible for us to get to know him and God the Father in an intimate way. He literally adopts us into his eternal family.

Finally, he offers a love that never ceases, ongoing forgiveness that is without limit, a source of peace and righteousness that can't be experienced any other way, and eternal life that can never be lost or stolen.

If this is the kind of relationship you want with God, you can begin now. Jesus said, "Come to me, all you who are weary and burdened, and I will give you rest. Take my yoke upon you and learn from me, for I am gentle and humble in heart, and you will find rest for your souls. For my yoke is easy and my burden is light" (Matt. 11:28–30, NIV). And Jesus made a promise in John 6:37 when he said, "The one who comes to Me I will certainly not cast out" (NASB).

So how about you? It can all start with a simple prayer. For more than forty years, I've had the joy of watching people enter into an eternal relationship with God and begin a new life for themselves. When I've prayed with them, they have acknowledged to God that they realize their self-centeredness and sin have prevented them from having an intimate relationship with him, and that they need his forgiveness. They acknowledge that they can do *nothing* on their own to deserve or acquire forgiveness for their sins. They then ask Jesus to come into their lives and be their Lord and Savior.

If this expresses your desire, you should pray and commit your life to following Jesus. If you do, he promises that he will come into you through his Holy Spirit and receive you into his eternal family and kingdom. It's not your words but the attitude of your heart that counts.

For those who do not find it easy to pray, I offer the following prayer. If it expresses how you feel, it can serve as an example that you can follow, or you can even pray it as you read it.

"Heavenly Father, I want to make you the God of my life. I confess that I am self-centered and sinful and can do nothing to merit your love and forgiveness—and yet that is what I desire. I believe that you sent your one and only Son to earth to sacrifice his life as a payment for all of my sins. I want to make Jesus the Lord of my life and follow his teachings.

"Lord Jesus, I open the door of my life and ask you to become my Lord and Savior. I believe that you laid down your life for me. I ask that you would accept me into your family and begin to make me the person you want me to be. Amen."

◉◉ What Should You Do Next?

If you don't own a Bible, I encourage you to go to any bookstore and buy a modern English translation of the Bible. My favorites are The New International Version (NIV), The New American Standard Bible (NASB), and The New King James Version (NKJV). Most bookstores will carry one or more of these versions, or you can go online to Christianbook.com and order one.

If a friend gave you this book, let that friend know you have committed your life to Jesus Christ and ask if he or she could help you find a good Bible study or Bible-teaching church to attend. Otherwise, you can find a Bible-teaching church near you by doing a Google search, entering "Bible churches" and your city and state. It is critically important that you meet with other believers who can help you grow in your faith. Jesus said, "Where two or three are gathered together in My name, I am there in the midst of them" (Matt. 18:20, NKJV).

Finally, realize that Jesus wants to have an intimate relationship with you—one in which you can experience his presence any moment of any day. To have this kind of relationship, it is critical that you have honest, two-way communication with him. He communicates with you through his Word, the Bible. I always recommend that new believers start by reading the fourth book in the New Testament, the gospel of John. As you read his words, you will be astonished by their wisdom and power for your daily life. That's communication that comes straight from Jesus.

At the same time *you* need to begin to converse with him, by praying. You can talk to him about anything. In fact, the Apostle Paul told us in Philippians 4:6–7 to hold *nothing* back but to talk to the Lord about anything and everything that comes into our minds. Even when you want things that you know are contrary to what God wants, he wants you to talk with him about them. As you share your heart and mind, you are having an *honest* relationship with God. You will find that your desires will begin to change as you keep everything "in the light" between you and the Lord (1 Jn. 1:7, NIV).

๑๑ What Does Jesus Promise, and What Can You Expect?

Jesus has made more than 108 promises to those who would become his followers. In my forty-four years of being a Christian, although I have broken so many of my promises to him, he has *never* broken even one of his promises to me. Here are just a few of his promises. (The full list can be found on pages 298–304 of my book *The Greatest Words Ever Spoken.*)

Jesus promises that as his follower, you have been given the gift of eternal life, you will never die spiritually, and no one can take you out of Jesus's care (see Jn. 10:27–29).

1. You possess eternal life, right now, and you have already crossed over from spiritually dead to spiritually alive (see Jn. 5:24).

2. The Holy Spirit has made your spirit alive to Christ by entering into a union with your spirit. Not only will you begin to experience a change in your heart, but your new life in Christ ("rivers of living water") will

begin to flow out of your innermost being and give blessing and life to those around you (see Jn. 7:38).

3. If you begin to read Jesus's words, you will receive all the "light" you need to guide your faith, values, and behavior, so you won't be deceived by the illusions. Instead, you can fill your life with the realities that bring joy to your daily life now and count for eternity as well (see Jn. 8:12).

4. As you study his words, Jesus promises that you will *know* the truth and that the truth will set you free from all the things that have held you captive—even the addictions you may struggle with (see Jn. 8:31–32).

5. Jesus says that as you discover and follow his teachings, God the Father will love you in a special way, and that both Jesus and the Father will live with you in a special way every day (see Jn. 14:23).

6. If you will read or hear the words Jesus spoke here on earth and begin to do what he says, your life will be built on such a strong foundation that even the greatest storms of life will not bring you down (see Matt. 7:24–25).

෧෧ Fact Versus Feelings

Through the years a number of people have prayed with me as they committed their lives to Jesus Christ. Some experienced tremendous feelings of peace and joy as they prayed, while others said they were surprised that they *didn't* have an earth-shaking emotional or spiritual experience. Whether you experience strong emotions or not, neither is a true measure of the reality that takes place when you make such a commitment. In 1995 I took my son and one of my film crews from New York to Paris on the Concorde. Once the jet was over the Atlantic, it climbed to sixty-five thousand feet and began to accelerate. At the front of the cabin a digital airspeed indicator counted upward toward the speed of sound. All of us watched excitedly as we anticipated going through the sound barrier. But when we reached supersonic speed we barely felt a shudder. In fact, some of us didn't feel anything. The speed kept climbing until we reached *twice* the speed of sound (mach 2) or just under fourteen hundred miles per hour. Still, we felt no different than we did when we were flying at five hundred miles per hour. We were traveling through the air faster than a bullet—nearly seven football fields a second—yet we couldn't even feel it. And because we were twice as high as most airliners fly, and flying over the ocean, we couldn't even *see* a perceptible difference—yet there we were.

What mattered most? Our feelings that we were flying at a normal airspeed of around five hundred fifty miles per hour, or the fact that we were flying at fourteen hundred miles per hour? At five hundred fifty miles per hour, it would take us more than seven hours to reach Paris, while at fourteen hundred, it would take us only three hours. If you had to bet your life on the outcome, would you bet on your feelings or the fact? The same is true in our relationship with God. Feelings are wonderful when we have them, but they are *not* what matters. Jesus said, "Heaven and earth will pass away, but my words will never pass away" (Matt. 24:35, NIV). What matters are the facts of God's Word—his statements and promises are more reliable than the earth and the heavens.

If you have prayed and committed your life to Christ, I invite you to visit the Web site www.greatestwords.com, where you will find a link labeled New Believers. Click on that link for information you can download that will be very helpful as you begin your life as a new follower of Jesus Christ. You've made the most important decision of your life, and the joy, peace, wisdom, and wonder that lie ahead of you will bless you and those who cross your path for the rest of your life—and beyond. May God continue to bless you with an ever-growing knowledge and love for him.

Appendix 1

◉◉ The Vision-Mapping Process at Work

Because a picture is worth a thousand words, I'll illustrate the vision-mapping process with one example from my past. In 1996, my partners and I decided to undertake a project in which we would market a piece of fitness equipment for which we had acquired the marketing rights. At the time, the equipment was a piece of strength-training equipment used by professional sports teams and medical rehab facilities. Our hope was to market it to consumers as a premier home-fitness unit. The name of the product was the Total Gym, and our hope was to recruit Chuck Norris and Christie Brinkley as our spokespersons. Chuck had been using the professional unit for eighteen years and loved it so much he had it shipped all over the world to every filming location he traveled to. At the time, Christie had never used it, but we knew she worked out to keep in shape and we believed that if she tried it, she would fall in love with it. Here's a glimpse of a *portion* of my vision map for marketing the Total Gym.

Vision-Map Example: Total Gym

Step 1: Clearly define your vision/mission.

Vision

Redesign the Total Gym into an attractive and practical piece of home-fitness equipment and create a marketing program that will sell millions of Total Gyms to consumers in America and throughout the world.

Step 2: Convert your vision into specific goals that must be accomplished in order to achieve your mission.

Vision Goals

1. Redesign the Total Gym to make it more attractive and practical for home use. Shorten it and take at least twenty-five pounds out of it. Change it so that it comes fully assembled and can be folded up small enough to be slid under a bed.

2. Recruit Chuck Norris and Christie Brinkley to be our television spokespersons, at endorsement fees that we can afford to pay.

3. Produce a thirty-minute infomercial and two-minute and sixty-second commercials to sell the Total Gym directly to television viewers.

4. Create a market test to test consumer response to the infomercial and commercials.

5. Create a media plan to guide the media purchases.

6. Find a marketing partner that can distribute the Total Gym through retail stores that sell fitness equipment.

7. Create the marketing collateral material to send to interested consumers and include with each Total Gym sold.

8. Create the program and scripts for the inbound telephone call centers that will be taking the orders.

9. Create newspaper ads to support the sales of retailers.

Step 3: Convert each goal into the specific steps that need to be taken to reach that goal.

Goals to Steps

Goal #3: Produce a thirty-minute infomercial, a two-minute commercial, and a sixty-second commercial to sell the Total Gym directly to television viewers.

Steps

1. Conduct prewriting research.
2. Write the infomercial script.
3. Write the scripts for the interior spots.
4. Block out the show segments.
5. Determine locations and staging.
6. Create a production schedule.
7. Produce the commercials.
8. Edit the commercials.
9. Do sound sweetening.

Step 4: Convert each step into the specific tasks that need to be completed to take that step.

Goal #3, Step 1: Prewriting Research

Tasks

1. Determine all of the advantages of strength training over aerobic exercise.

2. Research other strength-training equipment on the market.

3. Determine the unique benefits a user will receive from the Total Gym.

4. Determine the competitive advantages of the Total Gym over other strength-training machines, apparatuses, and equipment.

5. Determine objections and excuses consumers might have for *not* purchasing the Total Gym.

6. Determine the answers to consumer objections and excuses.

7. Determine and prioritize all of the sales points that could be used in the scripting of the infomercial.

8. Arrange interview testimonials and before-and-after user groups.

Step 5: Assign a target date for completing each task, each step, and each goal.

When assigning target dates, I usually start with my target date for completing the project, mission, or vision, and then work down, assigning target dates for each goal, then each step, and finally each task. Many people prefer to do the opposite, starting with assigning realistic target dates for each task, then working *up* to each step and then each goal, and finally deducing a target date for the completion of the project, mission, or vision. Starting at the top and working down is critical when you have a hard or fixed deadline for completing an endeavor. If you *don't* have a hard deadline, starting with the last task for the last step of the last goal and working *upward* will enable you to allow yourself ample time for the completion of each task, step, and goal. Either way works, and you should pick the way that best fits the circumstances and your personality and work style or lifestyle.

Appendix 2

Vision-Mapping in Our Personal Lives

You don't have to limit your vision mapping to work. You can use it in any important area of your personal life. For example, let's say you want a more fulfilling relationship with your spouse. Here's a snapshot of what a portion of a vision map for that dream could look like.

Step 1: Clearly define your vision.

Vision
To have an extraordinary, fulfilling relationship with my wife—one in which all of our greatest needs and desires are met, and one that will serve as an example to our children of how vibrant and emotionally and spiritually fulfilling a marriage can be.

Step 2: Convert your vision into specific goals that must be accomplished in order to achieve your mission.

Vision Goals

1. Do whatever it takes to provide my wife with a relationship in which her most important needs (physical, emotional, spiritual, financial, etc.) and dreams are fulfilled.

2. Discover the things that I do or don't do that hurt our relationship, and begin to make changes in my behavior to better fulfill my wife's needs.

3. Clearly communicate my needs, desires, and hopes to my wife so that she can fulfill or help to fulfill them in our relationship.

Step 3: Convert each goal into the specific steps that need to be taken to reach that goal.

Goal #1: Do whatever it takes to provide my wife with a relationship in which her most important needs (physical, emotional, spiritual, financial, etc.) and dreams are fulfilled.

Steps

1. Discover from my wife what her most important needs and dreams are, and ask for her suggestions on how to fulfill those needs.

2. Determine the best ways to meet each of those needs and fulfill those dreams.

3. Create a plan for meeting those needs on a regular basis and for timely fulfillment of those dreams.

4. Begin meeting those needs consistently, and become proactive in helping her to pursue and achieve her dreams through the vision-mapping process.

Step 4: Convert each step into the specific tasks that need to be completed to take that step.

> Goal #1, Step 1: Discover from my wife what her most impor-
> tant needs and dreams are, and ask for her suggestions on
> how to fulfill those needs.

Tasks

1. Schedule a time when my wife and I can spend an evening free of distraction to ask her to help me to clearly understand her most important needs and dreams.

2. Use "drive-thru" talking and emotional word pictures to gain a crystal-clear understanding of her needs, hopes, and dreams.

3. Take notes that can be used as a regular reminder to help me stay focused on making real progress in meeting these needs and helping her to fulfill her hopes and dreams. (It will also show her that I'm taking her desires as seriously as I would take anything at work.)

Step 5: Assign a target date to complete each task, each step, and each goal.

Here again, assigning specific dates is important, because if you don't have a timeline, you *won't* achieve your goal. If you have a hard time assigning specific dates in a personal area, assign a one- or two-week range. A soft target is better than no target at all.

Haven't you wished
you could ask Jesus any question
and get his immediate help?

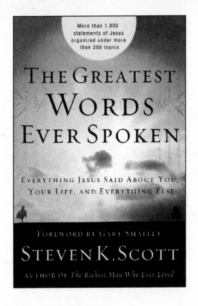

For the first time in 2,000 years, all
the statements of Jesus, organized
into practical easy-to-find topics.

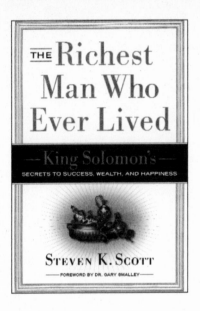